you're a [?]
already, you don't need
this at all!

But there might be a
few ideas we can use to
make things a bit easier,
but you are a <u>NATURAL</u>!!

all my love,

Aud.
x

The Fabulous Mum's Handbook

Grace Saunders has worked in fashion for many years, first as press officer and buyer for Whistles, then as a fashion journalist at *Elle*. She is now a freelance writer who regularly contributes to a huge range of national papers, as well as leading women's and parenting magazines. She lives in London with her husband and two children.

The Fabulous Mum's Handbook includes contributions from:

Jane Clarke on nutrition

Fiona Allen on exercise

Dr Tanya Byron on sleep

Gayle Rinkoff on style

Amanda Smith on home and living space

Camilla Palmer on work-life balance

Paula Hall on sex and relationships

The Fabulous Mum's Handbook

GRACE SAUNDERS

C

CENTURY · LONDON

Published in the United Kingdom in 2007 by Century

3 5 7 9 10 8 6 4

Copyright © Grace Saunders 2007

The right of Grace Saunders to be identified as the author of this work has been asserted by her in accordance with the Copyright, Designs and Patents Act, 1988

The information in this book has been compiled by way of general guidance in relation to the specific subjects addressed, but is not a substitute and not to be relied on for medical, healthcare, pharmaceutical or other professional advice on specific circumstances and in specific locations. Please consult your GP before changing, stopping or starting any medical treatment. So far as the author is aware the information given is correct and up to date as at February 2007. Practice, laws and regulations all change, and the reader should obtain up-to-date professional advice on any such issues. The author and publishers disclaim, as far as the law allows, any liability arising directly or indirectly from the use, or misuse, of the information contained in this book.

Century
The Random House Group Limited
20 Vauxhall Bridge Road, London, SW1V 2SA

Random House Australia (Pty) Limited
20 Alfred Street, Milsons Point, Sydney, New South Wales 2061, Australia

Random House New Zealand Limited
18 Poland Road, Glenfield,
Auckland 10, New Zealand

Random House (Pty) Limited
Isle of Houghton, Corner of Boundary Road & Carse O'Gowrie,
Houghton 2198, South Africa

Random House Publishers India Private Limited
301 World Trade Tower, Hotel Intercontinental Grand Complex,
Barakhamba Lane, New Delhi 110 001, India

The Random House Group Limited Reg. No. 954009
www.randomhouse.co.uk

A CIP catalogue record for this book is available from the British Library

Papers used by Random House are natural, recyclable products made from wood grown in sustainable forests. The manufacturing processes conform to the environmental regulations of the country of origin.

ISBN 9781846050435

Typeset by Palimpsest Book Production Ltd, Grangemouth, Stirlingshire
Printed and bound in Germany by GGP Media GmbH, Pößneck

To my lovely man, Michael.

Contents

Before It All Begins . . .

Remember this? You're thirty-six weeks pregnant, wandering around in search of the perfect buggy. You try (with the luck of a hippopotamus in a china shop) to avoid crashing your expanding tummy into all the other wandering bumps. You fantasise about the romance of it all, think about little Charlie (or Sam?) asleep on his sheepskin and snuggling angelic Scarlet tightly at your bosom in a denim Baby Björn papoose (loaned from your best friend). Your main worry at this point is how to possibly cram all fourteen hours' sleep (which are absolutely necessary for you to function as a blooming pregnant lady, of course) into your twenty-four-hour day, which Cadbury's chocolate selection to consume while flicking through *Grazia* magazine on a Saturday afternoon, and which sleeping routine (Ford, Leech or Hogg) will fit you best.

You may not be having riotous sex, but your partner regularly showers you with compliments about your 'radiance'. He cooks the occasional feast and knows where the Hoover lives. You book your favourite Italian on a Saturday night, treat yourself to a glass of house white wine and stay up way past your 10 p.m. watershed – let's face it, you know you can lie in with the Sunday papers and doze away the best part of the day. In all, top of the priority list is 'you' time – the odd trip to the local pool, the last-minute bikini wax, a good girlie natter with girlfriends (one builder's tea and a custard cream) and, of course, retail therapy (even if it is just window-shopping with a quick peep into the bookshop to leaf through baby names books).

This is how I remember it, anyway. Call mine rose-tinted glasses, but my memories of the pre-baby build-up are up there on a pedestal with my pre-graduation memories of Germaine Greer and Naomi Wolf: revolutionary, untouchable, sacred – and downright naïve. One minute, I am longingly staring at my twenty-week-scan picture for the fiftieth time that day (wondering in all sanity whether it's possible to get it tattooed to my left buttock). The next, I am looking at myself in the bathroom mirror at 5 a.m., horror in my eyes. I am a mother, I have given birth, and I'm in rapture, but I'm also grey-faced, bleary-eyed, two stone overweight, with milk and blood and exhaustion seeping from every orifice.

Cut to a few weeks later and I find myself asking myself, Where has my groove gone? And how the hell do I get it back? The weeks roll into months and my sleep quota rises slowly from zero hours per night to six – if I'm lucky. I learn to function, with my five-month-old sleeping safely snuggled between husband and me during the night and suckling from my 38E breasts during the day. I can only just about spell s-e-x I'm so exhausted, let alone think about engaging in it. My young, free and childless girlfriends call less and less, because they'd rather talk big nights, romantic weekends away and designer frocks (which incidentally might cost double what I spent on the buggy). All I can think about is whether I've sterilised the breast pump, whether to bin or worship Gina Ford, and what on earth I can wear because my size-sixteen drawstring trousers have died from overuse.

It's now three and a half years on. I not only have a wonderful and remarkably well-adjusted toddler (bar the occasional full-scale tantrum about wearing that Cinderella costume and clip-clop fairy shoes to Tesco), but I have also managed to balance a career of sorts, marriage, girlfriends, a scattering of holidays, Saturday nights out (yes, without the children!) and, somewhere in the middle of all this, a second child. Of course, I've had endless sleepless nights, many 'fat' days, weeks when I feel my house is not a home but an indoor play area and certainly hundreds of 'If I add one more thing to my "to-do" list, I will scream!' but I've also managed to salvage some of my identity and boost my self-esteem whilst I was at it. And what came out of all this is *The Fabulous Mum's Handbook*, a survival guide to making this parenting lark work and keeping wits, groove and sanity close by.

I began this journey by scrutinising my own mothering experience, the ups, the downs, the hurdles of balancing my role of mum with that of wife, friend, daughter, sister, colleague and self. I talked endlessly with my fellow mums (friends, neighbours, the mother sitting next to me at the sandpit, or behind me at the Waitrose checkout), and I sought out the advice of 'gurus' on all the topics close to our hearts, like eating right, exercising, making your relationships work, decluttering your house and wardrobe and going back to work. So it ended up truly being a book by mums for mums, and it's meant to be for *every* mum, whether you are new at all this or have screaming toddlers in tow, whether you believe in routine or laissez-faire, whether you just want a specific piece of hands-on advice to dip into or need all the details down to the last gory bit.

I don't think the 'have-it-all' mums would benefit hugely (you know the type, size-eight waist, a designer £800 buggy, fleet of nannies, cleaners and housekeepers tagging closely behind her and a blow-dry/manicure/pedicure and Botox to boot!); I think it's for those of us in need of simple, practical and attainable advice on how to cope as a parent, on being a (reasonably) good mum without losing our sense of self, our groove, humour, passion. And how to squeeze in a morsel of 'me' time amidst all of this.

Being a mum is a life-changing and life-enhancing experience, but it's also an incredibly overwhelming one. It's crucial for us mums to think about ourselves and to find that balance of adapting to a new life while retaining bits of our old identity. To give your life an overhaul, to pinpoint what it is that isn't quite working and to turn things around can sound like an overwhelming task, but with only a little effort and some commitment, I promise you can get some of your old life back, you can feel good in your skin and can start to feel truly fabulous.

Eat Well

Food and Pregnancy

Yes, there are some of those super-sensible women around, probably among your friends as well, whose pregnancy diets make Gillian McKeith's programme pale in comparison. An ultra-healthy nutrition plan, heaps of carefully selected vitamins and a teetotal approach to alcohol are their holy grail. I know more new mums than I can count who swear by excess broccoli, tons of folic-acid tablets and minimum passive-smoke inhalation for months (sometimes even years) prior to conception and carry on similarly during their pregnancy.

I'd like to say I was a wise mother owl and did the same, but that would be a not-so-small white lie!

We hadn't been actively trying to get pregnant when the stork decided to pay a visit. I'd been married for five months, and my husband and I were having a ball. We'd spent New Year in New York, redecorated our flat and finally got to unpack all those 'grown-up' wedding gifts – such as a real, not Ikea cutlery set, garden lanterns and blown-glass cake stand with matching candlesticks. We had nights out with friends, busy work schedules and romantic rendezvouses with one another.

Although we discussed kids a lot (would we call a girl Ruby or Rose? Would a boy have my husband's eyelashes?), generally the idea of becoming parents went no further than these lazy-Sunday-morning fantasies. As a whole, we felt like a lot of newly-weds in their mid-twenties: that it was too soon to start a family, and that we both still had a lot of living to do without a child in tow. A few glasses of my favourite rosé wine, a supper finished off with rich choco-late cake and truffles, and one steamy night in the country later and all that changed . . .

It wasn't, however, until some time into my pregnancy that I realised that my growing bump wasn't over-indulgence and a need for some extra sit-ups, but a beautiful daughter getting ready to rock our world. During those blissfully igno-rant few weeks, I kept up with our hectic and full life – socialising, eating out and generally working and playing to the max. Once I realised what was going on (I know, I know, but I just wasn't looking for it), my maternal instincts came tumbling down on me like a ton of bricks. I headed straight for the best health-food store I could find and shopped until I dropped! Overwhelmed and surprised though I was at the news of my unexpected pregnancy, I also truly felt that we had been blessed. I wasn't going to turn into a nutritional Mother Teresa overnight, but I was going to make damn sure that I gave this baby the best possible start in life. I felt guilty for those 'lost weeks', when I was carrying a tiny seedling of a baby and hadn't watched every mouthful (and glassful!) I consumed.

Well, I may have changed the quality of my diet, but in terms of quantity, I have to confess I did eat like a horse. Some of it, believe me, I regretted nine months later, when

I had to shift the extra weight, but the food I ate, well, most of it anyway, was nutritious and somehow gave me a feeling of satisfaction to have given the baby plenty to feed off. Leaving celebrities who stay slim throughout pregnancy aside (and, boy, don't they drive you crazy?), I don't think pregnancy should be a time for denial. It's mad to deprive yourself and your unborn child of nutrients just because you hate to see your upper arms wobble. An extra 200–400 calories a day was the gauge my midwife gave me, but if you have slightly more, don't beat yourself up either.

I found it really helpful to write down a rough eating and supplement plan that worked for me and gave me a sense of confidence in my ability to nurture this unborn child. Of course, I stuffed myself with cream cakes on occasion and ate a curry if I fancied it, but all in all, I tried to balance it out with a reasonably healthy eating structure. It was as much to fuel the baby as to keep my energy and the initial nausea levels in check as well. Here are some handy tips to bear in mind:

Take a good multi-vitamin

While you're trying to conceive, or as soon as you know you're pregnant, take a daily multi-vitamin with folic acid designed for pregnant women. I remember panicking when I found out I was already nine weeks pregnant and had failed the first crucial step in motherhood, taking folic acid. Bad mother strike one! Luckily for me, Jenny, a fellow *Elle* journalist at the time (and also known as one of the world's most hands-on mums) took the time to chill me out. During an extra-long lunch break, she took me to a huge organic health-food store nearby. Like a true earth mother, she stacked my basket with every tincture, tonic, pill and herb going.

That might have been going rather overboard and left me feeling slightly like a white witch (or an organic gardener at the very least), but at least I was reassured that I could start to give my baby a good dose of vitality in the womb. Once I began to look at the supplement market as a whole, I found that commercial chemists' pregnancy vitamins didn't have nearly as many essential ingredients as those bought at a good health-food shop. You don't need to go mad and stock up on every vitamin-booster on the shelf, as Jenny and I did; just make sure you look out for an all-encompassing multi-vitamin. Top natural pregnancy practitioner Zita West (and personal adviser to the likes of Kate Winslet) has a brilliant new range of 'Vital Essence' supplements designed specifically for pregnant women. And for all of us who hate to get the bus when suffering from the worst morning sickness known to womankind, they are available on the Internet (www.zitawest.com). The range is split into three essences, one for each trimester, and is packed with all the ingredients and benefits a new mum could need. Biotin (beneficial for the division of foetal cells), vitamin C (necessary for the absorption of iron) and magnesium (essential for energy production) are just some of the components. I know pregnancy vitamins can be pricey, but investing in a good brand is so vital it's worth cutting back elsewhere, if you can. (Just think of the money you'll save on alcohol and nights out!) It's also worth finding a multi-vitamin that can carry you through to lactation and those early months. Just like pregnancy, nursing a newborn demands a boost in vitamins and energy.

Foods to avoid

It can be a pain having to check the side of packets and order 'off menu' at your favourite fish restaurant, but some key foods are known to be potentially harmful to the unborn so it's good to be aware:

- **Liver and liver pâté.** These contain high quantities of vitamin A, which can cause deformities in babies. Pâté could also contain listeria, which can lead to miscarriage, stillbirth or premature delivery.
- **Caffeine.** Keep consumption moderate. It's a stimulant that gets your heart racing and so will do exactly the same to your unborn. (A speeding baby? No thanks!) A coffee a day isn't against the laws of pregnancy, but don't go mad. Most mums I know retched at the mere whiff of a cappuccino, anyway, but if you're among the lucky mums not plagued by nausea and strong smells, I would probably still abstain from that third extra-strong latte mid-morning.
- **Unpasturised soft cheese and cheese made from raw milk.** Brie, Camembert, Stilton, goat's cheese and Parmesan (deceiving because although it is a hard cheese, it's still unpasteurised) can all encourage the growth of bacteria, which can pass through the placenta to the baby. (Gosh, how I drooled over melted-Brie sandwiches in my pregnancy, if only for one small bite . . .)
- **Raw eggs and fresh mayonnaise.** Salmonella is the key risk here (it can cause severe sickness and diarrhoea), so just make sure all eggs are cooked well and check the ingredients on salad dressings, sauces and puddings. It's

worth consulting the waiter about ingredients if you're eating out.

- **Shellfish.** Shellfish are such a common cause of food poisoning that it's worth abstaining for nine months. (My first request after giving birth was for a pint of prawns. Not a good idea in an overcrowded, hot ward!) It's advisable to go easy on tuna, swordfish and marlin too, as they contain high levels of mercury. My nutritionally informed midwife advised two cans of tinned tuna a week as a maximum limit. Avoid sushi too (horrific, I know!).

The battle against nausea

If you get the kind of morning sickness I did, you may be wondering why it's called 'morning sickness' at all. 'Twenty-four-hour sickness' would seem more apt. Although I wouldn't dare say I know a way to alleviate it entirely, I do know many women who have found ginger, in any form, helpful. (My friend Lyn even slept with a stem of ginger beside her pillow!) I shaved fresh ginger into hot water, drank alcohol-free ginger beer (ice-cold) and blended up carrot, apple and ginger smoothies whenever I had the energy. I also found that by including extra vitamin B6 in my diet (nuts, poultry, fish, bananas and whole grains), it somewhat helped the constant feeling of sickness. Depending on the severity, you could even discuss with your doctor the possibility of taking a B6 supplement. These tips may not get you running around like a fabulous, sick-free mum, but they should help ease the nausea a little.

Keep it fresh

I know first-hand that during the initial three months what you fancy least is a bowl of steamed greens. All I felt like eating in my first trimester was cold gazpacho, baked beans, ice cream and peanut butter, sometimes all at once. (Make sense of that if you will!) Anything else made me feel sick as a dog, and even the thought of a lettuce leaf turned me a distinct shade of green. Saying that, I did manage to slurp my way through copious amounts of fruit smoothies and was certainly partial to a bowl of sugar-snap peas (with a dash of sesame oil and a sprinkling of sesame seeds) with my evening meal. Whether you feel nauseous or not, it's a good idea to try to get fruit and veg into your diet some-where, even if it's eating the same old carrot sticks with hummus day in, day out because that's all you can stomach (as my friend Sara did, until she turned a distinct shade of orange!). Once the sickness period has passed, you may find it easier to reach for the fresh produce. Fruit and vegetables are so packed with vitamins and minerals (and for those who suffer pregnancy constipation, they can do wonders in keeping you regular) that they are worth incorporating or hiding in other food wherever possible. Be inventive: avocado and banana on an oatcake, tropical-fruit smoothies, papaya and raspberries with a dollop of crème fraîche, broccoli and mangetout topped with melted cheese, or sliced tomato and mozzarella with a sprinkling of fresh basil and olive oil were some of my firm favourites and helped keep my intake of fresh goodies up. If you can afford the cost, keep it organic: the benefits of no pesticides go without saying, but no need to get completely obsessed . . .

If you're going to feast keep it healthy(ish)

It's all fair and well to advise women to 'eat healthily during pregnancy', but if you have a raging hunger that makes a dozen pancakes seem like a mere mini-snack, then it's a hard line to follow religiously. Let's face it, for many women, pregnancy is the one time when we can really go for it and indulge in a fry-up, followed by a whole apple crumble and a king-size Snickers bar whenever we choose. The trick is to have a little of what you love and a lot of what's good for you. It's an old myth that you should eat for two, and it's one that may get you into an awful lot of weight trouble. Don't deny yourself a triple-cheese deep-pan pizza (and make that a large), but try not to eat one every single evening. Don't bin the multi-pack of Cadbury's Flakes, but eat one after lunch, not the whole lot before breakfast. The key is to eat a balanced diet of everything – fruit, vegetables, complex carbohydrates and protein – drink lots of water and save the sugary snacks and refined white carbs for a treat. It will help you control your weight gain, but also keep energy levels constant (and this is even more important when you've got other children to look after). Go on, eat a buttered bagel piled high with bacon, if you fancy it, but make sure you have a good salad, some cottage cheese and an apple with it. Have that bag of crisps, but eat it with a vegetable couscous and some grated carrot and raisin salad, and if you fancy fish and chips, go for salmon (or another fish high in omega-3 oils – great for an unborn's brain development), baked potato and a heap of fresh garden peas. I'm a prize example in pregnancy of enjoying my share of yummy treats, but I also made my main meals pretty healthy. Mums, it's all about balance!

Little and often

Luckily for me, during my second pregnancy, one of my best friends (who happened to be a colleague too) and I were pregnant at the same time (Paula with twin girls!). At twelve weeks pregnant, we both confessed that we were often close to fainting prior to lunch – not a good look when it's face down on your laptop while in a meeting with a chief executive. It was then that we realised the importance of little and often. No longer could we run on reserve energy stores and wait until way past two o'clock for lunch, or have a hectic morning of meetings and appointments without a snack in sight. As well as the normal three meals a day, we also had to carry snacks for mid-morning and mid-afternoon (and sometimes in between these as well!). After arriving for a pre-natal scan ashen-white and shaking, my robust Scottish midwife advised me to 'carry a banana at all times, my dear girl'. And that is exactly what I did (that and nuts, dried brown apricots, coconut shavings and some Cadbury's Rolos!). Every time I felt hunger strike, I'd grab a quick fix and it would perk me up until the next meal. Bar the Rolos, I also found that it prevented me from grabbing a huge bag of Kettle Chips on the Underground when my tummy rumbled. Once Paula got towards the end of her pregnancy, she found that her bulge was so huge the little-and-often rule was even more essential. There simply wasn't room for a big meal any more, plus they gave her indigestion and kept her up all night, so eating lots of small meals worked wonders all round.

Booze, fags and the rest

There is so much conflicting advice about drinking in pregnancy that it's hard to know what line to follow. Some camps argue that a few glasses now and then won't hurt either you or the baby; others advocate complete abstinence throughout. My view is simple: smoking and drugs are definitely a big no-no in pregnancy; there is no doubt that even the odd cigarette harms the unborn child. Drinking in excess, too, is harmful (and new research suggests that even in moderation it can be damaging), but the choice to have the odd tipple (and by this I mean one glass of wine or half a pint of Guinness every so often with a nice meal) must be left to the mother.

The ideal is to abstain completely, and to be honest, alcohol actually made me pretty nauseous (not to mention weary), but I was pleased to have the occasional sips to mark out a special occasion. (I enjoyed a glass of champagne at a wedding, a glass of red wine on my birthday and one cold white-wine spritzer at a summer picnic.) My great friend Lyn drank half a pint of Guinness every six weeks throughout her pregnancy (it must be in her Irish blood) and swore blind it was a good iron-boosting tonic (with the added bonus of making her feel human again), so sometimes the odd drink can do wonders for a mum's soul. I'm not a health professional, obviously, so you must judge for yourself, but be sensible and mature, and remember, having to be good with booze won't last for ever!

It doesn't take an expert to work out that eating well and looking after yourself in pregnancy are crucial to a healthy baby, a healthy mother and being a fabulous mum throughout the early years of motherhood. I'm the first to admit I over-indulged in Ben & Jerry's vanilla ice cream and my best friend Katie's homemade chocolate-chip cookies on a regular basis. By and large, though, there were some golden rules I tried to follow wherever possible; I wasn't a stick-thin Donna Air lookalike in either pregnancy, but I knew I was doing the best for my baby and the best for me, most of the time at least!

Mother knows best

'With my first pregnancy, I went absolutely bonkers in terms of eating. I had always been on some sort of crazy diet and I felt pregnancy was a great excuse to indulge in all those 'forbidden foods'. I'd get up and eat four croissants, have a bumper sandwich and two chocolate bars for lunch and get a takeaway almost every night. The weight piled on. By the time Alice was born, I had put on four stone and I was really down in the dumps. The excess weight affected my mood and I started to feel depressed. It took me over two years to get back to my pre-pregnancy weight and a good state of mind. Now I'm pregnant again, I'm going to do it very differently this time. I've begun eating healthily and I'm sticking to whole grains, lentils, protein, oily fish and tons of fresh goodies. I'm never hungry and the weight gain is steady. I only wish I'd been this informed and disciplined the first time round.'

Lisa Lewis, shop assistant and mother to Alice (two)

Breastfeeding Hunger

Is there a mutual consensus amongst existing mothers to omit breastfeeding hunger from their parenting repertoire? When you're pregnant, fellow mums can't tell you enough about what to eat, what not to eat, what your specific cravings mean and exactly how to make a triple-chocolate sundae to gobble while you're up with the munchies at three in the morning. What they forget to tell you is how unbelievably hungry you get when you're breastfeeding. Pregnancy hunger is like a minor snack attack in comparison with the raging prehistoric dinosaur growling in your stomach when you're breastfeeding.

It first strikes when you're in hospital, just after giving birth. Any clued-up new mum will remember to take a separate hospital bag for her snacks alone. If you're lucky enough to be giving birth at a top private hospital, then I'm sure demand for caviar and Belgian chocolates will be catered for at any hour, but for the rest of us, hospital food leaves a lot to be desired. Even if the main meals are OK (but believe me, after one of those soggy Yorkshire puddings, I was ready to call and plead in person with Jamie Oliver to tackle NHS food), you are likely to be hungry in between meals. It's very hard to ask the nurse for a Jaffa Cake from your bedside at midnight, when family and friends aren't there to pop over to the local corner shop. After the Yorkshire-pudding incident, I made sure I had a good supply of food and snacks I loved and I knew would give me good energy stores. Brazil nuts, plain slightly salted popcorn, ripe peaches, raisins and oatcakes all proved to be winners for easy bedside access.

My sister-in-law Jo was even known to send her obliging mother to Marks & Spencer for the odd fresh salad, smoked-salmon bagel and fresh raspberry mousse (and that's before she put in her order for piping-hot homemade chicken soup).

Once I got home and the breastfeeding became more frequent (ten-minute feeds became half-hour feeds and sometimes it felt I was feeding more than the child was sleeping!), the hunger increased hundredfold. When you're not sleeping much at night, you're burning off far more calories just by being awake. Combine this with the fact that with every feed you burn off up to 300 calories, and you're left with one truly hungry mamma! For some reason, I found this to be even more apparent in the middle of the night. Just like in pregnancy, when I'd stashed some dry snacks by the bed for a 5 a.m. tummy rumble, the same applied for breastfeeding. My friend Catherine actually arrived one night just to give me a night-hunger bumper-pack of Jacob's Crackers. The last thing you want when breastfeeding is to traipse downstairs to the fridge when you'll be up again in a few hours. I'll never forget my sweet and ever-obliging lovely man getting up after only three hours' sleep to make me Marmite on rye toast and cutting it into squares (bless!). Without it, I doubt I would have been equipped for the next feed.

I learnt very quickly that the hungrier the baby got, the hungrier I got. Producing all that milk is hard work! Second time round, once you're running after a toddler as well, you need all the energy you can get. The irony is, you really need the most nutritious, home-cooked food to build you up and help produce rich breast milk, but this is when you have the least time in the world to do it. Try cooking a wholesome casserole with multi-grain rice and fresh-fruit compote whilst breastfeeding a starving baby and reading a book to an eighteen-month-old. The words 'impossible' and 'you're having a laugh' spring to mind!

This is where good planning and obliging friends and family come into play. The best advice I got from my pre-natal yoga teacher, Lolly Stirk, was to put aside a little time before the birth to cook meals that could be frozen. I cannot tell you how thankful I was for this pearl of wisdom. The last few days are a time when you feel housebound and slug-gish anyway, so what better way to use your nesting impulses than to cook for the weeks to come. Even just making extra portions of your evening meal would be helpful. Freeze it in one-portion meals and it will save you time and energy later. It's also a good time to stock up on your favourite dry snacks before birth. Don't go into war mode and buy up all the tins of baked beans on the shelf, but do buy slightly more than normal, especially of things like nuts and seeds. The last thing you want is to be trekking to the shops on day two of motherhood, when you feel like a zombie.

I built on Lolly's advice and realised that equally important is to enlist the help of well-wishers, close family and friends. Often, people will phone before a visit asking, 'Is there anything I can bring?' Instead of saying a polite 'No, thanks' (prompting them to come armed with a potted plant and some pink helium balloons), ask if they could make you a small something to eat. Obviously, there's no need to ask every Tom, Dick and Harry who rings to wish you well, but good friends and family will happily cook up a spaghetti bolognese or pick up your favourite quiche en route. After my first birth, an old colleague came over with her son. Sally had had a Caesarean the year before and remembered how even the simplest jobs can seem like a huge challenge during those first couple of weeks. She came armed with flowers (already arranged in a vase; one job saved), homemade flapjacks, a heap of fresh organic fruit and my favourite hard-to-buy American muesli. (The fact that her toddler had bitten big chunks out of the apples already was by the by; it was the thoughtful gesture that counted!) Flowers and pressies are lovely, but a few home-cooked meals are probably just as warmly received.

The snag about breastfeeding hunger is that it's never quite straightforward. You're hungry, you eat, therefore all is well and happy. Of course not, when is being a mother ever that simple? I found this out the hard way. While encountering my night hunger in hospital, I happily ate my way through a bag of dried apricots, a big bunch of green seedless grapes and four bananas. The result was a baby with serious wind and stomach cramps and a scream that had the whole ward after my expulsion. Some mums can eat pretty much anything with no ill effects; I'm afraid I (and 95 per cent of my gal pals) am not one of them. There is no hard and fast rule, so the best thing is not to omit all fresh food straight off, but work on a process of elimination. I kept a food diary and worked backwards from a bad night with the baby to see what the culprit may have been. Apart from the initial apricot-and-grape blowout, I ate pretty much freely, but in moderation. If I thought a food was too acidic (e.g. oranges, grapes, cherries and wine) or too spicy (e.g. hot curries and sauces), I'd eat a little of it and see what the reaction was. I was told by numerous mums that Thai food was off limits, but happily indulged in a good Thai seafood stir-fry at least once a week with no ill effects. However, grapes, which went down well with some mums, when filtered through to my babies' milk played havoc with their bowels. Just use your common sense, and when you know a food can cause upset, leave it out of your diet until you've finished breastfeeding.

Once you've established more of a rhythm with the baby, the overwhelming hunger does subside, but I found I still needed a few extra calories until I was done with breast-feeding. The brilliant thing is that all this suckling helps you lose a lot of your baby weight. Don't be fooled by the celebrity mums of this world who claim that breastfeeding alone had them back in their size-six jeans days after giving birth, but if you do it for a good period of time, it will help with a large proportion of the weight loss. Although many women find they hold a little extra weight on the upper body until the very last feed (me included), this should disappear pretty quickly once you finish completely. Well, as long as you don't substitute the extra calories burnt through breastfeeding with cream teas and lashings of custard on every dessert . . .

Mother knows best

'When I was breastfeeding my twins, I found I was ravenous twenty-four hours a day. I could no longer wait for my usual three big meals a day and just had to eat six small meals to keep up with the pace of my new mummy life. It was a cold winter so I asked my mum to make a batch of clear chicken soup (for mid-morning) and a hot, thick vegetable soup (for mid-afternoon). These were a lifesaver. I found eating a good protein lunch was also a brilliant way of staving off hunger and stopping me from snacking on fattening foods. A firm favourite was salmon or chicken with a quick, easy brown-rice salad. By the time my twins were weaned, I'd lost all my baby weight and more. Quick, small, nutritious meals throughout the day are the only way to go!'

Lydia Barker, portrait photographer and mother to Casper (one) and Lilac (one)

SOS Food Rescue

Let me ask you this: how often have you been famished, on the move, miles from a health-food store or fruiterer and therefore reaching for a bag of salt-and-vinegar crisps or a Mars bar? I'd estimate it would be way more than we'd like to admit. I remember only last week being out on a day trip with the kids at a petting farm. We'd left at the crack of dawn (hey, we were all up by 6.49 a.m., anyway), and before even reaching the motorway, the kids had finished all the mini-boxes of raisins, oatcakes and chopped grapes I'd stashed in the nappy bag for emergencies (and, I might add, my energy snacks as well as theirs). By the time we'd reached the horse paddock, it started to feel like a very long time since breakfast (which, in case you're interested, had been at 7.04 a.m.!). Luckily, the children were screeching so much at the excitement of stroking a real horse that no one heard my stomach rumbling like a Tyrannosaurus rex. Looking around, I realised that to fill this hunger attack, I had three choices; horse pellets, Mr Whippy ice cream or a large Kit Kat from the low-on-stock vending machine. A healthy way to satisfy an energy slump? I think not.

This anecdote reminds me of at least a hundred similar situations in the last year. First off, every day of the 365 days of the year, you're up and at 'em by eight o'clock in the morning at the very latest. No preserving energy with lie-ins, sleeping until noon, siestas or a lazy weekend in bed. Secondly, you're constantly on the run, burning energy (usually armed with the kids, their football kits, school bags and your briefcase). Thirdly, you're probably cooking for and feeding your brood for a large portion of the day, so it goes without saying that your own nutritional needs can go by the wayside while you dish up the third round of Marmite toast, fish fingers, fromage frais, fruit smoothies and chicken casserole, feeling like a dinner lady on a twenty-four-hour shift!

More often than not, darting between roles and responsibilities, you run very low on energy, often without noticing. If you're not prepared, the only answer will be an instant Mr Whippy fix or the guilt-ridden consumption of two large Kit Kats (washed down with a bottle of Coke). Not only does this give you a false burst of sugar-fuelled energy (followed inevitably by an almighty crash), it also firmly cements those extra pounds that haven't left your thighs since the birth of your firstborn. The only good thing about a sugar-laden mid-morning treat is that for those thirty-six seconds it takes to chew it, it tastes like heaven. The bad thing is that this high is followed by three hours of feeling like your head is fitted with a pneumatic drill, a couple of hours feeling vaguely dissatisfied and still peckish, and three weeks of wishing your jeans fitted better. (That roll of extra 'skin' didn't come from drinking just Evian, now, did it?)

Let's face it, we need all the energy we can get to fuel a normal day's work for us fabulous mums: broken nights/key client meetings/endless school runs/kids' tea parties/conference calls and third attempts at potty training. Without sufficient energy for all of this, I find myself getting short-tempered, exhausted, ratty and reaching for the unhealthy rubbish that I know will do me far more harm than good. (Like the other day – up since 5.45 a.m. with a teething toddler, preparing for a meeting with a magazine editor at lunchtime, followed by the school play at dusk, so weary that I can hardly string a sentence together, and then have to wear dark glasses throughout my daughter's first ever performance of *Hansel and Gretel* to disguise the dark rings beneath my eyes.) With kids, there is never a let-up in responsibilities and duties, so the only way to keep your energy levels truly up is to eat well.

I don't want to start banging on about routines, rituals and a little bit of forward-planning, but structuring even a tiny amount of your approach to food will go a long way to feeling good and staying in shape. It certainly has helped me – goddess of the large Kit Kat – to keep my energy levels high and my weight low(ish). If I get up in the morning and just go with the flow, things always go awry. Before I know it, I've skipped breakfast because my youngest has thrown a wobbly mid-egg-scrambling, I'm fancying lunch while in a PTA meeting (and it's only 9.45 a.m.), and I find myself scoffing the kids' mini shepherd's pies at teatime (OK, and their peas, sweetcorn, ketchup and apple crumble with ice cream). All this leaves me stuffed and shattered by the time the children are in bed, when what I really deserve is a nice meal and some adult conversation (or a rerun of *Sex in the City* at the very least).

Eating breakfast is one of the most crucial things in all this. If you eat the right breakfast, it keeps blood sugar levels constant and will prevent a dip in energy (and a dip into the biscuit tin!). I am addicted to my morning ritual of breakfast with the children. I've managed to instil a tradition of us all sitting down round the kitchen table and eating first thing in the morning (and believe me, this sometimes means getting up fifteen minutes earlier than normal to get it ready and put the kettle on). Don't get me wrong, we're not a happy stereotype of a 1950s family, husband in a suit, me in my floral pinny, but usually my two toddlers and I sit for at least ten minutes to gobble something fortifying and hang out a bit before the day ahead. My good friend Jennie similarly insists on starting the day *en famille*, and manages, God knows how, to whip up a boiled egg and wholemeal soldiers most mornings. (Failing this, her toddler munches the egg in a sandwich en route to her grandma's.)

More and more mums I know try to avoid a lot of the sugar-loaded cereals for family breakfasts (things like Coco Pops, Sugar Puffs, Honey Cheerios – you know the culprits), they've had enough bad PR for us to realise you may as well give your family a double-chocolate muffin followed by a bag of boiled sweets for all the sugar and refined carbohydrates they contain!

24

Things like Weetabix, plain Shredded Wheat or porridge are brilliant as they are absorbed slowly into the bloodstream and therefore give steady energy levels for longer. I love to start the day with a hot drink, so accompany mine with green tea, which is low in caffeine (and I'm told helps burn calories, yippee!). I'm not generally anti-caffeine per se, but I always find that if I start the day with a caffeine fix, it's hard to sustain that artificial energy throughout the day, which often leads to a crash at around 10 a.m.

Preparing breakfast the night before makes the pre-school rush far easier and means you're not panicking about getting out through the door in time. It always helps to know I can just open the fridge, bung some of the fruit-salad batch I make twice a week into three bowls (four, if my husband hasn't already left before the milkman arrives) and add the muesli or porridge. Instant food *with* the goodness left in.

Once the day is in full swing, I always try to carry a snack or two for that eleven o'clock tummy rumble. Many of you may last until lunchtime, but with all the mad running around we do, it serves you well to be prepared in case that lunch stop seems as though it will never come. Call it my own hang-up from pregnancy or call it an overload of diets that claim 'eat healthily every three hours and stay slim', but I function better if I snack healthily mid-morning. Same for mid-afternoons: I find that by eating a light snack with the children at their suppertime – a bowl of fruit, a yoghurt with a handful of breakfast muesli, or a light, clear soup, for example – I stop myself licking their plates clean and polishing off any discarded Mini Milks and half-eaten rusks while cleaning up! My sister-in-law Jo calls her snacks 'mini-meals' and has been known to have a mini replica of lunch at around four o'clock to stave off the hunger monsters until her evening meal. Even if your kids eat with you later on, then it's worth you all sitting down for a mid-afternoon snack attack to pick up weary souls. My girlfriend Amy swears by oatcakes and hummus to tide her and the kids over until supper at eight o'clock.

Now, when I say snack, I don't mean things that begin with 'cream-and-jam-laden' and end with 'scone'. Along with my recipes at the end of the book, I've listed a whole host of quick, easy, good snacks that will boost your vitality and hopefully help prevent you from diving for the digestives. They are also easy handbag snacks and ones that you could share with your toddler. You wouldn't believe it, but my three-year-old actually turned down a biscuit for a bag of dried apricots and raisins the other day. (OK, so she had indulged in a mini muffin that same morning.)

If you approach both lunch- and suppertime with the same consistent attitude, you should be on the way to reaching good, steady energy levels day in, day out and seeing some of those pounds drop off. Trust me, skipping meals in an attempt to lose weight only backfires. My friend Jennie (who has a metabolism faster than the speed of light) and I always laugh about how strung out and anxious we get when we miss meals. We're almost positive our metabolism actually slows down to preserve fuel. Only last week she missed supper because she was working late, and the next morning, when her daughter woke before it was light, she said she felt like an old carpet that had been bashed up and hoovered the wrong way. Too shattered to get up and have breakfast prior to work, she had to scoff a huge almond croissant and slurped a takeaway full-fat hot chocolate (extra large, topped with whipped cream at that). We've all been there; you hope that a quick-fix carb hit might revive you, but instead, the excess sugar and carbohydrate just make you exhausted. Top this off with a 9.30 a.m. work deadline and you've really got the day off to the wrong start.

To complement healthy, set mealtimes, I often take something called Floradix (a multi-vitamin supplement made with herbs and natural produce that is packed with iron). You'd be surprised how often low energy levels can be down to a lack of iron. (My good friend Gayle actually calls Floradix the 'magic juice', so sure is she that it is possessed with magic energising properties!)

As you can see from my three good meals a day and snacks in between, I'm no fan of food denial. I'm definitely not a fad-diet person. (The thought of Weight Watchers sends me into a tizz, and just the idea of the Atkins Diet, and all the bad breath and egg-white omelettes it entails, brings me out into a sweat.) Again, I think the key is balance. Of course, we all have days off and consume half a bottle of chilled white wine, a large slice of banoffee pie and a Thornton's truffle, following the virtuous steamed salmon and asparagus. But I know if I start making these treats an acceptable part of every day, I'll not only have wavering levels of vitality but could well be on a slippery slope back to my pregnancy size-sixteen drawstring trousers!

In the end, I'm very much into treating my body and nutritional intake with respect, keeping my enthusiasm for life high and having a figure I can just about live with. And it's not all that hard to do if you keep a few easy nutritional rules in mind:

- **Friendly carbohydrates and sugars.** Whatever the 1990s Atkins Diet drilled into us, not all carbs are bad. Avoid refined white carbohydrates and sugars (except fruit sugars), which give you false energy levels and make you hungry all the time. (My friend Luella, for instance, was thrilled to discover her constant hunger wasn't due to tapeworm, but down to her weakness for croissants!) Easy options are wholemeal or soda bread instead of a white loaf and sticking to sweet potatoes, not white ones. Lentils, beans and root vegetables always get the thumbs up.
- **Friendly fats.** I don't know if it's just me, but I find all the jargon about unsaturated/good/bad/trans fats very confusing. Basically, I think you just need to bear in mind that processed fats (margarine) and unsaturated fats should be avoided. Head for the olive oils and fish oils (high in the brain-boosting omega-3 oils and found in salmon and mackerel); butter is fine as well, and avoid too much fatty red meat (bacon, burgers and sausages). It should go without saying that desserts and full-fat ice cream should only be eaten in moderation, too!
- **Superfoods.** This is a term I love. The so-called 'super-foods' have anti-aging and disease-fighting properties. (My mother-in-law was so sure of this claim that she even binned her blow-the-budget face cream and invested the cash in the delivery of organic superfoods instead.) Avocado, blueberries, broccoli, carrots, live yoghurt, garlic, oats, onions, hemp oil, sardines, prunes, spinach, nuts and seeds are all superfoods that I try to weave into our family's diet on a day-to-day basis. (No one leaves the table without clearing their plate of broccoli, and that means me too!)

- **Processed precaution.** Ready-made meals that you bung in the microwave may be an essential part of the working mum's weekly meal plan, but think about making them an exception, not the rule. They are packed with sugar, salt, flavourings and chemicals. I'm not saying all meals should be straight from the farmer's paddock, but staying as close to the source as possible is a golden rule for the nutritionally aware mum.
- **Water, water, water!** Ninety-nine per cent of all the models and celebrities I have ever interviewed swear that water is the key component in their great physique and glowing skin. With all this positive PR, I felt it almost obligatory to try to stick to one and a half litres a day myself. Although I get the occasional mega-spot, I'm positive I can thank water for my generally clear skin and a lot of my energy.

We all need foods that feed the mind, body and spirit. The right diet should give us the energy and confidence to deal with sleepless nights, establishing peace with siblings in the midst of World War III and a clear head for some adult conversation when you finally catch up with your partner or friends at the end of a long day. Eating irregularly and whatever is available at the local corner shop, Underground kiosk or church playgroup can lead to problems with levels of exhaustion, excess weight and self-esteem. It's not neurotic to stick to the five nutritional golden rules to structure your meals and do a little planning of menus. If it keeps you energised, your weight constant and your sanity intact, surely it's more like common sense?

Mother knows best

'With three children under five, I constantly felt shattered. I was often up in the night, and my eldest started
each day religiously at 5.30 a.m. I would be so busy
getting the kids up and out to nursery and school that
my first breakfast opportunity would be a coffee at mid-
morning. I soon learnt that caffeine filled an initial hole
but left me grumpy for the rest of the day. It may not
be the best solution, but my answer was to pack a mini-
breakfast the night before of a banana, dry muesli with
a heap of dried fruit and a bottle of fresh orange juice.
I now eat it between school drops and have binned my
ten o'clock caffeine fix. It's not ideal, but for now I feel
100 per cent better and the kids still get to school and
nursery on time.'

Jo Slater, full-time mother to Samson (five), Layla (three)
and Talia (one)

Party-food Temptation

Like so many things in pregnancy and childrearing, it often
feels that food is sent to test us (and our willpower) to the
limit. When my second child was seven months old, I puffed
my chest out with pride (think robin-redbreast-slash-yummy-
mummy). I had (I thought) managed to go through the tears,
the sickness, the joy and the eating of a second pregnancy

and breastfeeding and had still managed to get back into one of my favourite pair of jeans. A few stretch marks, a slightly wobbly tummy and undeniably saggier breasts aside, I could still be a fabulous mum (and next year's pop idol, should my calling arise) and I was immensely proud. I'd learnt the tricks of eating healthily and exercising during pregnancy, I'd breastfed my son for seven months, and I'd come out the other side still looking like a reasonably groovy chick. Yes, I know: I should have been more humble. Don't be fooled, fellow mums – as soon as you take your eye off the ball, another obstacle is sent to try us. Birthday parties.

You won't believe it, but by the time the first round of parties roll up – from baby-massage classes, NCT reunions and christenings – you'll realise the true meaning of mindless snacking. Call it 'party-food temptation', call it 'mini Smartie cup cakes with your name written all over them' or call it 'fondant fancies – oh, just one, then', whatever it is, the end result is the same: sugar overload and calorie oblivion. Just when you thought your weight had stabilised and you'd managed to shift the extra two inches from round your thighs, you can't turn round without being confronted with the most delicious, delectable, desirable and sweetened treats you've ever seen. Unless you are a health-food obsessive (no doubt serving bean sprouts, pulses and wheat-germ juice at your child's first birthday), you are sure to indulge at birthday parties. Of course, there is always the odd bowl of uninviting cherry tomatoes, but these often look like they've done the rounds of every party in your neighbourhood over the last six weeks, and are the only things left at 5 p.m. when guests leave. What children's parties usually consist of are a large array of iced cakes, mini muffins, sausages on sticks, cheese puffs and the sweetest iced Noddy cake you have ever tasted.

Now I have two sociable toddlers attending nursery (which comes with the unwritten rule that every child holding a birthday party invites the whole class), the invitations come in thick and fast. Not a week goes by without Lily's princess-themed bash, Theo's soft-play party or the twins', Marni and Sienna's, first-birthday gathering. Weekends are no longer a quiet flow of Sunday brunches, the weekend papers and teas with the in-laws, but consist of wrapping presents, negotiating with a three-year-old which fancy-dress outfit to wear and stuffing oneself on party food (and that's as well as a roast Sunday lunch!). Unless you are careful, most Monday mornings start off with an extra three pounds in weight and a deep feeling of regret at all the pink cup cakes devoured at Samson's Peter Pan party.

I suppose it's a little bit like Christmas Day. You start the festive period with all the willpower in the world. You vow that this year will be different and that you will stick to turkey breast (no gravy), a mound of veg and just one roast potato. You read endless 'How to stay slim for the New Year celebration' features and clue yourself up on how to veer towards the carrot sticks and low-fat dips, bypassing the tortilla chips and honey-roasted cashews on your way. The moment you drink your first bucks fizz at lunchtime, however, all these promises fly out of the window and you find yourself gobbling the third mince pie and asking for seconds of rich cream trifle (and don't even get me started on that tin of Quality Street!).

The same applies to children's parties. You psych yourself up with willpower, reciting the mantra 'I will avoid the Dolly Mixture, I will avoid the Dolly Mixture, I will avoid the Dolly Mixture'. You arrive and head straight for the other mums, standing well away from the elaborate array of pirate-shaped iced biscuits and Captain Hook crisps. But slowly and surely, as the afternoon progresses, you find your hand dipping into the sweetie bowl, nibbling on the sausage selection and finishing off the remains of the stolen-treasure jam sponge cake. You stop, rewind and pause at the moment you arrived. How could one hour thirteen minutes and a thousand calories later have crept up on you so quickly?

It's easy to see how we come a cropper at kids' parties. Prior to children, you would rarely find yourself tired, in need of a mid-afternoon energy lift and surrounded by sweet goodies fit for Willy Wonka's chocolate factory. Sunday-afternoon barbecues may have offered a chicken skewer or a coleslaw salad, but rarely would they have tempting quick-fix sugar-filled goodies like praline-dipped flapjacks. Add this to the fact that you're sitting surrounded by kids stuffing themselves with mini sausage rolls (they must know it's back to organic beef casserole and greens once the party's over!) and it's all just too much to resist.

Fed up with myself for giving in to the fifth sugary treat and cross that my clothes were getting tighter as the baby got older (shouldn't it be the other way round?), I worked out that I needed to eat *before* the treats. Too often I would be so busy gift-wrapping the latest Angelina Ballerina book, feeding my kids nutritious salmon fishcakes for lunch and taking my eldest swimming (all before the birthday bash at three o'clock) that I'd miss lunch completely, arrive at the party ravenous and dive into the first cheese straw I could see. I now vow to structure my day so that I make sure I eat something small prior to a party. If I sit down for three minutes and slurp a hot vegetable soup with a chunk of bread (or steal a kid's salmon fishcake with a heap of peas), I find the party food doesn't hold so much immediate appeal. I'll still let myself have the odd mouthful of cake, but I don't feel hungry enough to pile my plate high with snacks.

If your own individual approach fails, then think safety in numbers. Ask yourself and your fellow mums this: if party food gives us a headache, what does gorging on additives and sugar every other weekend do to our little angels (who are drawn to sweetness like moths to a flame)? My daughter ate so many mini Cornettos at a recent summer garden party that she almost began singing *The Marriage of Figaro* with an Italian accent. Blame it on all that anti-fast-food hype out there, put it down to the *Jamie's School Dinners* phenomenon or simply call it the 'we're sick of hyper kids syndrome', whatever name you give it, appetising, fun and healthy party food seems to be catching on almost as quickly as the latest Louis Vuitton bag.

My fellow mothers and I were so taken with the fabulous mum's healthy-snack approach (for parents and kids alike) that we now have a 50/50 rule at our parties. Whoever holds a kids' party must offer 50 per cent treat food and 50 per cent healthy options. I'd like to say we started primarily because we wanted the kids to eat as healthily as Moses Paltrow and Suri Cruise, but it was as much for the mums as anything else; helping us stay in shape and keeping the kids' diet on the safe side of the health barometer.

It was my daughter's friend Tom's fourth birthday last week (or should I say my daughter's 'boyfriend'? – her term not mine). What made a change on the party table was that in amongst the chocolate muffins, iced gems and marshmallows, there were watermelon slices in the shape of boats, strips of wholemeal pitta bread with cream cheese and pineapple dips, and bowls piled high with fresh berries sprinkled with icing sugar. Believe it or not (she says smugly), my kids dived into this first ('Mummy, pink boats,' exclaimed my son when he saw the watermelon), and I was quick to follow. My fellow mums and I all agreed (as we gathered our face-painted children at bedtime) that we felt a hell of a lot better about ourselves than the same time last year, when we had stuffed ourselves silly on gingerbread men and jelly beans. Add to this the fact that without the excess sugar, the children actually went to bed on time and we decided that healthy parties were easily the best option for fabulous mums and kids alike.

Mother knows best

'I started hating children's parties because of all the overeating they induced. The best party I ever went to was one in which the children were given an individual packed lunch each that contained sandwiches in the shape of hearts, an organic yoghurt, fruit and a couple of icing-sugar-dusted biscuits. We parents had a small selection of nuts, olives, fresh dips and a glass of wine – perfect! The kids were happy and didn't throw up on the way home, the party-givers were pleased to have less clearing up to do, and I was delighted to have a glass of plonk and a handful of olives as opposed to a tummy full of icing. Genius!'

Lyn Holland, film producer and mother to Archie (seven), Isabel (five) and Martha (three)

Food and Self-esteem

Like many other times in my life, the food I ate during pregnancy and my children's early years wasn't just because of varying hunger levels. If life were that simple, we'd live in a society filled with glowing size-ten women. Sadly, there's a whole host of emotional issues to make sure food isn't just about hunger and fuel. I've suffered from bouts of near-anorexia (seven and a half stone at five feet ten inches while studying for my finals at university), and I have eaten a whole chocolate cake because a boyfriend dumped me. In between, I've eaten for hunger, but also boredom, fun, intrigue, sadness and excitement.

Pregnancy and parenting food comes with even more emotion, baggage and misconceptions. During pregnancy, the myth of 'eating for two' combined with feelings of sickness, cravings and the desire to eat well for your unborn can make food a minefield, especially when you're also fielding all those overwhelming fears and emotions about becoming a mum. Once you've given birth, breastfeeding hunger, getting up in the night, overwhelming tiredness, post-natal feelings of depression or baby blues and the sometimes difficult recuperation after the birth can all throw your eating and hunger patterns into disarray. Plus, there's the fact that most women hardly recognise their body with the extra pregnancy weight hanging on for dear life. While some women claim to be glowing and *über*-confident, a lot of us (myself included) feel about as confident as a two-year-old on their first day at nursery. Initially, I opted to sit at home with my new baby (wearing stained tracksuit bottoms, of course) rather than go out socialising with other parents. And when your self-esteem is low, eating can become a lifesaver and a vicious circle. You feel fat and tired, so you grab a bag of crisps for comfort, you then feel even more fat and tired, so you grab a chocolate bar to give you a sugar rush and tell yourself, Who cares! Feeling even more fat and tired, you are left unhappy, frustrated, gobbling biscuits and well and truly un-fabulous.

I'll never forget the moment I realised my very own vicious circle. My firstborn was six weeks old. I had boobs the size of a blow-up doll, thighs too big to fit into even my 'bad-day' trousers and a face with what must have been the chins of three grown-ups moulded into one. My daughter was feeding round the clock, I was shattered beyond all belief, and the rain slashed against the window in typical April-showers fashion. I was too embarrassed and self-conscious to even consider attending the Thursday-afternoon mother and baby group. Instead of getting out of the house and walking off some of my extra weight, calling a fellow girlfriend for moral support or devising a nice lean vegetable and turkey stir-fry for supper, I sat down in front of daytime TV and consumed a packet of digestives. Don't tell me you've never done something similar. Even if digestives and GMTV aren't your vices, I'm sure reruns of *Neighbours* and a large packet of buttered popcorn would tempt you in that direction!

We see far too many pictures in the press of new-mum supermodels (running around to glamorous lunches, stick-thin and skin glowing), which piles on the guilt when you feel like a sack of spuds yourself. Many women stuck in the low-self-esteem rut feel as though they're the only mum on the planet unable to contemplate getting out and about to live life to the full. So, you may ask, how did I get away from the digestives, TV cookery shows and post-pregnancy self-doubt? Well, the first step was identifying that food had become a big culprit in my diminishing self-confidence. I'd gone from super-fabulous, super-slim, super-chic fashion editor (with stilettos for every day of the week) to biscuit-munching big mamma in a matter of months. By delving for unhealthy food every time I mourned this old me, I just made matters worse. How on earth was I going to really relish my six months' maternity leave if I ate every time I felt tired/bored/sad or just in need of food to accompany the afternoon feed and the copy of OK! that went with it?

I found that once I'd identified food as an expression of self-doubt and a way of easing the inevitable feeling of isolation and, perhaps, boredom that comes with having your first child, I could then tackle it like a grown-up, coming up with solutions that would help me eat well, feel well and look well. The first bad habit I had to knock on the head was the constant snacking that had become way too easy now that I was at home for large chunks of the day. My friend Catherine and I decided to tackle this together (safety in numbers and all that!). We'd actually given each other the nicknames of 'Chunky Kit Kat One' and 'Chunky Kit Kat Two' to illustrate our ability to consume our favourite chocolate snack! We made two decisions. One, these sweet treats should be an occasional but not staple part of our diet. Reducing the forbidden items (organic milk chocolate being the exception, I have to confess!) and replacing them with healthy snacks, rather than totally banning them, seemed doable and reasonably realistic. A little, but not too much, of what you love is good for the soul, don't you think? Two, when we craved food in between meals, we made it the rule to wait an extra half an hour. We all know there are a hundred things a new mum can do to take up a little time. Before we started out on our venture, we went through our cupboards and stocked them with food high in slow-release energy, so that's what was in reach, rather than the biscuit tin (which, incidentally, we didn't refill when it was empty). Making these conscious changes as a team works well; you feel less alone and, if all else fails, can have a good giggle about the lure of the Kit Kat!

If snacking isn't your downfall, then identify what is. Is it when you pick the kids up from school and head en masse straight to McDonald's? Is it when you get up at 3 a.m. to feed your youngest and eat your way through the bread bin? Or is it when the biscuits are passed around at the baby-massage group and you end up taking a dozen (in the pretence they are for a group of fellow mums)? Once you've worked out what the main culprit is, you can see how to change it. Instead of heading for the burger joint, how about having a picnic in the park? Or if you've got pizza cravings, how about using your own toppings? These can be very healthy, especially if you include low-fat cheese, fresh tomatoes, olives, mushrooms, sweetcorn, rocket and lean ham. As opposed to a midnight bread-bin attack, try a corn cake with low-fat cottage cheese and pineapple, or a glass of hot skimmed milk. As for raiding the baby-massage biscuit selection, have a banana at hand to fill you up instead; make a joke of it with your fellow mums and maybe the lust of hogging the Hobnobs will be marred by the humour of it all.

Once you go back to work or your children start socialising more, the possibilities for a constant snack-attack decrease. (Unless, that is, you have a biscuit tin under your desk or on the back of your buggy!) You might still feel confused about your new role and down about your appearance, so being focused with regard to food is still important. Eat well, keep your energy levels high and try to think of a tasty supper with your partner in the evening or, if you're a single mum, the company of a good book, friend or favourite TV show as a reward for staying on the right food track all day. There really is nothing better than tucking the children into bed, opening a bottle of white wine, grilling some mixed seafood with aubergine and sweet potato, and discussing the day with my husband. No kids, no TV, no rushed, unhealthy fish and chips, just a relaxed way to unwind at the end of a day. I always find that my self-confidence is higher and I feel better when I've managed to plan the meal well, enjoyed the preparation and sat down to eat it slowly. It makes you feel in control and strong, rather than helplessly giving in to your cravings.

To pick up your self-esteem, you need willpower, but also good friends. You need to go out of your way to find fellow mums you can share all these new experiences with (over a fruit salad and not a cream tea!). You need to laugh about the madness of it all, like Catherine and me about our Kit Kat obsession, and share experiences and solutions that may help you come through what can be a battle with weight and food. I know it can be almost impossible to see light at the end of the tunnel when the baby weight just won't shift and you haven't had a good night's sleep for what seems an eternity, but talk about it! My initial answer to the digestive-fuelled rut? Call a fellow mum who also shares an extra stone in weight, is partial to the bakery cake selection and makes you laugh until you cry. Moan with her, thrash out the 'unfairness of it all', share the problem and remind yourself that you are not alone. Then turn to that gorgeous new baby and cuddle the reason for all this food angst. With all this love, how can your self-esteem not be lifted just a little?

Mother knows best

'I was under the illusion that once I'd given birth to my first, I'd be in a social whirl of other mums and be busily nesting with my baby. No one prepared me for the loneliness of the initial few months. All my friends were at work, and I felt too tired to forge out and meet local mums. This left me isolated and down in the dumps and I turned to food for comfort. After six weeks, I had a meltdown and cried buckets to my mum. The tears just kept coming. My solution? I decided to try the GI diet (a diet that focuses on food with a low glycaemic index level, such as oatcakes, porridge and lentils) as I'd read so much about it and it seemed to suit my nutritional needs as a new single mum. I made it my mission to be disciplined and eat healthily. I told myself I could have sugary treats at teas with fellow mums but not when I was home alone. The weight really did start to fall off and this gave me the confidence to get out and about and make a new social group of fellow mothers. I'm still a stone heavier, but I don't really care. I feel better about taking action, and now I'm a busy bee, I'm loving my new role as mummy.'

Clare Carter, nursery-school teacher and mother to Lucinda (six months)

Working With Food, Not Against It

Prior to this new world of motherhood, it was probably rare for you to be home alone, left to cook for yourself. I know from my experience that I would have eaten breakfast on the move, had a working lunch (which could be anything from a sandwich at my desk to a posh meal with clients at some fancy London haunt), and supper would more often than not be a meal I'd throw together in six seconds flat. I've never been a big fan of ready meals, but I certainly wouldn't come in from work and embark on a lamb marinade or a slow-cook pot roast. It came as something of a surprise, then, to be at home with a new baby, left to my own devices and needing to think about three wholesome meals a day. I pride myself on being a pretty good cook, but when for a lot of the day you are eating alone (in between feeds, nappy changes, phone calls and the washing machine whirring the whites at 90 degrees), it can seem pretty redundant to cook up three-course culinary delights for you and you alone.

I'm sure any new mum has been victim to the endless Marmite-on-toast cycle. When you've got a newborn attached to your boob and no one else about, it's only too easy to survive on toast and little else. After my sixteenth day of toast variations (and believe me, by day twelve I'd thought of a list as long as my arm), I began to think that my approach to food during my maternity leave and beyond needed refreshing. Each meal had become a chore and a burden, and had started to feel like an extra hassle and one more thing 'to do' on a list of endless mundane tasks and mini-shops for wipes, nappy sacks, wholemeal bread, milk and tea bags. Time, I thought, to start working with food, not against it.

Even though my breakfast tends to be pretty much the same day in, day out, I try to vary it at weekends, when my husband is around to man the fort. Even if it's just scrambled egg with toast and some roasted Portobello mushrooms, or soda bread with cream cheese and a slither of smoked salmon, just the smell of it cooking now makes me feel that the weekend's here. I love nothing more at weekends than eating slowly, reading the papers and letting the kids fight over the last mini croissant without their mother standing over them with a stopwatch. (Well, not quite, but you get the early-morning pre-nursery-rush picture.)

Equally as important was forcing myself to focus on making lunch a little more inventive. Because I know the children will be in bed in the evening and I'll have the company of my husband, I used to neglect my lunch completely, resorting to toast on the go and a few slices of ham while passing the fridge. It may seem weird to sit down alone to eat something exciting, but treating yourself to a good meal does wonders for your self-esteem. Now, many a new mum will be hooting with laughter at this point. 'How the hell will I find the energy and time to cook up a Michelin-star meal for myself?' I hear you cry. Don't get me wrong, I'm not saying beef casserole followed by stewed rhubarb and homemade ice cream; I'm really suggesting just making the food look interesting and varying it from day to day. If you're going for a sandwich, how about making it an open sandwich on wholemeal pitta bread? You could just as easily bung some cherry tomatoes in the oven with a dash of olive oil, stuff the pitta with lettuce and the warm tomatoes and sprinkle some feta cheese on top. It will look appetising, be colourful and enticing on the plate, and taste delicious. Similarly, instead of pouring hot water on a Cup a Soup, make up a huge stash of gazpacho when you have an hour to spare, freeze it in portions and you're sorted for a yummy, feel-good summer lunch that will last you a good few weeks.

What I'm getting at is the need for us mums to use food as a reward and a pleasure, not a chore and a battle. If you serve up something colourful and tasty for yourself, not only will you get the energy you need, you'll also give yourself a pat on the back for treating yourself with a little respect and self-worth. If you've got toddlers at home for lunch, or have fellow mums popping in for a bite, then there's even more reason to sit down to eat something that looks and tastes good. My friend Sonia's famous mum-lunch special (tuna steaks, green beans and sweet-potato wedges) got such a reputation that she even had mothers she didn't know inviting themselves over so the 'kids could play during lunch'! If you're a working mum, that's no excuse to neglect food in order to keep up with the treadmill of work-parenting responsibilities. I know heaps of working mothers who sacrifice their lunch break to leave on the dot of five o'clock and be home in time to catch their children before bed. They stuff a sandwich in their mouths while typing away at their desks, and it's almost as if that midday meal is just another item on their 'to-do' list. It doesn't have to be quite like that. I know one mum who now insists on leaving the house five minutes earlier so she can pick up an organic salad and a fresh quiche from a local deli. This means she can guarantee a good lunch at her desk without the lunchtime rush (and I know for a fact that she dreams about the type of quiche she'll choose for the whole bus journey into work; she often calls me to discuss the choice). A solution perfected by my friend Elaine was to team up with all the other 'working-through-lunch mums' in her office and take it in turns to buy a nutritious lunch for all (courtesy of Joelle's fantastic organic deli seven minutes' walk from the office). There were seven mums in all, so in the end, they only had to leave the office for lunch once every seven working days, but all had a fortifying meal on a day-to-day basis.

I know only too well that it can seem impossible to keep your spark with food alive once you've had children. Especially if the weekly supermarket shop is done *with* them in tow, it can feel like a military conquest just to get round the aisles and through the checkout in one piece. I'll never forget my most recent expedition to Sainsbury's. My son insisted on wriggling free of the trolley straps and getting out while my back was turned; the only way to keep him in was to ply him with snacks. Well, if *he* was getting snacks, then my daughter had to have them too, and of course pulling hair and screeching at one another was undertaken before a compromise was made on exactly which snack suited all. By the time we had reached aisle twelve, I wasn't sure whether there was more in my trolley or in my children's stomachs and around their mouths!

So it's no wonder we just grab the groceries as if we're on automatic. For many of us, Internet shopping proves the easiest of all, but even if the weekly shop is an enormous teeth-gritting chore, maybe you can squeeze in a mini-shop alone later in the week. My good friend Jennie has sworn by it since giving birth: doing a weekly shop online, then nipping out to the local independent while her husband watches their daughter. She loves looking at produce, being able to unhurriedly select some good meat, some seasonal fruit in a variety of colours, maybe some fresh fish and a bunch of blooming orchids. Sure, take your kids along once a month (I know plenty of children who adore the whole market experience, and in fact, it's not a bad thing to refresh their interest in food, too), but you'll be amazed at how many foods you'd forgotten were out there when you have time to browse without a toddler tearing out chunks of your hair. (Pomegranate, sesame oil or roasted fennel anyone?)

If our only opportunity for building a relationship with food is the dash around the supermarket, the continual rotation of kids' meals and the half-hearted consumption of a limp sandwich at half past one, then no wonder it's a battle. I know it's hard to squeeze yet another responsibility into already jam-packed diaries, but I can't emphasise enough how working with food and not against it is positive for the whole family. It makes you realise how you can make food interesting by just varying the colours of the ingredients on your plate; how if you can squeeze a calm fifteen-minute food shop alone to select some goodies, it may well inspire you to cook, and how if you see food as fuel (as well as a means to relax and enjoy), you may even look forward to cooking a chicken and cashew-nut stir-fry, once a long, hard day reaches its close.

Mother knows best

'I was always a terrible cook and never made more than a simple Chinese stir-fry for myself. Once I'd had kids, their eating became a priority and I made it my mission to cook them nutritious, appetising meals. I suddenly realised that while they were gobbling healthy, fortifying food, I was living off a bag of crisps and an apple. I decided to adapt the children's meals for the whole family and found myself loving the fact we all sat down to a good meal together. Even though it's hectic, it's worth it. Not only have the kids established better manners and we all manage at least five minutes' conversation, I'm also feeling so much more energised and have actually started to enjoy cooking.'

Sandra Choi, bank clerk and mother to Beatrice (five) and Hannah (three)

Top ten nutrition tips

1. Eat well during pregnancy (and through conception, if possible). Don't gorge yourself, but ensure weight gain is steady.
2. Throughout pregnancy and breastfeeding keep energy high. Make sure you have healthy snacks by the bed for night-time feeds.
3. Plan your meals prior to giving birth. Enlist help and support for cooking and shopping if you can.

4. Make kids' parties healthy affairs. Cup-cake overload is bad for kids and mums alike.
5. Try to stick to three balanced meals (and a few healthy snacks) per day. This will prevent sugar-level lows.
6. Keep sugar, white carbohydrates, fatty meats, excess dairy and booze at a minimum. Trade them for fruit, veg, wholemeal grains and lean proteins.
7. You really *are* what you eat. Don't underestimate how what you eat, when you eat and how much you eat affect your mood and self-esteem.
8. Take pleasure in shopping and cooking. If you design quick, easy meals that are healthy and low in 'bad' fats, you may well surprise yourself with your culinary skills and boosted energy levels.
9. Devise and perfect some quick, healthy recipes and snacks that you love. You can turn to them when strapped for time (or culinary creativity).
10. Make it a group effort. Family, friends and kids can all join in the eat-well, feel-well philosophy.

Grace's Guru: Jane Clarke

Jane Clarke is one of Britain's leading nutritionists with a highly renowned clinic in London. She is also expert nutritionist to *The Times*, a regular contributor to ITV's *This Morning* and *The Wright Stuff*, and is nutritional adviser to chef Jamie Oliver. Jane is working on her second book, *Yummy*, and devotes any 'time out' to her three-year-old daughter, Maya.

What are your main nutritional and diet tips for mums?

A mum with a newborn The golden rule for mums with a newborn is to forget any notion of dieting. The first four to five months are both physically and emotionally draining, and restricting calories is the last thing a new mum should focus on. You as a mother must be the primary concern; remember, a nutritionally strong mum is far more able to produce rich breast milk and cope with sleepless nights and exhaustion. Literally, the early months are about survival, and not about denial.

A big struggle for women in general is seeing calories as a friend, not an enemy. I've found women are scared of calories; and new mums seem to be no exception. The big mission in the newborn phase is to change this view and begin to see calories as energy and as a means of absorbing the shock of sleep deprivation. Mums need plenty of healthy, friendly carbs to munch on throughout the day as well as comforting starches such as wholemeal pasta, rice, sweet potatoes, squashes and root vegetables. Wholegrain is also crucial for maintaining high energy. I'd suggest dark rye bread covered with a pure fruit spread, hummus or almond paste – what better to snack on at 3 a.m.?

A lot of new mums go off animal produce. I suspect that after the raw experience of giving birth, the last thing women want is to chomp their way through animal flesh! This shouldn't be an excuse to discard animal produce as a whole, however. I'd recommend eggs as a good alternative. A simple omelette made with olive oil, Cheddar cheese and mushrooms couldn't be easier and is rich in protein and vital nutrients.

New mothers would also be wise to prioritise store-cupboard foods to save on time and energy. Dried figs, dates and apricots are high in calcium and ideal if you're breast-feeding. Likewise, muesli with a little soya milk can be easily stored and prepared in a flash. Big cauldrons of soup are also good for the same reason – they save time and can be frozen and reheated almost blindfolded. Tuscan bean, roast vegetable or even tomato and sweet potato are good combinations and contain heaps of fresh goodies to nourish the new mum. One last suggestion would be to bung a tray of vegetables in the oven (squash, peppers, sweet potatoes, courgette, aubergine, parsnip and turnip) slosh on some olive oil and rosemary and cook for half an hour. You can then snack on this whenever you feel hungry, and if you make enough, it could last several days at least.

A mum wanting to lose the bulk of her baby weight
The first thing a mum wanting to lose weight should do is keep a diary of her food intake and why she's eaten each meal or snack. Often when you have the evidence in black and white, you can see what you are doing wrong and how to correct it. So many of you, I bet, think you eat a healthy three meals a day, but when you look back over a week, you will start to see the other grabbed snacks (crisps, cakes and biscuits) adding to your food intake. The second lesson in weight loss is to control your portions. If you cut the normal amount of food on your plate by half, then you're bound to start losing weight.

When planning your daily meals, start with a nutritious breakfast. Porridge with dried sulphur-free apricots and cinnamon, muesli soaked overnight in dried fruit or a heap of berries are perfect. Follow this with a good lunch. In my view, nothing beats a healthy sandwich. Avoid white bread with tons of butter, mayonnaise and rich fillings; instead, make sure it's something more like dark rye bread, with a tiny amount of butter, lean ham and cherry tomatoes. If you need warmth, ready-made soups are a good choice; just search for a soup that's vegetable-based and not too creamy. Make your evening meal light, vegetable heavy, with lean protein, avoiding too many starchy foods. However, don't cut back too much if you've not had time for a big lunch, this will leave you light-headed and starving the next morning. If pudding's your thing, follow meals with fruit.

Make sure you avoid high-GI foods and try and cut out all chocolate. You don't need to cut out sweet things altogether, but choose pure fruit bars (I've even been known to chomp through a children's organic oat and fruit bar during meetings), dates, figs, dried apples or a small pot of yoghurt instead. If you must eat a biscuit, then try some kind of flapjack or something of the Rich Tea or digestive type, rather than one covered in milk chocolate.

A mum with little energy, little time and little cash
As simple as it sounds, increasing your water intake by 20 per cent will almost instantly raise your energy levels by 20 per cent. Tap water is fine; you could even fill up a bottle and put it in the fridge to make the distinctive flavour of tap water sink to the bottom of the bottle. Make sure that while drinking more water, you cut down on caffeine. Two hits of caffeine a day is ample, any more and you'll feel dehydrated.

Whilst fresh fruit and vegetables can be expensive, frozen

ones are a lot cheaper and retain more vitamins than the fresh variety. The same applies to soups. I constantly hear that fresh soups are far superior to tins, but in actual fact, a tin of Heinz tomato soup contains a lot more tomatoes than many pricey fresh organic alternatives. Just take the time to read the quantities of added sugar and salt and ensure these aren't too high.

Often, ready meals are the main culprit for busy mothers strapped for cash. I tend to avoid supermarket ready meals, as they are expensive and can contain a lot of added salt, sugar and often fat. My solution is a mezze of cold meats, cheese and some good rye bread, a simple risotto, some scrambled eggs with roasted Portobello mushrooms, wholemeal pasta with a tomato sauce or lentils and beans cooked with a tin of chickpeas. These are just as quick as ready meals, but are far more nutritious and less costly.

Whatever you do, try to stop, sit and savour whatever you are eating. Clear your head and try to eat slowly; I guarantee you'll enjoy each mouthful far more and feel less rushed because of it.

A mum looking for solutions for the whole family
Try your hardest to eat *with* your children. Communicating at mealtimes only adds to the whole family's enjoyment of a meal. Some winning recipes for mothers and children are a heap of wholemeal pasta, rice or couscous topped with either tomato or vegetable sauce, even simple meatballs in tomato sauce are likely to please all ages.

Slow cooking and casserole cooking are great for family meals; you might even want to invest in a slow cooker. This makes it so easy to throw something like chicken, lamb or beef casserole in the oven mid-morning and just let it cook until the family is ready to eat. You'll also find the leftovers work a treat for days afterwards (in sandwiches, salads or omelettes).

A mum in search of the key superfoods Broccoli has got to be number one, as it's accessible, pretty cheap and one of the richest sources of the powerful antioxidants carotenoids. The other green vegetable I love is curly kale. I can't get enough of it, steamed, drizzled with good olive oil, black pepper and goat's cheese on top.

I'm also a huge fan of oily fish – sardines, herrings, mackerel, salmon and fresh tuna – as they are very high in omega-3 fatty acids, which help prevent heart disease, stroke and some cancers (always keeping in mind, though, that mums should stick to just two portions of oily fish per week, as they might be exposed to too many toxins otherwise). I recommend to my clients that they grill a tuna steak (which is delicious with a salad and jacket potato) or mash tinned sardines in tomato sauce with lemon juice and black pepper and spread on hot, buttered wholemeal toast.

In terms of starches, I now automatically go for sweet potatoes, an ideal starch that releases energy slowly into the body, as well as lentils and beans – they are low in fat and salt and are cholesterol-free (as well as being a great source of fibre).

If I'm choosing superfood fruits, I go for red grapes (which, like cherries, contain ellagic acid, so they help fight certain cancers and stave off aging), berries, kiwi or papaya, all of which are great for vitamin C as well.

What are your top five foods for a mum wanting peak nutrition?

1. Good organic dried fruit
2. Water
3. Porridge (especially if you add linseed, hemp seed and pumpkin seeds)
4. Hummus (on top of steamed vegetables or piled high on an oat cake)
5. Bananas.

What are the key dos and don'ts for a mum wishing to promote optimum health and nutrition?

Dos

- Keep hydrated.
- Be prepared and stock up on essentials.
- Utilise online delivery services, especially for bulky items like tinned tomatoes and oats.
- Religiously have breakfast every morning.
- Watch alcohol. Half the time, you lose the will to cook healthily after a large glass of wine in the evening. Remember not to drink before a meal.
- Try to avoid cakes, pastries, sweets, biscuits, chips and fast food. Opt for wholegrain toast instead of a butter-laden croissant, for example.
- Go for easy-access food. Unsalted nuts are ideal.
- Enjoy food and the process of cooking and eating well.

Don'ts

- Don't become obsessive. Ruling yourself with a strict iron rod is bound to end in failure.
- Try not to feel you always have to shop with the whole family. They have years to learn about different types of mushrooms!
- Don't crash-diet or follow fad diets, healthy eating in the long term is a much better attitude to have.

Jane's secret . . .

Easy family recipe books:

Body Foods for Busy People, Jane Clarke (Quadrille Publishing, 2004)

Jamie's Dinners, Jamie Oliver (Michael Joseph, 2004)

The Kitchen Diaries: A Year in the Kitchen, Nigel Slater (Fourth Estate, 2005)

World Vegetarian Cookbook, Madhur Jaffrey (Ebury Press, 1994)

Fast food that's not forbidden:

Pizza margherita at Pizza Express

Clear noodle soups at Wagamama

Sushi and sashimi at Japanese restaurants

Jane's fabulous mum's nutrition mantra:
'When you eat, always ask yourself the question "Will this nourish me?"'

Is This Body Really Mine?

Big Is Beautiful

There's no point beating about the bush, I loved getting fat for my first pregnancy. Sure, I romanticise it now. I look back wistfully (all glazed-over eyes and those rose-tinted spectacles again) and remember myself looking radiant with a perfect bump, my upper arms wobble-free. However, anyone who knew me in my first pregnancy will tell you otherwise, trying to cushion the blow by coming up with something as nice as 'glowing' or 'blooming', but the fact of the matter is, I was pretty damn huge, and I loved it!

I'd spent a decade squeezing into skintight jeans, far too busy interviewing the latest 'I take myself far too seriously' fashion designers and attending catwalk shows (could it really be black *again*?) to eat more than a salad at lunchtime. I prided myself on the fact that I could carry off almost any trend (well, I *thought* I looked good as a goth-cum-prom-princess-cum-hippy-chick!) and I loved the summer, when I could wear itsy-bitsy summer frocks and strapless tops that showed off the kind of slim arms you can only possess if you are under the age of twenty-five or Nicole Kidman. All this attempted slim-line living can get rather dull after a while, though, and it's certainly lots of hard work, and there comes a time when the thought of another steamed green or a virtuous sushi takeout makes you want to run to the nearest ice-cream parlour, tear off your size-eight jeans and dive head first into the largest tub of double-chocolate-chip ice cream going.

My window for rebellion came the minute the pregnancy test showed positive. After revealing the fifth blue line in a row (it took five different tests before I could believe my eyes), I immediately felt sick with excitement, shock, nerves and euphoria. This was in turn followed by an onset of hunger that would take me through the next seven months. My husband and I had planned a night out with friends who happen to be partial to the odd cocktail (or ten). I immediately called to change the venue to the local Chinese as opposed to our usual bar. Miffed, my fellow friends obliged and proceeded to accompany me through stir-fried vegetables, prawn crackers, spring rolls, sweet and sour chicken and a large selection of sesame toast, no strawberry margaritas in sight! I managed to fake a vodka and tonic, so as not to give the pregnancy game away, but eyebrows were raised when I ate my third plate of beef chow mein and started eyeing up the pudding menu!

Waking up the next morning to the reality of my new pregnancy, I was still euphoric – and hungry. My husband and I cuddled up and discussed names in bed – Willow, Isabella, Rudy or Isaac? – followed by my rather long breakfast wish list. Pancakes, bagels, fresh strawberries, a huge bowl of crunchy, honey-covered muesli with full-fat milk? Or an English breakfast? The possibilities seemed endless. But the best thing was, they *were* possibilities! No more squeezing into drainpipe trousers for brunch with a fashion press officer on Monday morning, no more fighting in the changing rooms for that size-eight blouson top and no more waist-and-weight-watching, well, for seven months at least! I would be big and beautiful, pregnant and proud, and boy, oh boy, would I be the first one to suggest cream tea at four o'clock in the afternoon!

It was only two weeks after I had discovered I was pregnant (and all this culinary high jinks had begun) when not only my bump, but my thighs, upper arms, bust and face began to blossom. Friends and colleagues started to raise some eyebrows at this, still unaware of the main impulse behind it. As you've probably gathered by now, I don't do things by halves, not even three-quarters, oh, no, if I go for it, I really, really go for it! So it was around week ten, as I waited for the lift in the lobby at work, that a fellow fashion editor nestled up to me and asked, 'Grace, sorry, I have to ask, but are you pregnant? Your boobs are huge!' (She admits now she'd meant my whole body, but she was trying to be nice!) I'm sure you've heard how the fashion world can gossip (pretty much like any office, I'm sure), so it was precisely four hours later that the cat (who had obviously eaten all the cream) had to be let out of the bag.

Admittedly, after my initial food splurge, things calmed down somewhat in the Grace Saunders kitchen and sanity kicked back in, but I still relished the thought of eating many of the previously 'forbidden' foods. I loved the fact that for the first time, being big not only felt OK, it really felt beautiful. It's not that I looked in the mirror and caressed my curves with joy, and, yes, I faltered when I saw everything start to wobble and expand, but all in all, I did have a deep contentment when I looked at my changing shape. I felt I had no choice but to give in to my new body form and let the growing baby make its mark, even if this did mean thunder thighs and a chubby chin!

The best thing about pregnancy shape is that for the first time, you feel your size is representative of so much more than just you as an individual. You are now a pregnant woman and people tend to respect you and your shape for that (unless you're a celebrity and then your ballooning body is splashed across the tabloids, usually at its most unappealing moments). For some women, the weight gain is a huge struggle and the feeling of being 'fat' overshadows a lot of the joys of pregnancy, but most mums-to-be I know enjoy watching life grow inside them and being big is just another part of that. I did on occasion hold my head in despair when I caught a glimpse of myself in the full-length mirror or came across a photo of myself in all my blooming glory, but mostly, it was a chance for me to take a back seat on the vain fashion track and just listen to my body and what it craved – rest when I needed to rest, eat when I needed to eat, and enjoy a rich, creamy fish pie if it was fish pie I woke up craving.

The fact that my husband seemed to love (or at least be intrigued by) my changing shape helped immensely. He even insisted on taking photos of me nude for every month in the lead-up to the birth (the age of the baby written in lipstick on my ever-expanding tummy!). Maybe it was tact, maybe he couldn't face the thought of a hormonal outburst, or maybe he really and truly did love the fact that I was two stone heavier and carrying his firstborn child, it doesn't matter now. He supported me 100 per cent, which was a huge credit to him. (Admittedly, he also loved the extra biscuit selection, mature Cheddar cheese and soft, crusty, sun-dried tomato bread that started to appear in the cupboards.) My age-old buddy Clare was so impressed with this show of spouse support that she designed something called BFPO (best-friend pregnancy obligation). It simply means that the best friend of a newly pregnant woman is obliged to take the father in question aside and give him the low-down on what to say to his expectant partner. She had witnessed a good pregnant friend being told by her husband that her bum was getting a little 'more substantial'. This irritated her so much that she felt driven to write 'One hundred things to say and NOT to say to your blooming pregnant partner'. She happily gave him the printout for his next birthday present. (Slightly too late, I hasten to add: his wife ran off with a far more complimentary man shortly afterwards!)

So, here I was, three months pregnant and my fetish for food flourished. I let myself sample everything from whole-meal banana muffins for breakfast, Moroccan chickpea salad for lunch and my stepmum's winning paella for supper. It was at this point, though, that I realised I was going to need some muscle to carry all that new weight around. I know everyone talks endlessly about the benefits of walking and swimming for pregnant women, but, and I hate to admit it, they're right. Exercise during pregnancy is a lifesaver in the weight-gain and confidence-boosting battle.

I have always been a swimmer. I don't swim for hours, or for that matter am I interested in perfecting my butterfly stroke or underwater tumble-turns (unlike my pal Catherine, who was tumble-turning in the water at six months pregnant!). I like nothing more than a peaceful, twenty-five-minute stint of front crawl and breaststroke. In pregnancy, swimming was even better, bar the conventional breaststroke, which, I was advised, could tug on the pelvis. Instead, I devised a new style – keeping a float in between my knees. Great for the upper arms! Even though it was often an effort to get motivated (especially towards the end of my first pregnancy, when the snow was coming down thick and fast), I knew that once I was in the water, that feeling of weightlessness and calm would far outweigh the cold changing-room strip!

I'm sure it was to a large degree thanks to those four-times-a-week swimming sessions that I managed to stay sane and adjust to my changing shape. While lathering the almond oil all over my bump and drying my hair – incidentally, the best condition it had been in for years – I felt I could embrace those extra pounds and inches. It also made me feel a lot better about the apricot muffin that followed each swim, and it took away any feelings of couch-potato syndrome after a long commute to work.

'Swimming rocks!' was also a mantra recited by my great friend Sonia, who swore by a forty-minute swim three times a week (up to and even on her due date). She swears this exercise contributed to her manageable experiences of giving birth, claiming her brisk and tear-free experience was shaped by her supple muscles and relaxed mindset. Hers was a water birth, of course.

Exercise plays such a key part in staying in shape, having a positive self-image and feeling great that I don't think it really matters what form of exercise you do, as long as it's pregnancy-friendly and moderate.

Of course, it's a shame that as soon as we'd all begun to get used to this new body image, the whole concept was turned upside down and the minute our tiny squirming newborn was placed on our tummy, fat was no longer forgiven. Weirdly, it's as if society is turning the knife in women's self-identity, saying, 'As long as you're carrying new life, fat is fab, the second you're a mum, fat is forbidden.' No more guilt-free gateau-gorges, no more triple-decker club sandwiches. No, the new mum who lost all her baby weight during birth emerges the winner. 'Impossible!' I hear you cry? Exactly. So where do we go from here?

Mother knows best

'I found weight gain in pregnancy a nightmare. Initially, I was so sick I lost weight, and then once the pounds piled on my self-confidence plummeted. I hated feeling fat and dreaded losing the weight afterwards. I desperately wanted to be pregnant and glowing, but I just felt horrible. In the end, I teamed up with a pregnant mum in my office and we joined a Pilates and yoga club near work that ran courses for pregnant women. I felt doing some gentle exercise helped me feel better about my body and certainly assisted in the bonding process between Rocco and me. I think I'd been so used to going to the gym every day after work that just eating and feeling sick, with no physical exercise made me depressed. It wasn't easy, but by the time Rocco came, I had totally relaxed about my weight and even managed to continue with the classes once he was born.'

Isabel Pratesi, marketing executive and mother to Rocco (two)

The Pressure's On

Like most of you, I'm sure, I'd spent nine months eating up and basking in comments like 'Oh, don't you look radiant' and 'Your hair and skin are just glowing!' (OK, admittedly, the odd 'Boy, don't you look knackered' towards the end). Who cared that my fitted frocks hung gathering dust and my scales had been put in the local skip? I was nurturing a new life and I was proud. So it came as somewhat of a surprise, once I'd given birth the first time round, that this firm, perfectly round tummy immediately resembled a heap of wobbly jelly on a plate. Not only that, the rest of my expanded form seemed to get bigger as my tummy shrank and wobbled around for all to see. Wasn't the weight supposed to just fall off in the delivery room? Well, obviously not. OK, I thought, I can live with this, it's not as though I have any immediate wild parties to attend, requiring me to fit into a skintight little black number, and anyway, look at this delightful daughter I have to show for it. Aha, *you* may not care at that point, but for some ungodly reason, the world at large doesn't let you forget about it.

My girlfriend Luella swears that the second she returned from hospital, losing weight felt as much of an obligation as breastfeeding. She stepped through the front door with her daughter, Alice (the latter wrapped in a tight wool blanket, Luella wrapped in mega-sized loose wool drawstring trousers), and says the immediate pressure to fulfil the criteria of a fabulous scrummy mummy felt immense. She had the new Bugaboo buggy waiting for a stroll, a pre-planned tea date with five local mums and her in-laws coming over for champagne later that evening. She took one pleading look around her, asked her husband to cancel all plans for the coming week and retreated upstairs with Alice, closed the bedroom door and didn't come down for twenty-four hours!

Comments that are intended light-heartedly ('Back in your jeans yet?' and 'How's the tummy going down?') may be a form of making conversation, but please let me tell you, do not mention a new mum's tum under any circumstances! This sort of female camaraderie (combined with the fact that every women's magazine on the planet is showcasing one actress or another who's been 'back to size six in six days') makes you feel ready to jump from the top-floor window or bury your head in the Moses basket at the very least. As if new mums don't have enough to worry about with breast-feeding, sleepless nights and a crisis of identity – losing weight immediately after giving birth is certainly something we could do without. (As Luella quite eloquently put it, 'We need the pressure like a hole in the head!')

I have to say, I am somewhat miffed by those yummy mummies in the public eye who look fabulous within days. I'm sure the likes of Claudia Schiffer and Cindy Crawford managed it, because as super-super-supermodels they are quite obviously endowed with miraculous no-weight-gain prop-erties; however, how the rest of those celebrities manage it, I can't imagine. Tummy-tuck thrown in with the Caesarean section? Quite possibly. Anorexic pregnancy? Very likely. Personal trainer, dietician and personal cook in twenty-four-hour attendance? Definitely. It's very hard not to compare yourself with these miracle-workers, as you breastfeed your baby on day three, still waddling around, sore with stitches and three stone overweight. But try, try, try not to beat your-self up over what the media presents to you as 'normal' post-pregnancy weight loss. It's not normal, it's extreme, and many of these women have wasted their pregnancy (not to mention risked the healthy growth of their unborn) just to stay in shape. Believe me, I've sat next to enough ladies who lunch, at one fashion do or another, to know that even when pregnant, half a celery stick and two bites of noodle salad don't constitute a big meal.

Mums, be real. You can be fabulous, you can look good, feel good and get your life back, but it's just unrealistic to expect that to happen four days after giving birth. I'm sure in the memoirs of the next supermodel (whoever that may be), she will tell you otherwise, but, really, we all know that without a fleet of paid staff, a plastic surgeon and a huge selection of credit cards maxed out with ready cash, it takes a lot of dedication, hard work and time to get your life and your body back in shape. The trick is not to be too hard on yourself. In the end, I said to myself firmly, I ate well, bore healthy, happy, bonny and beautiful seven- and eight-pound babies. Carrying the extra weight post-pregnancy was just evidence of this commitment. I had to give myself time to get my energy levels and brainpower back on track before even contemplating strategically losing that weight. And as we talked about in the previous chapter, you'll need all the nutrients you can get (especially if you are breastfeeding) to sustain the long, hard nights without collapsing in a blubbing heap.

I found after my second pregnancy the pressure to look good, feel great and have your life back on track within a blink of labour was even more intense. So many fellow mums had told me before, 'Hey, it's so much easier with number two, you'll just pop him out and be back in your jeans and down the pub in no time.' Hello? Are you insane? I may have shed more weight in the first few weeks than first time round, but I still felt shattered, plump and the furthest thing from fabulous. Instead, the pressure and all the expectation made me feel vulnerable and self-conscious.

Once I'd come out of the initial haze of my second baby, the prospect of having to get back in shape was immensely daunting. Oh, the effort, the denial, the hard work; couldn't it all just drop off overnight? While breastfeeding both my children for seven months definitely helped, there is no denying that it is bloody hard work. I didn't want to succumb to the social pressure of being a cool, thin, new mum, but I did want to feel good about myself. It is a fine balance, I found (yes, again!), and one which we all inevitably have to find at some point after giving birth: how to stay energised, feel good, look good and start to lose that pregnancy weight. The only way you know when the time is right for you to take on this challenge is to tune out the world for a moment and work out what's right for your body.

Mother knows best

'I was so fed up of being confronted with pictures of glowing, skinny celebrities kitted out with designer buggies that I banned them from the house for the first month after giving birth. I'd just had twins and my main concern was to bond with them, not to lose weight. I couldn't bear the barrage of 'Lose your baby weight in a week' features, so my mother and husband were under strict orders to make sure I didn't see any of these. By

Body-image and Self-confidence

If you're reading this, babe in arms, toddlers running amok in the kitchen, and feel 100 per cent happy with your weight and body image, then lucky you! You can happily skip to the next chapter, bypassing this one, and give yourself a pat on the back for your achievements. However, if you're like a vast proportion of new mums and feel that your body image and self-confidence could do with a boost, then welcome, you are not alone! During my second pregnancy, the moment of truth came to me about two months into my son's life.

After the birth, the weeks raced past and turned into months. At first, I didn't even have time to wash my hair, let alone stand naked in front of the mirror and examine my new shape and the extent to which the pregnancy had taken its toll on my figure (and don't get me started on the four days it had been since I last attempted some pelvic-floor repair!). I was lugging around enormous boobs, trying to find discreet ways of feeding in public and generally attempting to keep my head above water with some air of grace. I found that once I'd battled the worst of mastitis, reflux and broken nights, my head was just about far enough above water to address the issue I had been dreading: my body. I was actually sorting laundry at the time. The sun was streaming in through the window, I was dressed in nothing more than a feeding bra, large knickers and a cool, cotton sarong. (I know, what a look! Don't tell the fashion police.) I'd been up three times in the night (which felt like a 'good night' in comparison with the eight times it had been a few weeks earlier) and was recovering from my sixth (and thankfully last) bout of the dreaded mastitis.

As I picked up armfuls of dirty baby vests, paint-splattered toddler T-shirts and my beloved's football kit, I suddenly caught the reflection of myself in the bathroom mirror. I admit I had a bit of a shock. Who was this woman? My hair unkempt (roots going on for miles), my tummy hanging down like a balloon half-filled with water, my upper arms twice the size they'd always been, and my face puffy and lifeless. I had to force myself to stop staring, and that's when I knew: it was time for the tide to turn.

The morning feed finished, the phone didn't stop ringing, and my toddler continued her endless requests for yet another Maisy story. I emptied the washing machine, cooked the pasta, called for a spare dishwasher part. It was boiling, I felt fat and lifeless, and to be honest, I just didn't want to make the effort. With all this positive energy and confidence-boosting (not), you can imagine what a bag of sparkling energy I was when my husband returned home from a business trip. 'You take the bloody baby and do the washing-up, I am going to bed,' would be an accurate summary, as he handed me a box of duty-free perfume and an extra-large Toblerone bar. Poor man.

As I traipsed upstairs, leaving a bewildered husband (still in his coat) in the hall, it was hard to see any way of feeling myself again. Would I ever swan around the children's Christmas party feeling glamorous and confident again? Would I ever feel ready to step out in my skinny jeans and wafty tops to enjoy a glass of wine and an Italian meal, arm in arm with my proud husband? Would I ever be able to stand at the school gates wearing a sleeveless top, chatting with ease to my fellow mums? And would I ever be able to build up my physical strength and energy enough to race my growing boy around the park? At nine o'clock that evening, as I lay in bed staring at the ceiling, my breasts leaking on the sheets, it truly felt as if I never would.

How could it be possible that so much of my confidence as a mum, as a wife, as a friend and as a writer was bound up in all this extra flesh? Sure, I loved my growing role as mum and had endless enthusiasm for the joys of new motherhood, but at that precise moment, all I felt was fat. Who wants to go out for a romantic meal when you can't bear your partner to show you affection in case it raises the prospect of making love? Who wants to chat at the local sandpit on a summer's day when the only top that fits is a thick roll-neck sweater? And who wants to play football in the park when even lugging yourself up the stairs feels like running a marathon?

I had been very happy to plod along with my firstborn, indulging in the odd cream cake and pushing my small-waisted black trousers to the back of the wardrobe way into her sixth month. It wasn't, in fact, until my return to work after seven months of maternity leave that I really felt I needed to get back in shape. A work conference, a star-studded banquet dinner and a best friend's wedding all loomed ahead, and there was no way I was turning up in drawstring trousers and an Arsenal football shirt! With my second child, the disillusionment and overwhelming body-image crisis crept up on me much earlier.

Whenever it comes for you (and you could even have a teenager in tow), this new-mum self-confidence crash calls for some serious action.

Mother knows best

'I was always so confident and, although a dress size eighteen, felt very happy in my skin. After the birth of my third child, I went up to a size twenty-four and that really got me down. More than anything, it was the lack of energy for all those physical things I love to do as a mum. Sports, long walks, piggyback rides, I just felt too big to enjoy them. I never wanted to be model-size – in fact, I hate that skinny look – but I did want to have more energy and enthusiasm for life. The moment I started to eat healthily and be disciplined about the sugary treats I love, my confidence was lifted. Taking action felt good. After a year of eating a balanced diet, I'm now a size twenty and much happier for it. Now I have more vitality, the whole family is exercising more, and it's had a knock-on effect for us all.'

Martha Matterson, lollipop lady and mother to Henry (seven), Luke (five) and Ellen (two)

Making the Change

Once you've had children, you long for the days gone by when the New Year rolled in and you could decide to join a gym or sign up for cross-country running and the only thing standing between you and optimum fitness was a hangover. A white wedding, two babies and a mortgage later, and even the thought of finding out where your local gym is seems as much a miracle as paying off your mortgage within the year.

For most of us new mums, finding the time to implement healthy eating and prioritise exercise just seems impossible. 'Who will look after little Riley while I zip off to the gym for two hours?' I hear you cry. 'Who's going to comfort the teething Katie and Ollie while I cook a nutritious salad?' and 'Who the hell is going to pick up my triplets from school while I go for a brisk walk in the countryside?' OK, OK, OK, did I say it would be easy? You should know by now that this mothering lark is never, ever easy, and making the time to get your body back is no exception. In fact, it's one of the hardest things in the battle to survive motherhood and stay fabulous. If you've reached the point where you are committed to making the change and are focusing some precious energy and enthusiasm into getting your body back in tip-top condition, then you're halfway there.

Following my washing-machine incident and the 'Who the hell are you?' reflection in the mirror, I knew the time had come to give my body an overhaul. How I wish this had constituted a week at a top health farm, a consultation with a dietician and make-up artist and a list as long as my arm of beauty treatments; sadly, it did not. Knowing that I desperately wanted to get back in shape, but also being realistic about the confines of time, I needed a solution and fast. There was no way I was going to get to a plush new gym every night or even once a week, not yet anyway. I needed practical fitness tips that I could do every day at home, and I needed to start eating for high energy and low body fat. No one said this would happen overnight, but if I didn't try, how would I know whether those fabulous clothes left to taunt me in the closet would ever be within reach again?

Now, when I tell you the next part of my getting-my-body-back-on-track story, you're going to scoff. I met a fabulous fellow mum in the form of a personal trainer called Fiona Allen. Her unique angle? Getting new mums looking great and feeling amazing from their own homes. I admit, once I'd seen her toned and trim physique and listened to her easy-peasy-lemon-squeezy approach, I was hooked. I went on to plot out a feature idea chronicling six weeks under her care, which ended up being commissioned by a parenting magazine. True, I was lucky to use Fiona under the guise of research, but before you scoff further, what I learnt and wrote about were techniques I could carry with me for life and were more than within reach for all new mums. So, while a personal trainer sounds glam and is not usually an option for everyone, what Fiona instilled in me was the discipline and skills to carry on with her fitness and eating rules way beyond the six-week feature. More about that in a second. First, once I'd made the decision to get fit and healthy, I had to make the time to actually do it!

Making Time

Like you, I'm sure, I don't have a fleet of staff willing to entertain my children while I get friendly with a treadmill for hours on end, so this is the part that takes some organisation. The best thing here is to make a regular date in the diary. If you make sure every partner, friend, family member and milkman knows about your time slot, there's no chance for confusion. Believe me, I've been there often enough: 'You're going swimming? Oh, I forgot I'd planned to watch the football on TV. Can't you go another day?' is not the kind of support that's going to get your motivation revved up, is it?

Over the past few years, I've learnt a few small must-haves that help make sure I get out through the door to do some exercise, and not only stick to it but enjoy it as well!

Enlist childcare you can trust

There is nothing worse than jogging halfway round the block only to turn back because you're worried about your toddler, who's been left with an obliging but not altogether trustworthy neighbour (and one who might just forget that your little cherub is allergic to milk and goes bananas when given sugar!). If you're going to leave your children so you can have a little time to get fit and pamper yourself, you need to be confident that you can relax about the care they are getting. Now, I'm not saying a Norland nanny is the only option, far from it, but make sure when you plan exercise you do it with the help of a trusting carer.

If your children are of school age, even better, you have

ready-made (often free) childcare! Likewise, if you are a working mum, lunchtimes can be a great opportunity to snatch half an hour at a gym, and many companies offer good deals and discounts with affiliated places.

Choose a gym with a good crèche

I appreciate that for many new mums, a gym membership can be an extra expense that seems unrealistic, extravagant even, but if you use it enough and it offers free childcare, it can work out to be pretty economical. So many gyms and leisure complexes have great crèches and it gives the kids an opportunity to play while you get fit. Many take babies from three months old, which can be a lifesaver for new mums locked into strict feeding with a maximum forty-five-minute window in which to work out. Even if it's not a plush gym, you may well find local community centres that offer mother-and-baby yoga or sports with willing helpers to assist with your offspring.

My sister-in-law Sue selects her leisure centre purely on the standard of their childcare. It's not just the availability of a water-aerobics class or the standard of the dance studios that gets her pen poised to sign a year's contract with a gym; it's the carers in the crèche. If the bouncy chairs aren't up to scratch or they don't offer nursery rhymes, then forget it!

Make a mum rota

My fellow mum pal (and next-door neighbour) Amy and I often help each other with childcare so we can get out through the door and burn off some calories. While she watches mine at the Tuesday parish playgroup, I occasionally have her sons over for tea so she can go for a run. Having the dates planned (bar chickenpox, hailstorms or work commitments) means 90 per cent of the time we get out and get going with maximum ease and minimum stress. So much so that another fellow mummy friend, Jennie, has started a rota in her neighbourhood. Her daughter is a real delight to boot, so a variety of NCT pals are more than happy to watch her on a Saturday while Jen swims. In return, their kids are looked after on a regular basis by Jennie while the mum in question goes boxing/cycling/pole-dancing. The added bonus? When all the exercise is done, the two new mums get to sit down to a large cup of tea and have a great catch-up about the previous week. A workout, a cuppa, a gossip and two happy children can't be too bad, can it?

Make it a group effort

While enlisting your girlfriends in your mutual plight to get fit, you may well find that you could all be doing it en masse. I know several local mums with newborns who have started a 'mum run club' (very similar to the near-cult fitness programme powerpramming). Seven or eight mums meet once a week, three-wheeler buggy in tow. They proceed to warm up in the local park for ten minutes, followed by a forty-minute run (and all with the baby gurgling from the pushchair). I've even seen them in summer doing floor-based exercises, often with the baby cooing happily on the mum's tum (to the fascination of the OAPs on their daily park stroll!). It seems a perfect way to get out, get fit, meet other mums with tiny babies, and the best part is, it's free and requires no separation from your tiddler!

Sadly, nothing so adventurous was on the agenda four years ago, when I gave birth for the first time. However, some girl-friends and I continued with the yoga we had done during pregnancy. Similar to the 'mum run club', the class was set up by true earth mother Lolly Stirk. She welcomed bringing babies, in fact the more the merrier! There would always be one baby kicking off and we took it in turns to help out. One way or another, we all got to do at least half an hour of yoga and caught up with our 'how to get more sleep' stories at the end. The teacher also made sure that family members and friends were welcome. One week, when my daughter was just eight weeks old, I took along my then child-free sister-in-law Sue, who had a day off work. We browsed around the shops, ate a spot of lunch and then she had a cuddle with my daughter while I enjoyed some yoga. Great bonding for them, brilliant time out for me!

No excuses

Now, it should go without saying that excuses for not exercising are banned from the fabulous mum's vocabulary. 'It's too cold', 'I'm too tired', 'I'm not in the mood' and 'I just can't be bothered' don't cut it for a mum wanting to look and feel great. OK, I admit I've dropped a few of these lines on an occasion when I'm just too pre-menstrual to consider a dip in the cold pool, or I've been up six times with a teething baby, but by and large, I live by the no-excuses rule. If you really and truly are committed to getting fit, healthy and looking great, then you have to be motivated and honest. There's no point in taking on the challenge and then bowing out at the first opportunity – hey, we would all rather sit at home and eat fish and chips, but this won't make us feel good and it certainly won't help us to look good either.

So you see, making the time to change isn't as easy as it was pre-children, but it *can* be done. I know I needed a vast supply of motivation, good friends and a hell of a lot of humour. When it's raining and you're running around the block with the knowledge that your husband is snuggled up with the children watching *Dumbo*, you need to be able to laugh. Failing that, you'll cry and that's the worst thing to do when you're out of breath with a mountain still to climb!

Mother knows best

'I couldn't afford to join a gym once I'd had my second child and was funding a nursery and a childminder. I was desperate for some exercise so my sister-in-law, Karen, who belonged to a local sports centre, offered to come swimming with me for an hour every Sunday morning. She splashed with my kids in the shallow end while I used a guest pass and got a good forty-five-minute swim each week. Karen loved her weekly kids play and said it was a great way of living out the mum experience without actually having to have any of her own! Not only was she happy, I was over the moon about getting a moment to keep fit. The fact it didn't cost me a penny was an added bonus!'

Lucy Williamson, secretary and mother to William (four) and Rosie (one)

Exercise and Endorphins

So, you've gone the full cycle of getting huge, deciding it's about time to get back in shape and working out a full one hour and twelve minutes per week in which to do it, now, what does one do next? I'm sorry to say the next bit is the really hard bit. We can all talk a good session on the running machine, but can we really cut it? And will we congratulate ourselves on our determination and willpower with an extra-thick slice of cheesecake? But the great thing about exercise is that once you begin on it, the benefits are often fast and fabulous. The endorphins you create by pumping blood around your body make you feel energised and wonderful (especially when previously the most exercise you got was sitting on the bus or at a playgroup eating a bag of crisps). Add this to the fact that when you see a little weight dropping off, or even the tiniest amount of arm definition (as opposed to the constant wobble that restricts you to long sleeves even in 80 degrees), you feel brilliant.

I remember vividly waiting for the first session with postnatal personal trainer Fiona Allen. Not only was she trainer to the stars but she had a reputation for not taking 'no' for an answer. I had given birth six weeks before, I could hardly see for exhaustion, and my body was in no state whatsoever for close examination by someone used to seeing *über*-stylish, ultra-slim A-list celebrities. Also, what the hell was I to wear? Mega-expensive tracksuits I had not; it would have to be a white vest (that had turned pink after being washed with my daughter's red sundress by mistake) and a pair of my husband's beaten-up old tracksuit bottoms. I'm sure you'll agree, not altogether a great first-impressions look! I nestled my son closer to my bosom and dreaded the doorbell ringing.

Nerves, low energy and a wardrobe crisis aside, what got me through that first session with Fiona was the feeling during and afterwards that I was actually starting to make a difference. I felt the blood pumping, I felt my muscles working, and I felt that with enough dedication I could really start to look and feel good. Sure, I could hardly walk the next day, after two hours of sit-ups, bicep curls and lunges (all done in my living room, while my mother entertained the children with lullabies and crown-making), but it felt great to know there was even a glimmer of hope of regaining a shape I felt confident with, even in the madness of those early months.

I admit there are days when even a trip to the toilet seems like a trek up the Himalayas. More often than not, though, I try to weave exercise into my day-to-day life so my endorphins stay buoyant, my confidence remains high, and my body can begin to resemble something of its former self. Between my mummy girlfriends and me, we've tried every sort of fitness scheme under the sun. A week of Pilates that ended with me skiving in the pub, a local t'ai chi group that left my friend Sophie in fits of laughter (so much so she was expelled from the class) and a dance class that had my buddy Amy swearing never to try anything Latin American ever again all spring to mind. With these shared experiences (and catastrophes), I've put together a crash course in the best kinds of exercise for busy mums, ones that can easily be combined with kids and family life and are flexible enough to fit our lifestyles. When it proved impossible for my friend Carolina to get to a gym, because she was breastfeeding a newborn round the clock, she took up the simple, day-to-day 'no gym required' practices. When my pal Lyn is doing the childminder/work-meeting dash across the city five days a week, she takes advantage of the outdoor exercises and bins a couple of gym sessions. Lastly, when the snow falls and Christmas treats tempt me, I resort to the ever-accessible local pool and the reward of a hot shower and a banana smoothie afterwards. So you see, rain or shine, newborn, toddler or teenagers in tow, you can always find a way (even if it's just an hour or so per week) to get fit and feel fab.

Types of Exercise

No gym required

One of the key tools that Fiona armed me with was the ability to see exercise as something I could do as part of my daily routine. If you have the discipline to work out at home (and that doesn't mean you have to splash out a fortune on high-tech equipment and a state-of-the-art running machine), then the goal of fitness is within reach. I found that especially once I was trying to cram my mothering and working roles into what seemed like such a short week, working out at home was the only way of guaranteeing a decent amount of fitness time.

Like most new mums, my target areas of improvement were my tum, bum, thighs, upper arms and pelvic floor. (Remember the midwife's rule: twenty pelvic-floor exercises every time you stop at the traffic lights, watch TV, go to bed, eat your breakfast. Yeah, right!) My main focus for two hours a week was to improve these. The one fitness 'tool' I invested in was a giant gym ball. (This actually came in handy for my second labour, which took place largely at home. However, I'll save this story for another time!) I've now really mastered the art of using the ball for squats against the wall. (Put the ball between you and the wall, rest it in the base of your back and move from a standing to a squatting position.) Although initially even three squats reduced my legs to a quivering mess, after a few weeks I really saw the thigh and tummy benefits and felt my leg muscles strengthen. Angelina Jolie, here we come . . . !

Sit-ups or 'crunches' and bicep curls are also pretty hard work, but require minimum planning or equipment. I'm no Victoria Beckham (who must surely do a hundred sit-ups with her husband every night to achieve that kind of washboard stomach), but post second baby, I tried to be disciplined about these exercises. Even with only a few sets, three times a week (believe me, I'd have died if I'd tried any more than that), I found they flattened the bulging tummy somewhat and made it resemble less of a kids' jelly at teatime. Bicep curls are also a good new-mum no-brainer. The muscles built up by structured bicep curls a few times per week (bringing your arm from a straight position at your side to a bent position at your shoulder using plastic bottles filled with water, kids' lunch boxes packed with sugar, heavy books or low weights) are then built on by day-to-day mum tasks. Lugging the weekly shopping bags from the car and up three flights of stairs, shifting the double buggy around and picking up a chubby baby twenty-four hours a day are all muscle-building exercises we do without thinking. (Make sure you keep your tummy tight when bending, lifting and pushing the pram; it will help strengthen the muscles and avoid lower-back injury.) The next great tip to bear in mind once you've got the exercises sussed is to make sure your *posture* is good. Standing straight and walking tall can do miracles for slouchy shoulders and a protruding tummy! Why not try it when you're trundling up to the local Co-op with the buggy? You'll be amazed.

Sit-ups, lunges, posture control, these may sound pretty gruelling, but because they're done from home, the effort can happen without too much turmoil. Who'd have thought that lifting Evian bottles for twenty-five minutes while watching soap operas in the evening (great for the biceps), taking the stairs instead of the lift four times a day (amazing for the thighs and bum), using a birthing ball for a few sets of squats twice a week (fabulous for bum, tum and thighs) or just walking with your back straight and your tummy pulled in would help me keep fit, lose weight and give the illusion of being four pounds lighter? Minimum hassle, maximum results – genius.

School-run fun

I was so sick of being yet another mum clogging up the local roads while taking my children to and from their respective nurseries/clubs/schools/tea dates that I thought I'd better do something about it. Instead of cursing the fellow mum in front (in her tank fit for warfare), it was time to take to the streets, no petrol permitted. The weather being on my side, I try to walk or cycle as much as possible with the kids. (I'd love to tell you I walk three miles, or cycle the same, in sleet, snow or thunderstorms, but heavy weather does call for the occasional exception. We're not superwomen!) When it was just my daughter and me, we would spend hours doing the relevant journeys with her on the back of my bike. (She was wrapped up like an Eskimo, I was sweating and ruby red in the face.) Apart from one occasion (when my Converse laces got tangled in the spokes and I landed in a puddle while protecting my girl from the fall!), all journeys were hazard- and tantrum-free. My daughter loved to whiz along and would squeal with delight as we flew down the hills. She even cried when the snow came and the bike was out of action for a week or two. Don't be fooled that bicycles must cost a fortune either; mine was so basic even the third gear was out of action (and there were only three gears in the first place!). It cost me less than six months' worth of petrol and was far more fun and ecologically sound than a car.

Once I had my second child, biking wasn't the easiest option (although my friend Rainbow has one of those pod-like contraptions that fits her strapping boys on the back of the bike; heavy work, but she is a devoted eco-fitness queen! Somehow I don't think my thighs are up to this.) When I could, I'd use the bike, but on other occasions I'd take to footwork. Now my children are a little older, my walking is accompanied by them whizzing at high speed on their micro-scooters. Even if your nursery or school is a little further than you'd like, making three or even two days a week to walk (or even scooter) could be enough fitness for the whole week. We mums can be in such a rush all the time that a car seems a huge necessity, but if walking the school run saves on exercise later in the week, surely it's worth a try? I love nothing more on a warm day than walking with my son to pick my daughter up from pre-school. He collects leaves and knick-knacks in the park (slugs, snails, dog hairs, you name it, he stores it), and we all do a detour to stop off at the swings on the way home. If it's sunny, I sometimes organise a picnic with fellow mums and the afternoon passes in an instant. The novelty of all this walking has even given me (and a handful of motivated mums) the incentive to raise money for charity. By walking the school run three times a week, we have decided to use it as training for the Moonwalk, a 13K walk that raises money for breast cancer. My sister-in-law Sue confesses that every time she feels like flaking out and taking the car, she thinks of the midnight walk and how terrible she'll feel if she can't keep up. Only a tiny bit of pressure, then!

If you're a working mum or a brand-new mum, walking can be the best option for you too. When my friend Paula went back to work after her first baby, she was desperate to get out of the morning-rush/slow-commute/stagnant-desk rut. She decided the best way to get twenty-five minutes' exercise was to walk from her home to the Underground station (instead of waiting for the number 102 bus, which was always late, fume coming out of her ears!). She'd pack her stilettos in her handbag and walk to the Tube in trainers. Ninety-nine per cent of the time, she'd beat the bus and feel good about getting some fresh air and exercise while she was at it. Likewise, a whole host of my mummy girlfriends found walking an ideal way of getting out and getting fit post-birth. It was not unheard of for my good friend Jennie to walk four miles a day with little Minnie in her pram, running errands, popping into a gallery, meeting a friend for lunch and stopping off at the baby clinic on the way home. She knew the local streets like the back of her hand and, boy, didn't she look amazing in her summer sundress three months after giving birth!

Swimming

Now, I know I can go on a little bit about my love of the water, so I won't elaborate much further here. But swimming does help keep my weight steady and my figure in OK shape. Not only does it tone more muscles in the body than most other forms of exercise, I find my mood is lifted beyond belief after a swim. I often find I have my best ideas (for the next book, for a good supper recipe or for a good strategy to get my son to hold a pen properly) while I'm doing my lengths. Belonging to a local pool or having access to a public one is also a great way of making exercise something for you and the kids to enjoy. My two children are both happy and fearless in the water (so much so that my three-year-old daughter has just received her five-metre badge – that's my girl!). In fact, show me a kid who doesn't love the water. Usually, swimming is a safe bet for all ages (newborn or newly adolescent alike).

Running

If I pretend to be the runner of three London Marathons or even the type to run to the local Co-op for a pint of milk, I would be lying. Even the thought of me in a pair of leggings jogging in the park seems to evoke fits of giggles in everyone who knows me. Maybe it's the sweating, maybe it's the stitches I always get when I attempt it, or maybe it's the thought of those sweat patches that appear on your crotch after a sprint around the block, but running has never been my first choice of exercise. Sorry, I'm putting you off and this wasn't my intention. Talk to my fellow mum and neighbour Amy and she will tell you a different story. Amy is not only super-gorgeous, super-slim and super-stylish, she is also the mother of two demanding boys who give her very little time to indulge in fitness. Running after the two of them surely burns a good 500 calories a day, but if you saw her size-ten waist and pert bottom, you'd know that chasing a toddler and a ten-year-old wasn't the sum total of it.

Amy swears by having the boys tucked up in bed by eight o'clock (or tucked up and reading comics at least), and then takes this opportunity to run a good forty minutes at dusk before getting down to the supper/housework/phone-calls agenda. When I see her pounding back as I tuck into my third slice of organic chocolate and a rerun of *Friends*, I often wish that running were my thing. The empty roads, the night sky, the time to think and the feeling of a cool shower post-jog must be very satisfying (not to mention the feeling of getting back in your size-ten jeans because of your hard slog!). I wish my attempts had been as seamless and romantic. (Think hair sticking to your face, a twisted ankle and a desperate pant for water and you'll get a better picture.) Even with a baby in tow, running can be a dead cert for getting back in shape. Many new buggies offer a safe way to run with the baby tucked up in the three-wheeler for an hour. Not ideal once your baby bucks every time you go near the buggy, but while she's happy to sit and watch the world go by, maximise the benefits!

Yoga and Pilates

I know that yoga and Pilates have gained themselves something of a celebrity reputation of late. Don't let this put you off, or the opposite – entice you with the illusion that they are an easy option. But they are great forms of exercise to do throughout pregnancy and pretty much immediately after giving birth (depending on the type of birth you have, of course). They are also toning and relaxing (breathing and slow movement are key to both), and they can be great ways to socialise and meet fellow mums. I bet nearly all of you could find a local gym/town hall/community or leisure centre where either yoga or Pilates is on offer. The great thing about yoga is that there are so many different forms and you can select the one that suits you best. My friend Danni is a complete convert to bikram yoga (where you do vigorous exercises in a room set at 100 degrees. The aim? To sweat out the calories and toxins). She looks amazing and dropped two dress sizes in what seemed like the blink of an eye. She enlists evening babysitting from her mother, goes with her husband once a week and could talk about its benefits (toning, firming, detoxifying, invigorating . . .) until the cows come home.

While I was pregnant, I went for a more moderate form of post-natal yoga. I was addicted to the muscle stretching and 'angry-cat position' (a position undertaken on all fours), which were a godsend for my aching back, and the herb tea and custard creams afterwards were a great way to sit down and chat with other first-time mums. All yoga incorporates a focus on your breathing and some form of intense relaxation (so much so I was often found actually asleep at the end of my ante-natal yoga class), and it goes without saying that every mum on the planet could do with a little extra time to relax.

Equally as dedicated to her chosen exercise field is my friend Rainbow. She's done Pilates for years (way before it made its way on to the fitness radar for celebrities like Gwyneth Paltrow) and has a body that proves it works. You've never seen upper arms like it, and although she's constantly playing handball with her two boys, these biceps took a lot more than a little ball play to gain that shape, I can tell you! Rainbow sourced a great drop-in class, which costs 75p to attend (almost less than a king-size Mars bar!). It starts at nine o'clock in the morning and ties in perfectly with her nursery drop-off and the opening of her boutique at ten o'clock. Cheap, cheerful, kid-friendly *and* offering good results – I only wish I'd got there before the class was fully booked up!

Pump and stretch

For many of you, the only real option for getting fit is to get back into a gym. I've always found gyms rather intimidating and hate to stand, all wobbly boobs and post-natal physique, next to the bronzed god who's just won 'Best Body 2005'. However, if the bank balance stretches to a monthly membership, gyms can offer childcare and structured classes that give an incentive to turn up and get pumping. My fit girlfriend Danielle has always put the gym on her agenda (especially in winter when the bicycle's gathering dust in the garden shed and the school is closed for Christmas). She works out religiously on the cross-trainer, the exercise bike and the light weights, and says she would go up the wall without them. Apparently, twenty minutes on the cross-trainer and bike and fifteen on weights twice a week is more than enough to make you feel positive about your attempts to get back in shape. Failing this, Danielle's gym partner, Sara, sings the praises of a good aerobics class (and there must be some truth in this because she looks pretty damn good for someone with three kids).

I'm sure you can think of another dozen forms of exercise to get you feeling good about your body (ballroom dancing, boxing, football, underwater diving), and if they suit you and you can make time for them, good luck! I've just touched on some of the most popular and ones that my fellow mums and I have done. The realisation we've all come to is that making fitness a priority helps you lose weight, maintain the shape you're happy with and feel energised and good about yourself. It also provides a fabulous base for getting out and about, and can be an ethos shared by the whole family. Many of the exercises I've discussed can be done with children, as a pair or in a group, and this makes it an incentive for everyone. My daughter was the first to ask for a bicycle from Father Christmas this year 'just like Mum's' (in fact, her Barbie model with glittery tassels hanging from the handlebars is the furthest thing from mine, but that's beside the point); soon we'll take up the whole road with bikes just for a trip to the post office. Never mind, it's got to be better than road rage in a people carrier!

Perfume and Pampering

Any woman who's been out on the razzle straight from work (with no shower, no change of clothes and no make-up handy) will know how much better she could have felt with five minutes of prior pampering. Now, I'm not a huge fan of lengthy make-up regimes, daily exfoliations and clutch-bag essentials that cost the same as a week in Ibiza, but I do appreciate the value of a little pampering in feeling good about one's body. For me, a little Vaseline (with added aloe vera) for the lips, a touch of bronzing powder for the face, a good, smelly body lotion and a puff of my favourite scent constitutes pushing out the boat in terms of making myself feel body-beautiful. However, after years working closely with one of the country's top beauty directors (yes, Rosie, that weakness for luxurious face creams is thanks to you!), I also know how oils, potions, lotions and a bit of beauty indulgence can work miracles for a girl who feels in need of a boost.

In those first few weeks after giving birth, even stepping into the shower without hearing the hungry cries of your newborn can seem like an impossible feat, never mind slow, careful body exfoliation and face packs that require a minimum of one hour to work. I always used to try to take a shower first thing in the morning after the early daybreak breastfeed, even if it meant enlisting my husband to help or leaving the baby under the play-gym on the bathroom floor. If I didn't do it first thing, chances are it would be put off for a while, and this way I could shave my legs, apply a little gorgeous shower gel, moisturise, bung on some 'puffy-eye eliminator' (even if it did nothing more than soothe the black rings) and a dab of perfume. It doesn't have to be mega-expensive. Don't be fooled by the myth that spending more will miraculously get rid of all cellulite, stretch marks and age lines. I go by the principle that if it smells nice, doesn't cause a bad skin reaction and is within your price bracket, it serves its purpose. I do tend to spend slightly more on products for my face, simply because with the wrong face cream I end up a blotchy, puffy, allergic-reactive mess!

Once you have a little more rhythm to your life, and possibly more time to pamper yourself, a little 'me' time in the bathroom or gym changing room is central to the body-image issue. If you come home from work, put the kids to bed, go for a run and return home to a hot shower and a long lather of your favourite body cream (even if it's only once a week), I guarantee you will feel at least a little more like your old self. You're sure to feel better than if you'd rushed home, put the kids to bed, eaten a fatty supper, hoovered the living room and fallen into bed knackered, frustrated and wound up like a spinning top.

Although I have great suspicion of beauty companies' miracle claims like 'lose a dress size in three weeks', 'look ten years younger in a month', 'become Kylie with two applications', you get the gist, I do think your body can benefit from exfoliation, moisturising and the occasional beauty treatment. You only have to exfoliate with some form of salt scrub in circular motions all over your body to feel the difference in your skin texture. I am constantly flabbergasted by how smooth my skin feels after treating it to a gritty scrub. Likewise, moisturised skin looks and feels better to both the eye and the physical touch, and who doesn't glow after a treat facial or massage at a local spa?

Feeling good about your body isn't just about shape, size, weight or fitness levels, much of it is also due to a feeling of looking after ourselves, making time for *us*, something that is even harder once we have children. Nothing beats the feeling I had a few weeks ago, when my husband put the children to bed (yes, all on his own!) and I got ready for a night out at our favourite Italian restaurant. I locked the bathroom door, ran a hot bubble bath and sank into it with a glass of white wine. I applied a face mask, scrubbed myself with a loofah, shaved my legs and armpits, and then washed my hair. (I confess for the very first time in a whole week!) I then covered myself in rose-smelling body moisturiser (just a supermarket brand, but it smelt amazing!), gave myself a manicure and pedicure (well, trimmed my nails and painted them, anyway) and applied a sample of 'glowing face booster' that I'd nabbed from a magazine earlier in the day. By the time I was dressed, lip-glossed and ready to scoff some yummy Italian food, I felt as glowing, fresh and special as any girl could feel. And that can't just be from the freebie face pack!

Every woman (especially a new mum) needs a little time to pamper herself. The best Christmas present my mother ever gave me was a facial at her favourite beauty salon plus an afternoon of babysitting so I could actually take her up on the gift. An hour to lie down and be pruned, pricked and pampered was an utter luxury and one that made me feel great about my appearance. A healthy diet and some moderate exercise can only go so far if you don't allow yourself some space to refamiliarise yourself with your face and body from the outside in. Getting a good beauty regime (even if it's just a hot shower, a simple face moisturiser and a great lipstick) can be as important as structuring your fitness schedule. Who can deny they get a tiny boost when someone comments on how 'your skin is glowing', 'your lipstick really works' or how 'amazing you smell today'? Come on, ladies, reclaim that bathroom for ten minutes per day at the very least!

Wow! Is This Really Me?

After giving birth for the first time, my post-natal quest for a reasonable body was probably just like yours. Post-natal bodies are a great leveller, actually; in the end, whatever class, race and income bracket we come from, our bodies post-birth all share the same qualities. (Wobbly tum, saggy bum, lactating boobs – ring any bells?) Three and a half years ago to the day, the snow fell hard and fast, my stitches were yet to heal, and my nipples were cracked and sore. Even the mere words 'keep' and 'fit' in the same sentence made me fall over with laughter! Like nearly all the mum friends I've ever known, my body felt pretty alien to me and yet mustering the energy to change it seemed impossible. However, once my daughter was around five months old, I started my quest for a body that wasn't perfect, but one I could feel comfortable in. Once she was seven months (and I'd returned to work on a part-time basis), I really stepped up my goal for better energy levels and a fitter body. (And, boy, did I need it. Cramming in six commissions for articles, eight trips to the park, a supper party and a visit to the other side of the country to see relatives in one week demands optimum energy levels.)

I tried my best to eat a healthy diet low in sugar, alcohol, caffeine, saturated fats and processed meals. I vowed to cut out (or at least cut down) all those foods made with refined white sugar and carbohydrates that gave me a high and then a sudden, long low. (Bagels, crisps, non-wholewheat pasta, biscuits, patisseries and cakes were out. Ouch!) I combined this with some relaxing, productive exercise and wonder over wonder (so those health gurus were right all along . . .), I really started to win the battle against the bulge. Yes, I had plenty of days off from exercise and virtuous eating (a good golden rule; always have one day off a week or you may turn into Gillian McKeith and scare off all your friends!), but largely I tried to stick to an active, healthy lifestyle as much as possible.

So, when do you really start to see the results? Using my first baby as a gauge, I'd say around six months would be a good starting point. Talk to my friend Tanith and she'd say the nine-month mark would be an honest goal for getting back to your pre-pregnant form (nine months to go up and nine to come down). Ask my sister-in-law and mother-of-two Sue, on the other hand, and she'd tell you not to expect any miracles until your child is at least twelve months old. Whether it takes six months, a year or more, as long as you are consistent, it should start to happen gradually, once you make subtle changes to nutrition and exercise. It's best not to go headlong into a punishing diet and fitness regime from day one, killing your enthusiasm for sure, not to mention personality and libido, plus it goes against all health advice on when your post-natal body is ready. Remember, the rule is no exercise before the six-week mark and only once you've seen your GP. Whenever the time comes, I can guarantee you'll feel great for investing a little time in yourself.

You never forget the moment you look at yourself in the mirror post-baby (or -babies) and no longer think, Oh, hell, is this body really mine? but, Wow, is this really me? (Or at least, OK, I can now undress without the lights off!) I remember clearly the moment this happened after giving birth for the first time. My daughter was nearly eight months old and I had finished breastfeeding three weeks previously. One of my closest girlfriends Lyn was getting married at a beautiful service in the country and the sun was sure to shine. I'd focused very hard on getting back into a gorgeous flesh-coloured frock with lace on the hem that my husband had surprised me with on our honeymoon. You know the kind of dress? We all have it – one of those 'slim-day' dresses that you only dare wear if you feel great and confident about your figure.

My husband and I had decided to be child-free overnight for the first time. My mother was equipped with all the baby paraphernalia and had a mammoth list of all the nap timings, meal plans and 'what to do if she screams'. Armed with a pair of new gold strappy stilettos, that frock and no nappy bag (hurrah!), we headed to the countryside, the sun blazing down as we waved goodbye to our daughter, who was dribbling into my mother's hair. After a long bath (the first one since giving birth that had lasted for longer than six minutes) and a little session with a make-up brush and tweezers, I stepped into the dress that hadn't seen daylight for almost two years. I shut my eyes and stood in front of the mirror. Opening one eye slightly, and then the other just a crack, I saw for the first time in ages a body and person I recognised as myself. My confidence sky-rocketed. Sure, there were still lumps and bumps in places that were once as flat as a chopping board, but I had a beautiful baby to show for it and I certainly looked a lot fitter and more fabulous than I had in my drawstring trousers seven months ago. It goes without saying that the wedding was heavenly and the bride's outfit (all body-skimming white silk and intricate pearls) knocked spots off my frock, as it should, but my husband and I danced all night and I felt goddamn gorgeous!

Just two years later, Lyn had her first outing as a feel-good-factor mum herself. Although it didn't come close to her wedding day (it was a trip to Tesco in the rain that marked the Fabulous Mum Day), she remembers vividly fishing out a pair of old jeans 'just in case', only to find (to her apparent disbelief) that they practically buttoned up. Her son, Riley, was three months old, her bust was still on the page-three end of the scale, and the bags under her eyes had some way to go, but the button fastened and she felt amazing. With a little gentle exercise (walking and Pilates were her thing), she felt that the old her was somewhere within reach. We can all share that feeling. The day my jeans did up after my second baby, I felt it symbolised so much more than just a button in a hole.

There are no rules about size or shape that fit all. Many of you may just want to lose a pound and gain the independence brought on by attending an aqua-aerobics class once a week; others may be on a mission to lose two stone and be able to beat your seven-year-old at football. For me, it was simple. I wanted to feel great, look even better and be able to run around after my two toddlers without reaching for a coffee-and-Snickers fix at four in the afternoon. I wanted to have the stamina to climb trees in the park with my children (or attempt the first branch at least) and still be sparkling company for my husband or a girl-friend in the evening. To top it all off, I wanted to set a good example to my kids about healthy, happy eating, living an active life and being comfortable in one's skin. I'm sure that half the time I fail miserably, but 50 per cent of the time at least, I feel pretty good in my wafty tops and jeans (even if they have Play-Doh moulded into the back pocket and aren't quite the blow-the-budget designer pair I once owned). Did anyone say it's about time for a Saturday night out on the town?

Mother knows best

'Compared with some of my fellow friends with kids, it took me quite a while to lose all my baby weight and feel great. I wanted to take it slowly and couldn't bear the thought of a diet as such. Thanks to a twice-weekly jog in the park and a meal plan that included tons of fruit, vegetables, fish and nuts, on my daughter's first birthday I finally bought a size fourteen. Although I'd always been a size twelve, I passed all my skinny clothes on to my younger sister and invested in some great new outfits in my new size. My body felt slightly bigger, but definitely more defined. I had buckets more energy, I had great skin and hair, and I wasn't constantly wishing I could squeeze into my old clothes. The new me was fit, healthy, a happy mum proud to step out into the world.'

Janet Choi, restaurant owner and mother to Hanoi (two)

Top ten health and fitness tips

1. Don't diet and exercise to extreme during pregnancy. Eat healthily, try out swimming, yoga, walking or exercise classes designed for new mums.
2. Try to find the right time for you to get fit and lose weight. Don't succumb to peer pressure or celebrity role

models; it is impossible to shrink back to a size eight in three days.

3. For many women, body image and feeling good about one's size and shape are inextricably linked to self-confidence and self-esteem. Devoting a little time to fitness will inevitably boost your self-image.

4. Work out a little separate time for fitness in between your family and social life.

5. Make sure you can stick to your fitness plan by ensuring the kids are cared for or can come with you. Better still, make exercise a family effort.

6. Focus on the type of exercise you enjoy and will tone the 'problem' areas. There's no point in signing up for aerobics if you hate group classes, likewise, there's no point in jogging if it's arm definition you really want.

7. Remember, there are lots of mini exercises you can do at home, at work or even while walking the kids to school. Lack of time is no excuse.

8. Exercise alone is not enough. You must combine this with healthy eating and a controlled indulgence in caffeine and alcohol.

9. Do reward and praise yourself when you make the time and effort to get out and get fit. The endorphins alone should give you a boost, even if the results take slightly longer.

10. Once you start to regain your shape, stick at it. Exercise and healthy eating should be a way of life.

Grace's Guru: Fiona Allen

Fiona is a fully trained YMCA personal trainer specialising in anti- and post-natal training who boasts clients such as Jools Oliver. When she's not helping new mums get back into shape, she's keeping up with her three-year-old daughter, Zadie.

What are your main exercise and fitness tips for mums?

A mum with a newborn Ensure you wait the full six weeks before starting any form of exercise (ten weeks if you've had a C-section). When you do start gentle exercise, do it in short spurts and by no means push your body too hard, this will deplete your energy levels and could add to the risk of getting run-down and unwell.

Once you've passed the six-week mark and feel less like a zombie, for most new mums, the tummy seems the main area of focus. A good starting exercise is to position yourself on all fours and pull your abs in slowly. Do this for as long as it feels comfortable – remember, it's absolutely essential not to hold your breath. You can even do it while making faces to the baby on the play-mat or when watching TV in the evening. A similar alternative is one you could try when lying down in the bath, or on a mat on the floor between feeds. Lie flat, bend your knees and pull your abs down until your spine is totally flat on the floor. Once you've done this ten to fifteen times, holding for five to ten seconds on each lift, move on to bringing your arms and head towards your knees, and repeat ten to fifteen times. Always make sure when doing this to think of pulling your belly button inwards and remember that abs go right from the pubic bone to the ribs. Believe it or not, the whole ab area is around twenty centimetres long! Progress on to sit-ups with your hands either crossed in front or behind the head. When doing these exercises daily, let the baby watch, you'll be amazed how interesting a four-month-old can find it!

Some mums have told me that their baby likes to sit on their tummy during gentle sit-ups. Just lift your upper back and head off the floor ten times, repeating for three sets and I promise you'll feel those tummy muscles working. If you have the energy and stamina, combine these exercises with some walking or power lunges and some arm curls. For the lunges, simply step forward so both legs are at right angles and push back up to both feet. Repeat on each leg twenty times for two sets. For the bicep curls, grab a tin of soup or baked beans and use as weights; if you can do fifteen repetitions for three sets, give yourself a pat on the back!

If exercising at home seems too much like hard work, make it your mission to get out and about. Fast walking with your pram for around half an hour a day, three times a week will really help improve fitness, and it's brilliant for a new mum's state of mind as well. (Come on, we all know how feeding and changing a baby within the four walls of the nursery can make you go a little stir-crazy!) You could also try swimming with your babe in tow. Even if you're not doing laps in an Olympic pool, you could join a mum-and-baby swimming class and get moving in the water, it's amazing how much you burn off singing nursery rhymes in the shallow end!

Even when you're not working out, keep posture at its

best, especially when you're carrying the baby for long periods or feeding a lot, make sure you do your pelvic-floor exercises too (which can be done standing up or sitting down).

A mum with an out-of-shape tum, bum and upper arms A good exercise for all-over toning is swimming. Just remind yourself to pull your abs in while doing breast- or backstroke. Combine weekly swimming with the following exercises, aiming for three sets of ten to fifteen repetitions.

Reverse curls – great for the lower abdominal muscles. Lie yourself flat on the floor, keeping your head and shoulders firmly on the mat, legs bent up at right angles and hands beside your bum. Raise your bum off the floor and then lower it down again. I'd suggest three sets of ten to start with, adding more as the weeks go by.

Squats – ideal for toning your bum, legs, thighs and hamstrings. The best way to do squats is the gym-ball squat, increase the benefits by adding hand weights or filled water bottles.

Press-ups – the best press-ups are the old-fashioned box style, starting on all fours. Begin slowly, aiming to get your nose right down to touch the mat each time, before pushing up to the starting position. At all times make sure your back is straight and your abs held tight.

Leg raises – I love these for their ability to tone the outer thighs and bum. Lie on the floor and tie an ankle weight, dynoband or just a strong, thick piece of elastic between your ankles. With both legs bent, rest your elbow on the floor and place your head on the palm of your hand. Raise the top leg up and down for fifteen repetitions; do this for six sets. Change sides and repeat. I know this sounds a lot, but without this repetition you won't feel the burn!

Floor cycling – lying flat on the floor again, raise your head and shoulders off the mat. Kick your legs out one at a time, keeping them as low to the floor as possible. Make sure your opposite elbow comes in to meet the knee, twisting from side to side. It's a tough one, but it does work!

A mum with two very young children I find that for mums with young kids, brisk walks with the buggy, especially hilly ones, are brilliant. Cycling with the kids or an hour on an exercise bike are also a good weekly challenge, and it can be fun for all. Being active in your children's music, dance or even mini-football classes are also good, easy ways to get fit. Join in; the little ones will love it, too (as long as they're not old enough to be well and truly embarrassed by a very enthusiastic mum!).

If you're serious about fitness, you must try and delegate three forty-minute sessions a week to exercises at home as well – even twenty minutes is better than nothing. Press-ups, sit-ups, squats and lunges are all useful and have really quick benefits. I call these workouts my 'home toning routines', as you can actually do a lot of these exercises using everything from stairs to sofas so it couldn't be easier for the new or stay-at-home mum. For the warm-up, I'd recommend staircase step-ups. Explained simply, you just go up one step, join up both feet and back down. If you repeat this between twenty and thirty times on each leg and for three sets, you should start to feel your pulse racing without over-exerting yourself. From the stairs, go on to the sofa for some squats and sit-ups, even watch some morning TV if you feel bored and need to take your mind off the exercise.

For a sofa squat, start with feet hip width apart and attempt to sit down on the sofa, but just as your bottom is about to hit the seat, come right back up to standing position. It sounds like torture, I know (especially when you've just glimpsed a cookery show on Sky), but if you repeat this fifteen times for three sets, you'll feel your hamstrings start to strengthen in your thighs and buttocks. For the sofa sit-ups, have your legs bent and raised up on the sofa, back flat on the floor and arms behind your head, then raise your upper back and head off the floor. Hold this for a second and lower gently back down. Breathe out on the way up and in on the way down. This is a tough one, but if you can manage this fifteen times for up to four sets, you'll be doing brilliantly.

My suggestion would be to devote two nights a week (and possibly one morning, if you can bear it) to the home toning routine. You could always fit in a session while your baby is snoozing and your toddler is at nursery, or even when they potter in the garden on a summer day. Maybe try doing them with a friend who also has kids. You may find you have more motivation getting fit as a pair. I have many clients with two, and sometimes more, young children and after a month or so of three-weekly sessions using these exercises as a guideline, they really start to look and feel better.

A mum with two or more stone to lose Although one and a half to two stone is pretty much the average amount of weight left to lose after giving birth, I know women who've had up to four stone to shed. The principle is the same whatever the weight gain: take it slow, and remember it takes far longer to lose the weight than to put it on (and it's worth bearing in mind that muscle weighs more than fat). I would suggest a slow, pound-a-week goal for mums, less if they are breastfeeding.

Begin the weight-loss and fitness programme with long daily walks if possible and, if you have access to a gym, build on this walking by doing fifteen to twenty minutes on the cross-trainer as well. Work at a rate that challenges you so you can feel your heart rate increase. This will encourage your metabolism to speed up, therefore aiding weight loss. This walking must be teamed with some resistance or weights work for toning the body; bicep curls are perfect and can be done with water bottles when you have a spare twenty minutes, three times a week. The way to stay on top of weight loss is to stay active; make walking up and down stairs, to the corner shop and back via the bank part of your daily routine. If you combine this with healthy eating, you should see the pound-a-week rule work instantly.

A mum wanting to increase her stamina and physical strength Any mum wanting extra stamina and physical strength should work out a fitness routine that incorporates many of the exercises I've discussed. The secret is to do fewer repetitions of an exercise but with more weights or heavier resistance. I find that many of my clients are mums with a whole brood of kids, many well out of toddlerhood, who now need extra stamina to keep up with the energy levels of active schoolchildren. For these women, I suggest jogging for twenty to forty minutes, three times a week. Alternatively, power walks for one hour, three times a week have the same positive effect. Basically, these really energise mums and contribute to tip-top fitness, but I also find they can be done easily without taking a large chunk out of a busy mum's day. To aid physical strength, you may well need to do more concentrated exercises than a forty-minute jog around the local park. I advise press-ups and sit-ups.

If you can spare enough time to join a class at the local gym or sports centre, you can't beat body pump for toning, strengthening and increasing stamina. Likewise, spinning classes are great for stamina, and if you can squeeze in a body-conditioning class for added toning, all the better.

1. Try and do some sort of moderate exercise throughout your pregnancy.
2. Remember to do regular pelvic floor exercises.
3. Once your baby's born and you've begun to establish a good routine, prioritise a little time for exercise each week, and each day if possible.
4. Choose exercises you'll enjoy and look forward to doing. If you hate jogging then how about walking or water aerobics?
5. Don't leave until tomorrow what can be done today. Exercise and keeping fit will lift your spirits I promise!

What are the key dos and don'ts for a mum wishing to promote optimum fitness?

Dos
- Wait until six to ten weeks before you start.
- Get a qualified doctor or fitness instructor to do a recti-check so you can monitor abdominal separation before you launch into exercise.

- Start with gentle tummy pull-ins – even while lying in bed.
- Breastfeed for as long as possible, in my experience, it really helps pull the tummy back in.
- Remember, breathing is key. Breathe in on the exertions and out on the relax.
- Try to include lots of bicep curls and light weightlifting. Arm strength is essential as babies get heavier.
- Start gently with short periods of exercise, then build up day to day.
- Walk every day.
- Push yourself enough to feel the muscles working, but not so you are in agony.
- Think 'posture' all the time – keep the spine lengthened and stand tall.

Don'ts
- Don't start until you feel well enough. Try not to exercise before breastfeeding, and if your breasts are heavy and sore, stay away from lying exercises and wide arm exercises.
- Be careful not to overstretch your body in the first few months. The relaxin hormone can stay in the body after pregnancy for up to five months, making you feel more flexible than you really are.
- Never overwork or overstretch the abs until you know they are starting to knit back together.
- No need to rush out to a gym until you have done simple exercises at home to build up your strength.
- Try not to get stuck on the same set of exercises. Aim to vary them and set yourself a new challenge every week.

- It's crucial not to compete with other mums. Everyone is different and their bodies recover at different paces.

Fiona's fabulous mum's fitness mantra:
'Set yourself small, easy targets and vary them from week to week. Most of all, enjoy this time to get fit and try not to think of it as a chore!'

Sleep and How To Get It

Sleep and Pregnancy

It's one of the biggest ironies of motherhood: it's a job that requires absolute clarity of mind and a sane brain while providing less than the minimum amount of sleep and rest in which to achieve this. If I had known this prior to having my first baby, I am absolutely convinced that I would have given up my job and insisted on spending all nine months of my pregnancy sleeping in preparation for the next eighteen years. Instead, I fell for the hype. As my bump grew, I looked at gorgeous sleeping babies on the covers of glossy parenting mags and peered into buggies on the high street, both of which revealed newborns snuggled up in the land of dreams. Little did I know that this four-hour midday nap was probably replacing their night sleep or was the result of a hefty dose of Calpol!

During my pregnancies, once my initial morning sickness had passed (which, I'd like to add, involved passing out on Tube trains, drinking carbonated water by the gallon, eating homeopathic ginger supplements like Smarties and lying down post-work feeling like I was on a boat in a storm), I chose to live life to the full. Instead of taking the twelve-hour sleep quota available to me, I took on the role of Superwoman. I could be pregnant, a social butterfly, super-journalist *and* hostess with the mostest all at once, couldn't I? Work parties, supper with friends, shopping trips, cooking for twelve at the weekends. Hey, I was radiant; why not show off that bump?

It was in my twenty-fourth week of pregnancy, sitting down at one of these mammoth dinner-party extravaganzas that I met an old acquaintance who had just given birth. Puffy and bleary-eyed, she held little Tom to her breast for what she said was the fiftieth time that day. She had waited years for his arrival and the joy was obvious to see, but boy, oh boy, did she look knackered. A twenty-two-hour labour, twelve stitches, mastitis in both breasts and an over-zealous mother-in-law who had decided to move in to 'help' were all taking their toll. 'Grace,' she said, wincing at having to shift her bottom along the sofa. 'For goodness' sake, take it easy. See yourself as a badger stocking up on sleep during hibernation. Spring is exhilarating, but you'll need your rest supplies by the truckload.'

By the time the baby and then my second pregnancy came around, I realised the shattering truth in her badger advice. Any expectant mums out there, I'd urge you to stock up on your sleep. I'm not saying hide away and wallow in it, I'm all for an active pregnancy, but knowing your limits and enjoying a time when you can bow out of many of the social demands of a hectic lifestyle has something to be said for it. There's nothing wrong with nurturing this time and resisting the desire to push your natural resources to their limits.

They say that sleep breeds sleep and nowhere is this truer than in pregnancy. Especially towards the end of mine, it seemed that the more I slept, the more my body craved it. I eventually had to limit myself to one evening out a week, and those were usually very low-key. I wanted to see friends, aware that it may be a while post-birth before I was able to escape to a night out with girlfriends, but a pizza, a video and bed by eleven suddenly was more than enough. And I wanted to make sure I had some intimate dinners or just a movie with my husband, who would soon enough feel second fiddle to the new arrival. In between these bits of social life, the routine of work and the slow preparations for the baby (which in my case meant not a lot more than buying a Moses basket, some white Babygros and some newborn nappies), I finally managed to take it easy with a capital 'E'. Sunday lie-ins, Saturday afternoons reading a novel and munching Brownies (OK, and Maltesers, Rolos and my mother's ginger cake) and early, early nights. I even took it upon myself to get rest on the work agenda. Three other women in my department at work were pregnant so we organised a spare meeting room as a 'chill-out zone'. Instead of charging around the high street in search of a perfect sandwich, causing our feet to expand to yet another size, we took it in turns to bring lunch and put our feet up for forty minutes. Invaluable zone-out time, great for office/new-baby gossip and even enough time for a few midday zzzzs. Male colleagues were none the wiser, and our female editor at the time was even tempted in the last lap of her pregnancy. Genius.

I know so many women for whom after the seven-month mark, night-time sleep (let alone napping in the day) becomes increasingly difficult. My sister-in-law Sue swears that from month six of her pregnancies she slept no more than fifty minutes at a stretch each night. So much was the indigestion/discomfort/anxiety and general tossing and turning during her pregnancies that she has sworn she will only have two kids and she isn't budging! Other women are so exhausted they manage six hours at a stretch. I come somewhere in the middle, apart from the three-hourly pee-stops (which I'm sure is meant to prepare you for the initial three-hour feeding) and a constant repositioning of pillows between the legs to prop up the bump (which I confess has become a habit I still have two years after my last birth), I would eventually get to around about eight hours in total.

Of course, by your second pregnancy, grabbing rest whenever you can is almost impossible. No more sleeping until midday on a Sunday or spending the weekend curled up on the sofa watching *Beaches* while the husband plays football. There's no denying that being up with number two, three, four or, more relentlessly, rising at 6 a.m. makes sleep even harder to come by. Eventually, after two pregnancies and an extensive poll among my girlfriends, I sat down and made an 'essential sleep hit list':

- **Get an early night whenever possible.** If you have other young children, have an uncomplicated meal once they're asleep and then feel free to hit the sack. Even if you read or unwind in bed first, just resting with your feet up will help. I'm a great believer that the sleep you get before midnight is twice as valuable as that after it. It wasn't unheard of for me to be in bed by 9 p.m. in the last stretch of my pregnancy. (I'm sure my husband had a parallel life going on between 9 p.m. and when he came to bed at midnight!)

- **Rest in the day.** If you're a working mum, resting during the day is pretty much out of the question; however, taking a chilled lunch break (and that doesn't mean daily trips to Top Shop's accessories department via the packed number 39 bus) and resting at weekends all count. Likewise, if you have other children who nap in the day, you could use that time for yourself, or grab an hour or so while they are at nursery or school; the shopping and cleaning won't do itself, but you'll manage it even better without one eye shut. If all else fails, my good buddy Sara swears by lying on the sofa for forty minutes in a half-comatose state while her toddler watches *Noddy*. I'm not at all saying bung them in front of the box and hit the sack for the afternoon, but just stopping to breathe and be still for half an hour is enough to help you get through the day.

- **Share your responsibilities.** If, like me, you find it hard to ask for help, then pregnancy and birth are one of life's milestones when you have to improve on that. It doesn't make you seem incapable or needy in the least to ask your partner, family, friends or neighbours to help you pick up the slack. Not many of us have a house-keeper, personal shopper or a fleet of nannies to keep the household going during this time, but there are probably at least a couple of obliging family members or friends. During my first pregnancy (after my cravings for gazpacho, baked beans and cookie-dough Häagen-Dazs had passed), my husband cooked more than his fair share of meals. He's no Jamie Oliver, but he does make a mean seafood pasta and the best roast chicken (bar my mother's, of course). I would often take the leftovers to work with a salad and this would save on trawling the supermarket for lunch the next day. Similarly, with my second pregnancy, my sister was a weekend lifesaver at entertaining my one-year-old, so I could put my feet up and dream of tiny newborn hands and water births. She would regularly trek over from the other side of London to take her to the park and push her on the swing for an hour, or treat her to sausages and smoothies to save me from cooking supper. You'd be surprised at how much people want to help . . . My advice is, let them!

- **Enjoy at least one lazy weekend away with your partner or a good friend.** Even if a five-star hotel is out of your reach, a nice country B&B will do the trick. The idea really is just to get away, either with your partner or with a good friend and savour some serious R & R before the birth. No cooking, cleaning, working or answering the telephone. Take a stash of magazines, a good book, a face pack and your favourite box of chocolates and just get away. Even if it means bribing your in-laws with the first framed picture of the newborn so they'll look after your toddler (or threatening to name the child after your husband's favourite Tottenham striker as my friend Kate did – a brilliant way of gaining help from her Arsenal-supporting in-laws), it's worth it. A good cash-saving trick is to choose mid-week breaks, it keeps costs lower, as hotels are often offering special deals (extra champagne in the room sound tempting?). It may be a while before you can get away again after the birth, and you, the new baby and the person nearest and dearest to you are worth it.

- **Make sleep as comfortable as possible.** You may feel like a beached whale and the baby's back flips are making you squirm and fidget in your bed, but the more comfortable your sleep space is, the higher the chance of achieving some rest. I always found that to try and do some form of exercise in the day (walking the last bus stop, going for a swim) will help your body wind down at night. A long bath before bed will also help (not too hot, though!); and stock up on pillows and props for the bump. Having a sheet on hand if the duvet feels like it's 100 degrees is useful, and if you can nab a back rub before you hit the hay, then do it! If it's your mind not your body keeping you awake at 3 a.m., stash a pad and pencil beside the bed to write down your fears or 'must dos' in order to let them go until morning.

The rest (excuse the pun!) is up to you. Just remember that those first few months as a mum are like a rollercoaster and you'll need as much rest and calm as possible to cope. Make sleep and a little 'you' time top of your priority list and everything else will follow.

Mother knows best

'I already had a two-year-old when I found out I was pregnant again with twins. I had been incredibly active in my first pregnancy, but this time round the demands of my high-energy son and a full-time job just zapped me. I was huge and desperately tired all the time. To make life easier on me, I worked out a rota with some fellow mums to help get Semai to nursery in the morning. My boss agreed that I could start work an hour earlier and could then leave an hour earlier. This meant I missed commuting in the rush hour and got home with enough time to nap before picking Semai up at the end of the day. Those forty-five minutes of day-sleep were a lifesaver and always revived me enough to give Semai the warm welcome he deserved and stay awake for a TV dinner with my husband.'

Manira Brivarti, travel agent and mother to Semai (three), Jennal and Caal (both six months)

Those First Few Weeks

It's almost impossible to describe the multitude of emotions you go through in those first few weeks. You've waited nine months (and probably more) for this moment. You've dreamt about it, fantasised about it and prepared for it in every way. You've written the birth-plan, bought the muslin squares, heard the birth story of every mother you know and had your hospital bag packed and beside the front door for at least the last month. You will never forget the moment that all this waiting finally reaches a crescendo and labour starts. Whether yours is a three-hour home-birth breeze or a thirty-hour ordeal followed by an emergency C-section, it takes it out of you. The emotions, the lost nights' sleep, the pain and the euphoria all take their toll. Combine this with spending the night in a packed NHS ward (where the sound of newborns crying and the hubbub of new arrivals being wheeled in means a permanent high noise level) and there's even less chance of having a rest. Once the endorphins had worn off and I realised how desperately I needed sleep right then and there, my daughter had woken up, found her voice and wanted instant feeding and attention at least every two hours. This is where mother and child are at loggerheads. Mother needs sleep, and baby needs mother and she needs her awake. If you are among the 2 per cent of the population who can rely on a maternity nurse to get you through this, then you can skip this part and head for a relaxing hot bath and a full night's sleep! For the rest of us non-fully-staffed mums, delirious tiredness is part of the whole motherhood package.

The baby may sleep in the bed with you (as my firstborn did for the first six months of her life), in a Moses basket beside the bed or in a cot at the end of the corridor (as my neighbour's son did because there was no other space left in a house with two older siblings!). I always found that having the baby close made things infinitely easier. Not only does it mean you don't have to traipse around the house in the early hours, but you can see and hear your baby at any time. There can't be a mother on the planet who hasn't rushed to her newborn sure that it had stopped breathing and prodded it just to check. If you're breastfeeding, having the baby near means you can easily feed without too much disturbance and can do it from the comfort of your own bed. I certainly found that when I was learning the breast-feeding ropes, I needed endless pillows to get the positioning right. A night-light is a great saviour during all this nocturnal activity. My good friend Catherine lent me a very nifty model that dimmed as you fed. I often found my daughter latching off as it went dark, and in no time we were both back in the land of slumber. No getting up and turning off the switch required.

If you are bottlefeeding, best be prepared. Keep a bottle-warmer by your bed and then the only real hassle is getting up and grabbing the ready-made milk from the fridge (unless you are my friend Kate, who invested in a tiny bedroom fridge so she didn't even have to leave the bedroom at night!).

It's not an easy situation for the guys, with their full day's work (and with an eighteen-month-old and newborn to look after, what the hell would you call my day, a bloody holiday?), but it's best to try and work out a compromise early on. If you express, he could feed at the weekend or one night a week.

The key to those first few weeks is to make it easy on yourself. Keep the baby close, have water and snacks beside the bed for night hunger. (If you thought pregnancy hunger was bad, wait for breastfeeding hunger!) Keep a spare sheet handy – night sweats post-labour can be ferocious. (I woke up most nights feeling like I'd been trekking in a tropical rainforest.) Likewise with your bottom sheet, keep a spare or sleep on a towel (preferably not white – those sweat stains are hard to shift). For those with post-birth bleeding, nights can feel like a heavy menstrual cycle times a hundred (or 'like your insides are falling out whenever you move' as my friend Kate so eloquently put it). I hate to go on, but have

I mentioned the leaking breasts? Wearing a specially designed night-time nursing bra might look unglamorous, but with pads in each side, it can save you from a drenched bed. Mums, let's face it, things will be uncomfortable for the first few weeks, and the best way to get through it is to be prepared and have all the necessary equipment and sustenance on hand.

The trick in those early days is not to expect miracles. Be kind to yourself and your newborn and leave it up to those close to you to help with everything else. Limit the amount of visitors and get those willing to help to assist with cooking, cleaning and the childcare of siblings. One of the best presents I received after my first was born was a week's worth of hot meals. My sister-in-law Jo (easily one of the best cooks in North London) came to see me with an armful of dishes. (I can still taste her delicious shepherd's pie, moussaka and vegetable couscous.) We froze the lot and saved on cooking during those precious first few nights. My friend Lyn's mother came up with the genius idea of arriving at Lyn's home armed with vases and arranged all the well-wishing bouquets around the house. She also handed Lyn a box of thank-you cards, envelopes and stamps, another thing that would have taken her time to organise and instead left her free to tend to the demands of nurturing a newborn. All this fabulous well-wishing can be exhausting, and combined with running the home, does seem like a huge feat when you're low on energy, so pulling the ranks together is a hit formula.

Once you have a support system in place, I found that you just start to learn to catch rest when you can. Most of your friends with children will advise you to 'sleep when the baby sleeps', and unlike a lot of other annoyingly well-meant advice, this probably is a wise one to take on board. It's easy when your baby naps to rush around making calls and doing the ironing, but no one will fault you for easing up for a while. Taking the opportunity to rest in the day helps you catch up on the sleep lost at night. When I got home from the hospital second time round, I somehow felt an enormous amount of pressure to be the superhuman mother of two. 'It's soooo much easier after your second,' people would say. So I entertained, played with my daughter, breastfed my son, did the food shop, went swimming, even offered to cook Sunday brunch for friends. Until I hit a wall; exhausted and burnt out I got the most excruciating bout of mastitis and had to say, 'Stop!' I was so anxious I wouldn't be the wife/mother/friend/daughter I had always been that I ended up bedridden with a high-grade fever and couldn't be anything to anyone. It was a learning curve and one in which I had to train myself to limit visitors, chores and play-dates and concentrate (for the first few weeks, anyway) on my immediate family. This wasn't only essential for my well-being but also came as a blessing for my toddler. She had, after all, just been presented with her brother who was attached to *her* mummy's breast every time she wanted a cuddle!

Advice Overload

The best advice I was ever given was to ignore 90 per cent of all advice. You've probably noticed that ever since your bump became slightly obvious, the world and its neighbour had an opinion on it. One morning, when I was six months pregnant with my son, I counted the amount of comments I had received on my hour-long journey to work in Central London. Eight in total, in just one hour! The guy at the Underground news-stand reckoned, 'It was due any day.' (Was I really that big?) The lady who offered me her seat had a good feel and exclaimed in the silent Tube carriage, 'Aaaahhhhh, bless!' The bus driver reckoned it was 'Dead cert to be a girl'. (Yeah, right!) And the checkout woman at Sainsbury's Central told me in great detail about giving birth to her twins three years previously. Good intentions aside, everybody will give you their twopence about your baby, their baby and any other baby they know or will ever know.

And the topic of sleep and children seems to prompt more advice than any other parenting issue around. Every mother and father has been a victim of sleepless nights, and even if their kids are now well into school age, their day is likely to start with the pitter-patter of tiny feet at 6 a.m. or earlier, day in, day out. Their seven-year-old may be wetting the bed again, and their nine-year-old may even have been up for the last four nights with chickenpox. I've yet to meet a parent on the planet who can't relate to sleep deprivation on some level.

Sleep (or lack of it) is one of the most fundamental issues and touches a nerve with every one of us. I hadn't taken that fully on board until the moment I stepped over our threshold with my newborn and it fell on me like a ton of bricks. Every family member, every fellow mummy pal, every visitor, every neighbour, every mother at the bus stop will offer you some sort of advice on how to get sleep. 'In my day, we left the little rascals to cry,' was the advice of one helpful old aunt who came armed with a potted cactus. (A cactus – that says it all, doesn't it?) 'Skin to skin at all times; haven't you heard of the attachment method?' said a yoga buddy, who kept her three-month-old strapped to her in a New Age papoose for the entire three-hour visit. 'The baby's starving: top up with formula,' said a pro-bottlefeeding relative, who clearly felt that someone breastfeeding openly put her off her almond macaroon. If this wasn't enough, every birthing and baby book, from Ford to Ferber and back to Hogg, offers you advice on getting your baby to sleep, keeping it asleep and managing to do so when you want to. In the end, I just wanted to scream, 'Let me find what works for me!'

No infant is the same and their needs vary. Some are touchy-feely and for the first six weeks just won't be put down; some feed efficiently and then sleep happily for three-, even four-hour stretches from the very beginning; some just cry and cry and cry and all you can do is soothe them and wait patiently for this stage to pass. (I know it doesn't seem like it, but it will, I promise!) As mothers, fathers, co-parents and family members, we try to work out the needs of our children, whether newborns, babies, toddlers or fully fledged schoolkids, and the advice overload, at times, can seem like just too much.

I was the first of my siblings and the first in my peer group to have a child. While bewildering at times, I loved the challenge of forging my own path and working out a family structure and routine that worked for my husband and me, regardless of what everyone else was doing. We were going to travel with our daughter, breastfeed her in public, take her to Sunday lunches and make her part of our world.

That sounds quite nice, doesn't it? Well, once she was born and began to grow, we quickly realised that we had to adapt a lot of our plans to suit an inquisitive baby who loved routine. And that was fine; what was crucial was having the space to carve out this structure for ourselves.

From the moment my newborn latched on to my breast, people asked, 'Is she sleeping in the bed?' (For now, yes), 'Is she feeding on demand?' (Ditto), 'Are you following a strict routine of feeding, sleeping and playtime from birth?' (No, not yet), 'Are you going to express milk?' (Yes, but not immediately), 'Are you really taking her on holiday at four months?' (Yes, yes, yes!). I'm surprised I wasn't asked by well-wishers for a full inventory of her nursery and schooling up until the age of eighteen. My method of managing this was to stay calm – and to tell people what they wanted to hear. 'No, of course she wasn't sleeping in the bed,' 'Routine, of course, from day one, Gina Ford all the way,' 'Yes, she's down for Monkey Music, Tumble Tots and Ballet, who cares that she's only six weeks old!' It sounds strange, but it makes people back off and gives you a bit of space to breathe and find your way. By the time the baby is a few months, and you've begun to get your life back together, you can then work out exactly what you want to tell people about your childrearing methods. In the end, the choices you make are personal, and if you are too honest and anxious with everyone about your approach, the tirade of advice and the list of 'dos' and 'don'ts' will be endless.

That said, even before giving birth, you may have worked out your inspirational advisers and mentors for bringing up children – central friends, family and colleagues who share the same approach to life as you and whose opinion you trust. (You know you've found one when you can call them at 3 a.m. with a possible contraction, or fifteen times a day with your toddler projectile-vomiting across the living room.) I always admired (and still do) my mother's methods for bringing up my three siblings and me. Hands on, full of love, creative, playful and imaginative, and through it all she always maintained her own skills, identity and life. (She could make the best chocolate brownie in town, but on occasion missed bedtime for an opening at her gallery or the launch of a book she'd worked on.) Likewise, my good friend Jennie, who is a youngish mum (twenty-eight for her first), and maintains a good job as well as a strong family unit, is someone I can turn to for advice on everything from colic to schooling. Her daughter is one of the happiest and most robust in the neighbourhood, and her tips on those early years are always received with open arms: 'Love them, listen to them, let them play outdoors, don't spoil them and teach them to clear up after themselves, especially the boys!' was a nice contrast to all the other erratic advice on night terrors, bed-wetting and gastric reflux. There are those who will surprise you: a distant acquaintance who gives birth the same time as you and shares your ethos on feeding and childrearing, a relative who supports you in a way you'd never have seen coming before giving birth, and new friends who pop up as your kids grow (like my new pal Tanith, whom I met at the school gates. Her tips on everything from sleep to combining freelance work with two under-threes have been insightful and inspiring to say the least). Slowly but surely, you'll build a network of important women who share your values and whose advice you seek and relish. They will be your saviours!

Mother knows best

'My best advice, and something you never get sick of, is to follow your instincts. My three-year-old was a good sleeper and suddenly she was waking up and crying in the night. People advised me to use the controlled-crying technique, try a night-light or to put her to bed later. I tried everything, but my instinct was that something was wrong. On the fourth day, I took her to the doctor and he diagnosed a deep-rooted ear infection that had been giving her nagging pain in the night for what could have been weeks. We treated it with some antibiotics and some homeopathic remedies and within days she was sleeping like a dream.'

Georgina Cape, full-time mother to Edie (six) and Rosemary (three)

Routine

Routine is a funny old thing. For many women, routine is their religion. It means they get a set structure that can be followed like a winning formula for life, passed on to friends and family whenever they are 'in the family way'. They live it, breathe it, love it and can't imagine life without it. For others, routine is like the anti-Christ: bad, rigid, controlling, oppressive and to be avoided at all costs. Luckily, I have been resident in both camps, so I can see the good and bad in both. My method has been to try to find some form of structure that while it can be considered a 'routine' as such, doesn't bind us into so strict a ritual that we cannot step outside it even for a second.

When I had my first child, I don't think I'd ever considered how much our lives were bound to routine. Most of us get up at the same time, probably eat the same breakfast and get the same bus to and from work, and then repeat again until the weekend. It then came as a bit of a shock to me when my two-hour-old daughter didn't really fit into my routine. She slept when she wanted to (usually not at night), ate when she wanted to (twenty-four hours a day), cried when she wanted to (although not much – what's there to cry about when you're always attached to the breast?) and filled her nappy whenever she desired (which was usually once we'd arrived at the supermarket, or just run out of the last nappy on a day out). For the first three months, I very much let her lead the way. She slept in our bed at night and in her Moses basket in the day (on the kitchen table, under the shade of our garden tree, beside the bath while I bathed). She breastfed on demand (and this was occasionally when I was sipping a cup of tea in a local café with friends, or once all the way through a supper party at a neighbour's).

A quick note on routines and feeding on demand

Personally, I feel that yes, routines are beneficial, and yes, eventually they will help you and the baby get a good night's sleep, but for the first few weeks, making a baby fit into a rigid structure will only end in tears (both yours and the baby's). It's great to have a rough idea of when the baby tends to feed and for how long. It's also ideal if the baby can space the feeds every two to three hours, feeding for around twenty-five to forty-five minutes per feed (the fore milk the baby gets first isn't nearly as rich as the hind milk reached after around fifteen minutes on the breast), and after several months, you could even try to push this to four-hour stretches between feeds.

Deciding whether to feed on demand or implement a sense of routine immediately after the birth is such a personal choice, and each new mother and family unit must decide what suits them. My gut feeling, from the experience of my own babies and those close to me, is that for the first few weeks you must really let the baby guide you. You know that it is best to space out feeding and naps, but you can't force a baby to feed for exactly twenty minutes on each breast, take four ounces at each bottlefeed or nap for two hours precisely at lunchtime, not yet anyway. You only end up feeling frustrated when the baby falls asleep after every ten-minute feed and then naps for three hours just before bedtime. Focusing on learning the meaning of each cry, getting feeding to work for you, holding, touching and bonding with your baby is the key to those early days. Responding to the baby's needs and working out when he cries from hunger, pain, tiredness or boredom will go a long way towards helping you eventually implement a successful sleep structure that suits you and your child. Feeling fabulous three days after giving birth is a pretty impossible feat, but feeling calm, in control and not overwhelmed by choices and demands is the first step!

The long term

I found that feeding on demand in those early weeks definitely helped me bond with my daughter. But nurturing aside, I admit I was also knackered, and around three months, once my wounds had healed and my baby weight had begun to reluctantly drop off, my longing to get out and really explore life with baby in tow was growing. The only trouble was, I never had any idea when she was going to want to feed, and boy, did she scream when she was hungry! Visits to the local shops could be a nightmare with a 'starving' baby screaming for her milk, and she seemed to know every park bench between here and the corner shop upon which I could whip up my top and feed her. While I didn't want to force her into a strict structure, I was in desperate need of some sort of predictable routine to enable me to reclaim some life outside my own four walls. By this point, I had roughly worked out what each of her cries meant, how long she liked to be awake and how long she would feed for. I knew when she used my breast for comfort and when she really needed that milk. I knew that she liked to sleep on her front with her head to the left. (I know, I know, not ideal.) I knew that she liked a massage from her dad towards the end of the day, and I knew that her favourite lullaby was 'Lavender's Blue'. The time had come to work on that dreaded concept 'routine' and get my life back on track.

Over the weeks, months and years that followed, my husband and I worked out a structure that suited our family's needs. At four to five months, the routine was based on the certain knowledge that she *could* go for longer periods without a feed. She'd progressed from feeding in the night at 7 p.m.,

11 p.m., 2 p.m. and 7 a.m. to just needing one feed in the night at around 2.30 a.m. By six months (and a bonny eighteen pounds), she was skipping this feed. (First, she still woke looking for milk; occasionally, she'd cry a little, but I'd leave her for a bit and eventually, wonder over wonder, she'd resettle herself.) At this point, we moved her out of our bed and into a cot in her own room. We kept the same bedtime routine and all the closeness this involved and she loved her new cot. (It was me who cried the first night about not having her in our bed!) It felt like an unbelievable breakthrough to get a full night's sleep alone at last. It hadn't happened immediately, but I was glad I'd been patient and hadn't rushed it.

There are so many structures to choose from – Gina, Tracey, Ferber and so on – but if you're like me, you'll find that it comes down to creating your own in the end. And if a child is sick, for example, you need to go with the flow and let them eat and sleep at will. Likewise, if you are a working or single parent, time schedules will vary and you may not get home until 7.30 p.m., or you may be alone putting four children to bed. Finding your own routine is more than worth it: it will help you feel more in control of your life and give you a formula for happy children, happy families and a good night's sleep for all. Hurrah!

This is a structure I mapped out between my babies and toddlers, and all those of my girlfriends, and it seems to work for quite a few people, so there might be something here for you as well:

- **Waking up.** My children wake up at around 6 to 7 a.m. My sleep-loving daughter can sometimes sleep until 8 a.m., but my skyrocket of a son is ready for action religiously at around 6 a.m.! Obviously, some kids do need less sleep and may wake up slightly earlier, or you may need to wake them if you take them to a carer before work, but waking any earlier than around 5.30 a.m., in my book at least, is still the middle of the night and is a problem – see the next section, 'Common Sleep Problems'. Both my children have black-out curtains in their rooms, and I am confident that by keeping the rooms dim, it helps them sleep longer, especially in the summer.

Once the children are up, they usually come into our bed for a drink of diluted juice, water or milk (for the youngest). It's nice to have a moment to chill out, time for a cuddle and a few jokes in Mummy and Daddy's bed, before the day starts, and it also reiterates that they are allowed in the bed in the morning, to play, but never in the middle of the night.

- **Daytime naps.** If you have a child under two, 11 a.m may be a good time to let them nap. Younger babies may benefit from a sleep for half an hour at around 9 a.m. and then again at around 1 p.m. Older toddlers who still need to crash in the day may also hold out until 1 to 1.30 p.m. I would advise only letting them sleep for a maximum of an hour to an hour and a half (and some may only need forty minutes or so) and no later than 3 p.m. I know a few mums who let their toddlers sleep and sleep (one friend often lets her three-year-old go to the three-hour mark), but we all unanimously found that this tends to interfere with night sleep or means they wake at 5 a.m. If it doesn't affect the night, lucky you – enjoy the time off!

Many toddlers will sleep anywhere, and sometimes

this works well if you are out shopping, in the car or out for lunch. I always envied the mother having one glass of Pinot Grigio at a Sunday-brunch al fresco with friends while her children slept soundly in the buggy. Mine always got overtired and ran around like maniacs, leaving me to fret and get indigestion. Most of the time, I found that letting them have a quiet, deep sleep in bed (whether this be at your home, at the childminder's or at nursery) actually meant they were on better form for the afternoon. My fellow mums and I all agree that our children tend to nap better in a quiet space that holds positive sleep associations, and the quality of their sleep is higher. (No grouchy, screaming toddler sore from a buggy-induced cricked neck!) If you have siblings around at the same time, set them up with a quiet game, story or creative play. It may be a nice moment with them, which you couldn't have enjoyed with a younger sibling around.

- **Winding down for the night – bath time.** Depending on your working life, I think it's good if one or preferably two adults are around for bath time. Personally, I love the idea of a bonding pre-bath ritual. We listen to music, chat about the day and have a cuddle on the bed while the bath is running. My friend Gayle devotes the time to a ten-minute massage ritual that helps her engage with her twins before bed. It's also great to involve children in bath-time preparation (pouring in bubbles, selecting bath toys, choosing night clothes). This will get them excited about the whole pre-bed process. Bath time is part of the winding-down process, and making it calm and relaxed is crucial, I think.

- **Story time.** Not counting the time when both children finally go to sleep, this is the best part of my day! If your children are close in age, you could read to them together; if you have older children, it may be an idea to let them have quality time with a partner, play quietly in their room or even assist you with the younger siblings' bedtime. This will make them feel older and slightly special, giving them time with you alone once the youngest are in bed.

  Story time is relaxed and calm, preferably in their bed. Draw the curtains and dim the lights and children will start to understand that this is a time for sleep. Give them a small drink of milk or water if they want it.

  Ensure older children go to the toilet before bed, hopefully preventing them from needing to go in the night or wetting the bed.

- **And finally . . . bedtime.** All kids have different bedtime rituals; indulge them – most of the time, they're there to make them feel safe. My friend Kate's son can't do without a recital of all the family members he loves, for example, and my niece Layla insists her mum 'zaps all the big bad wolves' out through the window before she goes off to sleep! And put the toy or comforter they need in reach.

Routine is such a double-edged sword, but if you make it work with you, it can change your life. And I think children actually thrive on it. They need us to impose some kind of structure on their day, however rigid or flexible you decide for it to be. It's crucial to listen to each child's needs and follow their lead on how they like to sleep, what food they prefer to eat and what games they enjoy playing, but it is also up to us to guide them. We've been far longer on this planet to learn that eating chips all day isn't a balanced diet and staying up all night makes you ratty. They may resist it and fight you all the way to the sack, but being strong, consistent and loving, and letting them know with a kind but firm tone that you are the boss means they as much as you will reap the benefits.

Having content and happy children who sleep well (and I'm not saying every night, all year around – hey, we're all human!) gives you the chance to make time for all those other areas of your life that are important to you. It doesn't take a genius to work out that if your kids are in bed by eight (and you know they are likely to sleep through until a decent hour in the morning), you can start to get your own life back on track. Evenings and kids' naptimes are for you and your partner, for exercise and, yes, household chores, for girlie times and relaxation or just a quiet meal and a good soap opera. Getting your groove back takes a while, but you need to make sure that the time is there – without the kids screaming or sneaking into your bed at 3 a.m.

Mother knows best

'Goodness me, I'm an old hippy so the idea of a routine scared me rigid. My son, Tiger, was up most of the night, would regularly gatecrash our dinner parties and would eat pretty much whenever he pleased. This suited me fine, as I was often known to have lunch at 4 p.m. myself! Once he started nursery and I gave birth to his sister, Violet, however, things started to get difficult. He fell asleep at nursery, became ratty and bad-tempered because he'd missed breakfast and would then be up all night while I breastfed V. I was at the edge of despair and beyond exhausted, so decided with my partner to start to get a rhythm into his life. At first it got worse, but we persevered, especially with the bedtime routine, and in the end he thrived on it. He now takes himself to nap at 2 p.m. every day and will be the first to strip off and jump in the bath most evenings. I now teach special-needs kids at home in the evenings. Thanks to a simple routine to his day, we all sleep better and I'm expecting my third!'

Tanya Lewis, teacher and mother to Tiger (three) and Violet (eleven months)

Common Sleep Problems

The day I finished the first draft of this section I felt wonderful. I'd made a list of all the sleep problems I could think of, then, with a feeling of utter satisfaction, I jotted down answers to each of them.

Of course, as always, bad-sleep demons are there to remind you never to get too smug. The next morning, my two-year-old son was up at 4.55 a.m., wandering around the landing looking for 'Mummy'! By the time I had resettled him, it was close to 6 a.m., bright sunlight was streaming in through our bedroom window and the dustmen were clanking around outside. Since then, I have had several months of Sleep Hell (a son with 2 a.m. tantrums, also occasionally found wandering around at midnight, and inevitably up at 5 a.m., with a smile that says, 'Hello, I'm awake for the rest of the day'). It goes to show – whether you're struggling with sleep issues or think you've sussed them, common sleep problems always, always lurk in the shadows, ready to raise their ugly head whenever they please, and from one day to the next, you'll spend the whole day (or months in my case!) in zombie land.

So, what was my approach to this sleep setback? I tried (even though I felt like getting down on my hands and knees, sobbing) to stay calm and consistent. My brief was to reassure my son, offer him love and security without over-stimulating him or letting him rely on me to go to sleep. A fairly steep task, I agree! But even when all I really wanted was to retreat to a Balinese spa and never come home, I tried my very best to offer my son that extra play and mummy attention in the day, hoping it would divert his need for extra attention at night. Admittedly, it took almost two months (and not three days as some parenting gurus suggest!), but in the end, the night-waking stopped and we have reached the compromise of a 6 a.m. start. (Believe me, after getting up at 3 a.m. for eight weeks, this feels like a lie-in!)

As babies grow to toddlers and toddlers grow to children, they will inevitably pass through phases of illness, insecurity, bed-wetting and pick up some bad habits and irrational fears along the way. I think the trick is to stick with the routine you've come up with and be consistent when working through the sleep issues. I've jotted down some of the main problems my fellow mums and I have encountered along the way and outlined some techniques we've used to combat them. Some of these work for babies, some for toddlers, or both, but however tried and tested, they are suggestions only, compiled from mums who've also been up half the night, tearing out their hair (and reaching for a double vodka at one time or another). In the end, all families are different, so this is just a guide or, better still, a voice that says, 'We've all been there too. Keep calm, bear with it, things will improve. Eventually!'

Early risers

Let's face it, for many of us new to this parenting lark, even 7.30 a.m. seems like the middle of the night. Only now do you see that the world is full of bleary-eyed parents, up at 8 a.m. on a Sunday, desperately trying to find something to do with the kids. (The only other people crazy enough to be up at that time in the morning are those still partying from the night before. Not long ago, that was us!) Soon we come to realise 7 a.m. feels like a lie-in. For me at least. If I could guarantee that the kids would sleep until then, every day and every weekend, I would pay for it by direct debit without question. As I mentioned earlier, however, for many families the day can start much earlier. I often hear mums complaining that their children 'Wake up religiously at 5 a.m. every morning' or that 'Little Johnnie starts his day bright and perky at 4.45 a.m.'. A few tips and tricks might come in handy:

- **Ensure the child isn't going to bed too early.** It turned out that little Johnnie, the 4.45 a.m. riser, was being tucked up at 6 p.m. Stretching out bedtimes slowly over a week or so, adding fifteen minutes every night for a week, may help; 8 p.m., in my view, is as late as it should go, though, as letting bedtime run into nine, ten, or eleven o'clock at night could actually have the opposite effect. Believe me, my friend Sophie tried it and almost tore out all of her hair. Both child and single mum were overtired, strung out and grumpy and calming an over-stimulated toddler consumed that nine o'clock window Sophie used to do the ironing.
- **Ensure the child isn't napping too much in the day.** If your three-year-old is having a mammoth sleep in the day, then try cutting this down. A good friend of mine, Sonia, loved having the afternoon off while her toddler slept the day away (she chatted to friends, caught up on work emails and read the latest *Vogue*), but was distraught when he suddenly started waking up before dawn. A child only needs a certain amount of sleep over a twenty-four-hour period and most of that should be at night. They will hate you at first (no tired child likes to be woken from a nap), but coax them out of it with a quiet story, a cuddle or a cold drink. On the other hand, if your child desperately needs half an hour of shut-eye to make it through the rest of the day, make sure she gets it. When I cut out my son's day rest as an experiment to get him sleeping better at night, I found that it only exacerbated the problem. He was dropping by six in the evening and fell into a heavy sleep for the first part of the night. He'd then come out of his deep sleep

at around 3 a.m., and what do you know? The day would start for the whole family then. What was I thinking?

If your child does wake early, it's important they don't crash again at 9.30 a.m. They may be using this as the last part of their night-sleep, leaving you frayed at the edges. Again, try and stretch this nap, until eventually it reaches the 10.30 a.m. mark at the very least.

- **If they are old enough, insist they stay in their room.** For many families, early rising is just a fact of life. After trying every technique imaginable, your children may still insist on waking with the lark at two, three or older. If this is the case and you've resigned yourself to it, you must be firm but kind in instructing them to stay in their rooms. Make sure quiet toys are accessible. (I'll never forget when my nephew went through a stage of early waking; he managed to discover the noisiest electric drum with Walt Disney sound effects at 6 a.m.) Also, perhaps leave a drink or a piece of fruit beside their bed. The idea is to be clear about what hours are acceptable for waking, and at the same time to redefine your bed and bedroom as out of bounds during the night hours.

Separation anxiety

I've been through intense separation anxiety with both my children. (Not just at night – even going to the toilet has been a serious issue at some stage!) I am still heartbroken when a child passes through this phase. The sound of them crying and calling out your name goes straight to the core of your being. But the thing to remember is that children have to learn how to put *themselves* to sleep, on their own, without crutches. If you are in bed with them, holding their hand (an old favourite of my son's), or sitting beside them until they fall asleep, it can begin to rob them of the ability to go to sleep alone and that's where you come in – at twelve or three or five o'clock.

- **Try not to get into bed with the child from the very beginning.** I know so many couples who sleep with their children for at least half of the night. One high-flying girlfriend would regularly tuck herself up in bed with her twins to help them go to sleep, more often than not finding herself fully dressed and still there in the morning. I don't need to tell you how, in the long run, this led to dependent children, a disgruntled husband and zero evening 'you' time.
- **Slowly separate yourself at bedtime.** Instead of getting into their bed, give them a favourite story, turn off the lights, have a nice long cuddle, some kind words and then sit close to them (on an armchair or the floor) in the room. Each night, sit for less time and get further towards the door. You'll probably find (as I did with my son) that the moment you get outside the door they lurch up and begin to cry. Go back, lay them facing away from you and tell them you love them and that it's time for sleep. Then go through the procedure again. Once outside the door, make sure they can hear you breathe and, once they seem calm, creep away. (I now know every creak in the floorboards to avoid.) Eventually (and be prepared, it took me three weeks!), you will get there. Believe me, we opened a bottle of champagne once we'd done it!

- **Try the praise method.** If you have a particularly tricky toddler, you could try a technique recommended to me by an acquaintance (and professional kids' sleep expert), Andrea Grace. She suggests tucking up your child in bed, reiterating how warm, cosy and snug it is, and telling them clearly that you will go and tell Daddy/Grandma/or a friend how good they are at staying in their bed. 'I'll be back in five minutes' is her mantra. Come back every few minutes as promised, repeating the process each time. More often than not, praising your child for staying in bed alone will be motivation enough to go to sleep themselves. Her method has worked for at least three families I know, so surely it could be worth a try?

Night wakers

Just the thought of one of my toddlers calling out 'Mummy' at 2 a.m. makes me tired. As anyone with kids knows, it can take hours to get them back down and then another hour to get yourself back to sleep. In short, you feel wrecked. As mums, we tend to know when that persistent waking is for separation anxiety, illness, teething or a horrible bad dream. There are still many other complex reasons why children wake at night. (Let's face it, as adults we wake with fears, worries, anxieties ourselves, or indigestion after a Chinese takeaway.) My daughter woke up only last week in a flood of tears, clutching her snowy bear for dear life. There was no doubt in my mind that she had just had the worst nightmare, and it took a good ten-minute bear hug to stop the whimpering. More often than not, though, night waking is more a case of MINA (Mummy, I need attention). My trick is to follow the rules for separation anxiety and reiterate through your actions that night-time is for sleep and sleeping alone. If your child is particularly anxious, try to bring in a favourite soft toy, blanket or comforter. My daughter won't ever sleep without her snowy bear, so it has become an invaluable tool in getting her back to sleep (so much so I have two of Snowy's 'sisters' stashed in my bottom drawer ready for that inevitable day that Snowy I loses an ear or gets left on holiday).

If the night waking seems to be due to a recurring bad dream, then it's worth trying to get to the bottom of those fears. Silly as it sounds, my friend Sophie eventually realised that her toddler's bad dreams were due to a fear of the nursery toilets (bless!). A daily visit to the loos with mum at drop-off time (and the painting of a jungle mural on the toilet walls) soon solved this and her two-year-old sleeps better than ever. Likewise, my niece Layla's wolf fear got so out of hand that she was waking almost every hour in tears. My husband devised a great 'wolf-zapper' (an emptied lemon-shaped Cif decorated with heart stickers, if you must know!). He instructed Layla to keep it by her pillow and if a wolf came into her room she had to 'zap' him with it, therefore turning him into a fairy. Two weeks later, she is sleeping tons better and the Cif is still safely tucked under her pillow!

Night wanderers

This will sound ridiculous, but I often wonder why they don't make cots for six-year-olds! OK, I know they need independence and the free will to come and go from bed, but do I have to find my daughter sitting at the top of the stairs in her Tinkerbell outfit and ballet shoes at midnight? Once children go into the 'big bed', they are bound to wander around at some point, so establishing that their bed as the place to be is important right from the start.

- **Make their bed special and sacred.** When my friend Jennie's daughter received her new girlie white bed, her whole family made a huge fuss of it. They talked incessantly about the big-girl bed in the lead-up to its arrival; she chose her new bedding and went with Grandma to pick a new soft toy. By the time it arrived, she was so excited that Jennie had to talk her out of going to bed at 3 p.m.! (Well, let's not make the bed too fun, a bleeping car model with neon lights will imply playtime, not sleeptime!)

  The trick is to make a big deal of this growing-up phase, but not to do it when they're too young. (Many parents can't wait to get the room done up, but a nine-month-old is unlikely to be ready for the toddler phase.) If you are forced into the transition by the arrival of a sibling, consider a cot-bed. At least then the child can stay in a cot until they are ready and you can simply take off the sides at a later date.

- **Returning in silence.** Once the child is set up in their bed and you've done all the right things with your routine, you've established the wind-down ritual and your approach to separation anxiety and you *still* find them up and about in the middle of the night, the trick is to return them silently and swiftly. Pick them up, give them a cuddle and tell them it is 'bedtime'. Don't chat, fuss, stimulate or be overly affectionate; this will be just another excuse to get up again. Do this from the very first time, as often as is needed. Even after your twentieth attempt, try not to give up. I know it's exhausting, but you'll reap the rewards in the long term. Turning on the TV, or getting in bed with them just to get an extra hour of shut-eye will only exacerbate the problem.

The same applies if they come to your bed. If you are a heavy sleeper, you may not wake up as a little body slips in beside you, but the minute you do, follow the returning-in-silence method. The key, as it seems with everything to do with children, is being consistent. Doing exactly the same thing every time will teach them that getting up doesn't have the effect they want – if you let them into your bed once, they'll think that if they just try long and hard enough, you'll give in. I promise you, with a little hard work on your part, they will stop trying and resign themselves to their own snuggly bed for good!

I also try to focus on praising and rewarding good behaviour (and I mean really piling it on!). This only works for toddlers or older kids, but heaps of congratulations and a sticker chart, treats, a coin for their money box, even a present at the end of a rough period can do wonders for a restless child! My pal Elaine even went so far as to offer a weekend at a theme park and it worked a treat! Encouraging a child to be proud of the fact that they've stayed in their own bed is a really useful thing to remember; emphasising that it is their choice (not something they are forced to do) helps many a stubborn toddler from losing face (and as any mum knows, children hate losing face!).

Mother knows best

'My three children were all terrible sleepers. My eldest was up wandering the house at all hours, my middle child had hundreds of comforters and if he lost one in the bed, he would scream the house down, and my youngest would only sleep with me in my bed. I was run ragged. We decided to try sticker charts and a reward system, which really helped. Each child got a sticker if they slept well for the night. If at the end of the week they had six or seven stars, they got a small reward (a toy, a favourite chocolate bar or an outing to the swimming pool). The bad sleepers hated missing out and things really improved. We still get up some nights, but it's got 99 per cent better in a matter of weeks.'

Ruth Nyman, accountant and mother to Leo (five), Zac (three) and Talia (two)

Cry-baby

I'm sure that if you have a difficult sleeper in the house (or four), you sometimes feel like just locking their bedroom door and letting them cry until the cows come home. Some children won't wander, they won't wake early, they will just cry and cry and cry until you come to their rescue. And sometimes you can try all the sleeping techniques in the world, be consistent and loving and all that, and a child will still be crying in her cot and nothing will soothe her but you by her side.

For some kids, it is a simple matter of feeling insecure, for one reason or another, and needing some good quality time. Recently, we had a series of huge emotional upheavals in the family: one grandmother died, I went to freelance at a magazine for a few months and ended up with insane hours, and my eldest began a new pre-school. My daughter (who could usually sleep for Britain) started to play up before going to bed and woke up in the night. She is a sensitive child, so I soon realised that she felt shaken and unnerved by everything that had been going on. I made it my mission to take pains to reassure her and gave her some special time, just the two of us. I took half a day's holiday and we went alone to a local children's theatre. At the weekend, my neighbour minded my son in her garden for an hour and my daughter and I went and had ice-cream sundaes at a local ice-cream parlour. I think it was simply a matter of helping her through a stressful period, giving her that extra bit of one-on-one whenever I could, reassuring her of how much I loved her and that changes in life would never affect that. In a matter of weeks, she was sleeping better and had regained much of her confidence in the world.

Controlled crying

From time to time, night crying won't be about insecurity but may have become a nasty habit that kids find hard to shake. Once you've ruled out that quality time won't combat your sleep issue, you may have to turn to controlled crying to help you through it. When my son was younger and had a period of bad sleeping, nothing, and I mean nothing, seemed to work. On the eighth day of broken sleep, I decided to resort to the infamous controlled crying. It's not pretty, and most of us don't like to do it — hate it, in fact — but sometimes it is the only way to break the cycle. If you are the type of mum who would rather have no sleep at all than listen to even a minute of your child crying, then I suggest you skip this part.

My son began crying for no apparent reason in the night. After ruling out illness, teeth, bad dreams and so on, and after numerous attempts to soothe him, I decided to give him an initial five minutes before going in, stroking his head and telling him I loved him and leaving the room again. Inevitably, this would get him going again and the noise levels would rise. Even at the risk of waking my daughter, I'd leave him for a further ten minutes before going back and doing exactly the same. I increased this by five minutes each time until it was, say, fifteen minutes of crying before I'd return. This sounds harsh and brutal, and believe me, at some points tempers were running high enough to lift the roof off the Saunders' house. (My husband and I regularly threatened divorce and emigration at this point, but as a rule, all conversations during controlled crying must be ignored!) It is the worst, most heart-wrenching process to go through, but after a day or two, things start to get better. In our case, after a week, we found our son sleeping perfectly again. In the morning, I always gave him that extra bit of love and a long cuddle, praising him for sleeping until morning. He's now a toddler full of love and energy and he doesn't seem to hold a deep-rooted hatred for me! I think the rule is, be wise. Use controlled crying as a last resort and never as a means of punishment.

You'll know if it's right for you as a family. Just trust your instincts as a mum, they are rarely wrong!

Sleeping Children Mean Time for You!

It's so easy to say, and terrifically hard to actually do, but getting your children to sleep well is one of the central cogs in enabling you to get your groove back. If you are up half the night, still sleeping in bed with your toddler or entertaining your whole brood way into the evening, you end up feeling shattered, depressed and the furthest thing from fabulous. Even after just one broken night's sleep, I feel completely disorientated and incapable of adult conversation. One fellow mum I've been talking to has not slept through the night for the past five years. Even though her children are now at nursery or school, she feels too knackered to work out, see friends, get back on the career ladder, let alone try and rekindle the flame with her husband. Sleep deprivation is a form of torture, and working out a formula for getting more of it should be top of your priority list. The other day, my sister-in-law Jo said to me, 'Forget being fabulous, just a good night's sleep would be a start!' We all know that without sleep, everything, even the washing-up, seems impossible.

I'll never forget the first night my son slept through the night. I was still breastfeeding, but I'd managed to get him to drink enough at 7 p.m. to make it through until early morning. That milestone was a revolution for us. The first night we thought it was fluke and we didn't dare think it would happen a second time. Then it did, and then a third and a fourth. 'Book a restaurant,' I told my husband on the phone, as I rummaged through my wardrobe for something even semi-glamorous to wear. Although we'd managed a few nights out since his birth, we'd always be half watching the clock, anxious to get back for his eleven o'clock feed. Now the world felt like our oyster. OK, so we only went to the local Thai and drank a little too much wine, but for the first time in ages, we felt like our old selves again.

Of course, it's not like that every night, but the thought that both children are tucked up in bed for the night by 7.30 p.m. is enough to bring a smile to any mother's face. The evenings become yours again and you feel like wearing a T-shirt bearing the slogan 'Reclaim the night'. Just having the knowledge that your day as being a mum has come to a close, that you can, if you choose, see a girlfriend, cook a special meal, gas on the phone or have friends over for a takeaway means that you are getting back a bit of yourself. Mums we may be, but that's not all we are, and we need space in which to remember that.

Top ten sleep and routine tips

1. Rest during pregnancy whenever possible; it may be your last opportunity for a while!
2. The first few weeks are a time to bond with your baby. Getting to know her will help you later on establish a routine that works for you both.
3. Take advice with a pinch of salt! You'll be overloaded with it so use a little, file a bit and bin a lot.
4. Work out a rhythm that suits you and your family and stick to it. Routine will help all of you sleep better.
5. Remember, the wind-down rituals for bedtime are key to the whole day.
6. Approach sleep problems with calm, consistency and clear boundaries.
7. Work out your stance on crying. Controlled crying can be a solution for a troubled sleeper.
8. Praise and reward children when they make it through a rough sleep phase. A little treat for good behaviour goes a long way.
9. Enjoy family life, spend quality time with your children and make them feel safe and secure enough to sleep well.

10. Use the time they sleep well productively. Make sure you reserve some of it for pleasure. Enjoy!

Grace's Guru: Dr Tanya Byron

Tanya is a consultant clinical psychologist who has been working for the NHS for sixteen years. Specialising in child and adolescent behavioural issues and sleep problems in particular, she was snapped up by the BBC to work on and present their parenting shows *Little Angels* and *House of Tiny Tearaways*. She also tackles the nation's family problems via her weekly column in *The Times*. Tanya has two children, Lily (eleven) and Jack (eight).

What are your main sleep and routine tips for mums?

A mum with a newborn The first thing I would say to a mum with a newborn is, don't have unrealistic expectations about creating perfect sleep behaviour immediately. In my experience, the first six months are primarily about bonding and attachment, not about enforcing regimented sleep routines. I know many well-known parenting preachers will argue with this method, but I truly believe getting to know your baby is more important than following a rigid formula on sleeping and feeding.

Having said that, we do shape our child's sleep behaviour from very early on, so there are a few obvious sleep no-nos to avoid. Letting the baby fall asleep regularly on the breast before moving her asleep to her cot will only lead to a dependency on suckling to fall asleep; instead, try and put your baby down awake. Similarly, try not to let the child rely on you as their comforter; they need to learn the cues and associations of putting themselves to sleep alone, or you could run into problems later on. After a few weeks, try and differentiate between feed-times, naptimes and night sleeptimes – this will eventually help you find a rhythm that suits you and the baby and shows your baby the difference between the three. At the end of the day, a baby needs adequate sleep but must also fit into your life, so don't beat yourself up if she naps in the buggy or in the car every so often.

Above all in the first six months, rest when the baby rests and remember, you don't have to be 100 per cent efficient all the time. I found initially when I had my daughter that I wanted to be busy when she slept – you know, making calls, cleaning up and opening mail. In the end, my mother said, 'Stop!' I began to see how much it was wearing me down, and forced myself to sleep when my baby slept. As your baby approaches the six-month mark, start thinking about a routine that suits your lifestyle, your family and one that you'll be able to stick to for the next few years. The trick is to be consistent and loving while remembering to make time for *you* in all of this.

A mum with siblings close in age If you have trained your first child early on, you should have a healthy sleep behaviour that shapes the whole family and rubs off positively on siblings. Focus on involving all siblings in the bedtime routine, which should always be calm, quiet, soft and relaxing. I know many dads come home from work straight before bed, then engage their children in frenzied play – don't do it! This only works kids up and makes it harder to get them to sleep. Instead, keep siblings together and encourage a hot bath, soft clothes, stories and cuddles. I still follow this pattern with my children and they are way past toddlerhood. It's a great time to bond, relax and unwind as a whole family. Make the routine the same every night and this should give all the right positive sleep cues. I would suggest making sure all siblings under five are in bed by 7 p.m. and over-fives by eight o'clock (even if the older ones want to read or, like my daughter, write a diary).

If you have siblings sharing a room and one develops bad sleep behaviour, see first if the good sleeper can ride it through before taking drastic action. Often, good sleepers will sleep right through cries, wails and even night-time tantrums. If a bad sleeper is waking a sibling, move the good sleeper out of the room on to a mattress in your bedroom, while you sort out the behaviour of the bad sleeper. Once the week (or weeks) of sleep training is over, you can put the siblings back in the same room.

A mum with no support partner at home A lot of single mums make the classic mistake of having the child in their bed, often out of loneliness. Although it's so easy to see where the comfort is in this, you mustn't use your child as an emotional comforter. Kids need their own identity and they need space to grow up without the intense attachment that sharing your bed will induce. As a single parent especially, creating boundaries is crucial.

If you are responding to bad sleep behaviour by letting them share your bed, or even indirectly by allowing negative sleep habits to continue, you need to gather extra strength to break the pattern. Get a parent, friend or someone you can trust to support you, whether that's by being on hand to comfort you when the going gets tough or just to talk to on the phone when you've had a particularly bad night. Chat rooms and websites are also a great way of gaining support, advice and tips.

A mum with a child who refuses to go to bed or is up endlessly in the night The ideal approaches for such sleep problems are either 'rapid return' (where you settle your child in bed and then return them gently and swiftly every time they get out of bed) or my 'gradual withdrawal' (which involves you staying close to the child, but not actively involved as you withdraw from their presence slowly). Both have worked equally well for many families under my guidance. The former is a 'tough-love' behavioural technique and works well for severe sleep problems, especially when they come hand in hand with other distructive behaviour such as kicking, biting, spitting, arguing and tantrums. The latter is an especially good way of getting children to settle themselves to sleep calmly, and I find can be a perfect method for older children who are unused to their own beds, for children who may need your physical closeness as a sleep cue or for those who are anxious about being in an unfamiliar structure or place.

Remember, when attempting either method, be firm that this isn't about playtime or 'fun'; it's just about you being there to provide a comforting presence or to take them back to their own bed. Being utterly boring at all times is key to success here. Look away from your child and not in the eye. Above all, when withdrawing or returning a child to bed, make sure you avoid cuddling them, playing with them, turning on the lights, bringing them downstairs or entering into any form of discussion or aggression.

If you have a case of chronic sleep problems, you may have to repeat your chosen method throughout the night. It will be exhausting to begin with, so share the load with your partner (if you have one), but ensure you follow exactly the same line and that neither one of you decides independently to give up at 3 a.m.!

A mum in search of incentives for positive sleep behaviour Whichever sleep technique you decide to use, some serious bargaining and rewards may be needed in the early phase. One piece of advice, don't be too proud to negotiate a deal that promises a treat tomorrow in exchange for good behaviour today – but it shouldn't become a habit. If your child has done well and has achieved the targets you have set – e.g. has slept through the night, or has stayed in their own bed – be liberal with praise. Then move on to set new goals and involve them in a sense of their own achievement.

I love to use a sticker chart, so that a child can see how well they're doing. I find that a sticker chart makes a brilliant visual aid, and also gives kids a good time frame, a useful incentive and a tangible reward at the end to indicate success. Even if you're no artist, a simple sticker chart can be made in moments and doesn't have to be a sophisticated diagram – although it helps if they are child-friendly and colourful. For sleep, I would suggest having a chart divided into each night of the week with a sticker space for how well they settled and each hour they stayed in bed. I always try to involve the child in designing and decorating their sticker charts so they have a sense of ownership and involvement. This always promotes positive feelings and the idea that the process is done with the child, not to them.

Two other positive reward systems are the 'jigsaw' and 'Night-time Fairy' methods. For the 'jigsaw' reward approach, all you need to do is place a piece of jigsaw on the pillow or next to the child's bed each night. In the morning, they can add the piece to their ever-growing bedtime puzzle. My 'Nightime Fairy' concept is ideal for slightly older children and I've found works brilliantly to encourage good sleep patterns. It's so simple and involves you explaining that this fairy will be waiting to see how well they go to sleep – and when they do, the fairy will add a sticker to the sleep chart.

A mum in search of a good night's sleep for the whole family It's crucial in my mind to establish a good routine for kids from around six months. Make sure kids are happy, healthy and well fed, and that you encourage good sleep training early on. Simple stuff like making sure kids go to sleep in their own bed, feeling safe and secure are so important in getting the whole family to sleep well. As a parent, stay calm, consistent and focused, and make your sleep boundaries clear. Remember, it is your behaviour that influences your child's actions.

Try, too, to be creative and inventive. Use rewards and praise, and make sure you show them positive feedback; often, this will encourage even better sleep in the long run. If you have a child with bad sleep behaviour, follow my tips and remember you won't damage them for life!

What are your top five tips for promoting healthy sleeping patterns?

1. Recognise that as a parent you are responsible for your child's sleep behaviour.
2. Make sure you have a good bedtime routine (supper, play, bath, pyjamas, teeth, story, bed).
3. Put your children down awake.
4. Don't reinforce behaviour you don't want.
5. Make sure they get plenty of sleep. Sleep is essential for cognitive and physical development.

What are the key dos and don'ts for a mum wishing to have kids that sleep well?

Dos

- Make sure your kids exercise.
- It's up to you to ensure they are eating a healthy balanced diet.
- Help to make a child's bedroom a special place so they look forward to being 'in their own space'.
- Help to 'introduce' the child to his or her own bed (especially if they are unused to sleeping there).
- Have a bedtime routine you stick to, even if you're away from home.
- Ensure they are getting enough sleep at night. (Eleven hours is good, anything less than nine and they will be sleep-deprived.)
- Prioritise your relationship with your partner or time off alone.

- Aim for your child to be able to put herself to sleep at six months old.
- Remember to reward good behaviour.
- Try to keep a log of sleep training; draw a graph with the results and you'll see the improvements.

Don'ts
- Try not to let children rely on a bottle or dummy to put themselves to sleep.
- Be careful not to let children rely on you to soothe, comfort or rock them to sleep.
- Avoid letting them fall asleep for the night anywhere but bed. (In front of the TV, in the car or on your lap are all out of the question.)
- Don't have unrealistic bedtimes; choose a time appropriate for your child's age and stage and stick to it.
- Try not to lose your temper!
- Stay away from giving them drinks in the night.
- Be aware not to shift the boundaries on what sleep behaviour is acceptable. Saying one night they must sleep in their own bed and the next welcoming them into your bed at 4 a.m. will only confuse matters.
- No need to be unrealistic in your goals, radical change overnight is virtually impossible to achieve.

Tanya's fabulous mum's sleep mantra: 'Sleep is essential for healthy child development and for the ongoing health of your relationships, so make it a priority to teach your child good sleep habits.'

Dress Stress

The Good Old Days

In a not-too-distant memory (and one which I happily daydream about while I clear up the remains of my son's Cheerios and Marmite sandwich from my collar), clothes were a delightful hobby, dare I say, even a treat. Rather than being a chore and sometimes an embarrassment, clothes offered an endless source of fun and entertainment, and were a form of self-expression.

A bad week at work was soon put right by a Saturday morning spent wandering around the high street, trying on the latest designer rip-offs. A Sunday morning lazing around with the husband was so easy in a pair of perfectly fitting jeans and a snug lambswool sweater. And let's face it, who hasn't basked in the glory of wearing a gorgeous, all-singing, all-dancing top to a Saturday-night house party and revelled in the attention it brought you for the rest of the evening?

I remember clearly the final part of my honeymoon in Positano, Italy. My husband and I would eat al fresco and then wander, stuffed, around the cobbled streets, peeking into boutiques and trying on frocks (well, me trying, him finishing the ice-cream trio). Clothes shopping was a pastime, a pleasure and a leisure activity. Similarly, I remember working and reworking my outfit as I went to meet a hip celebrity for a glossy magazine feature. Would it be flats or three-inch? Would I go for jeans, cords or even a low-key dress? Underwire bra or camisole? Thong or panties? Goodness, the choice was endless. What was always the same, though, was the feeling of satisfaction and confidence when I got it right. In the 'good old days', you had the time to get it right.

I spent years working on *Elle* magazine, but I try not to remember the free Prada bags, the Alberta Ferretti evening dress 'loans' and the platinum discount cards for every store on Bond Street, because the fact that I write this in battered Levi's and a plain white cotton T-shirt will seem even more of an identity crisis. The truth is, pre-children, clothes were entwined in so much more than merely function. Whether you wore a sharp suit by day, skintight jeans and a designer top, a collection of the best bargain buys around or even your 'safe' black basics, clothes symbolised who we were and the message of confidence we gave to the world.

Similarly, we had conversations about them and any bit of popular culture surrounding them. We've all sat up late with girlfriends (polishing off yet another glass of Pinot Noir and eating yet another Kettle Chip) talking with immense passion about a new purchase, Kate Moss's latest look (and latest boyfriend!) or how to find the best high-street copy of *that* Mulberry bag. For many of us, clothes and fashion (whether that be the couture collections in Paris or the best catwalk rip-offs for under a fiver) provided the foundations for much of our leisure activities. The minute the blue line appears, it all changes. You suddenly become much more interested in conversations about sleep routines and the advantages of reading stories over Walt Disney videos, and bypass the fashion pap-snaps in favour of seeing pictures of a C-list footballer's wife at home with her newborn.

It's weird how clothes play such an important part in shaping our identity and our lives and yet they seem to sink to the bottom of our 'to-do' list once we have children (even below descaling the kettle and signing our youngest up for a swimming club). Imagine if you had a job interview for a position you desperately wanted; would you really sling on your husband's tracksuit and a stained Puffa jacket and hope for the best? Imagine you are anticipating your first date with a guy you've drooled over for months (come on, girls, it can't be that hard); would you tie your hair back in a messy bun and get dressed in the dark? I don't think so. But I think it is really important not to let this happen. Like exercise and nutrition, clothes have the power to make you feel good, fabulous even. Girls, it's time to make clothes work with us, not against us and to construct a new formula for dressing for success.

Mother knows best

'It's not fair! One moment I'm dressing like a catwalk queen, the next moment my two daughters have nicer wardrobes than me! I really miss the old days, but I try to remember that I can still look stylish and I should prioritise my own clothes too. The other thing I keep reminding myself is that my beautiful girls are the best accessory a woman could ever dream of!'

Katinka Malvonoso, advertising executive and mother to Petra (six) and Sasha (one)

Pregnancy and Clothes

Seeing as we've established how it used to be (oh, Top Shop, how we miss you), it's now important to work out where the shift in focus began. Look no further than the remains of that round, glowing, pregnant tum.

Before I knew I was pregnant with my first, I was shopping for a bikini with my sister, Fleur. The fitting-room conversation went something like this:

Me: [Shuffle, shuffle, groan, stretch.]
Fleur: Gosh, your boobs look huge in that! What size is it?
Me: It's a large!
Fleur: If I didn't know you better, I'd think you'd had a boob job. [Long pause.] When was your last period . . . ?

The rest is history and this fitting-room bikini moment became a landmark: it was the last time I've shopped for a two-piece in years, maybe ever.

I don't know about you, but in pregnancy my bust became catastrophic and my tummy began to hide any knowledge of the world below my waist (and this was before I'd even reached six months!). I tried to embrace the hippopotamus look and started to build a staple wardrobe of low-waisted jeans and empire-line tops, wrap dresses and stretchy T-shirts. I accessorised with great coats (worn open) and funky flat pumps and made sure I had great jewellery or a sequined belt to distract from my disappearing waist. By the end, of course, it all became a blur. Less and less choice, and more and more comfort. My four key 'looks' soon became two, then one, until

I really couldn't wash any of my clothes for fear of being left with nothing to wear! (This is not uncommon – my friend Jennie actually wore her stretchy hot-pink V-neck sweater every day for the last five weeks of her pregnancy!)

Somehow, it's this final trimester that shapes the way we dress after the baby is born. For some reason, our fuzzy, new-mum brain doesn't remember the glowing, experimental bumpy lady; it clings instead to the comfort of the big, the baggy, the plain and the 'I really don't care any more'. Those first few weeks you are so overwhelmed with the exhaustion, the bleeding, the lactating and the adaptation to the new arrival that to wear a dustbin bag would seem a success. Numerous health visitors and midwives reminded me in that first stage that in many Third World cultures women are bed-bound for the first month, forbidden to leave and waited on by the extended family. As I struggled into a pair of old linen drawstring trousers (which had gone at the knee), wearing the biggest knickers I could find in the plus-size range, I wished somehow I'd been born in the villages of south-east China and didn't have to make clothes choices on top of everything else.

Looking back, I think the best tip for new mums is to try before the birth to organise trusty items to wear in that precious first month. A common mistake is to resort to slinging back on our maternity clothes, simply because there's nothing else to wear. This should be against the law! Even if you have children already, set aside a little time to wash, iron and store in the most easily accessible place clothes that will offer ease, comfort and confidence. If you know in advance you are having a C-section (or think it may be a possibility), opt for bottoms that have a low waist, leaving the wound free to heal. If you are hoping to breastfeed, make sure you have easy access. Personally, I found that a vest top or camisole (in a stretch fabric with a lace edge or beading detail) with a cardigan (buttoned only at the top) was a good solution. It meant I could feed the baby by pulling the vest up, leaving the cardigan to cover my exposed bust. Alternatively, my friend Esme swore by long or three-quarter-sleeve T-shirts in a pale shade or with a pretty motif (avoid big, baggy, bloke's T-shirts at all costs!) with a muslin square or lightweight pashmina – a great way to cover herself and give the baby some privacy to suckle away. Even if track-suit pants seem like the only solution, try to choose a fabric that is soft on the skin and makes you feel slightly more special than a pair of baggy joggers. I still love my velour set and vividly remember snuggling up for feed-times with my first (born at the height of winter) in a pair of beloved wool-mix drawstring pants. None of these have to be expensive, but if chosen carefully, can make all the difference. From that first sign of a bump (whether it's your first or fifth), you need comfort with a little imagination. You have endless visitors, you are blinded by tiredness, and you may even be doing the school run on day one, so it's key to feel respectable and good inside!

Sure, there is no point in buying a whole new wardrobe for post-birth that will be way too big once the nipper is six months (OK, a year!), but equally, wearing the clothes that you have bulged and busted in, day in, day out for the last three months is the ruin of grooving. You could work those clothes you wore in the first trimester into your first-month-with-baby wardrobe. You might find that the cross-seasonal clothes you bought or wore in slightly bigger sizes than normal will be fine for this transitional phase. (Obviously, bulky jumpers won't work for summer and flimsy tops for winter, but the in-between items should be OK.) I hated anything remotely tight or figure-hugging (there were just too many of those excess rolls), and some of the great loose dresses I'd loved while preggers were out because of breast-feeding. I opted for low-slung baggy jeans (rolled up to reveal a glimpse of ankle, the one thing that had almost gone back to normal), floaty fabrics (kaftans are great for cool, unstruc-tured appeal) and high-necked sweaters for winter and three-quarter-length sleeves for spring (far better than tank tops or vests for arm flattery). Choosing those pregnancy trousers with built-in elastic might seem like the easy option, but in terms of feel-good factor, it scores *nil points*!

Don't get disheartened: that weird space between preg-nancy and the new you really is one of the hardest times clothes-wise. You have gone from glowing, blossoming preg-nant woman (who got seats on the Tube and an excuse for wearing the same outfit every day) to a mess of hormones whose tummy is like a wobbly jelly on a plate. You just don't have the time to make yourself look and feel stylish; you barely even have time to brush your teeth! This is where planning and organisation are vital. We have already estab-lished that you need trusted basics ready and raring to go, even before going to the hospital. The other great tip is to get dressed in the morning. Now, yes, you may chuckle, but anyone who has been caught short in their night clothes when a neighbour comes wishing well at three in the after-noon won't be laughing. (Cue my pal Sophie, who was in her pyjamas at 4 p.m. when I went to visit her and her newborn armed with a breast pump and some soft-scoop ice cream!) It seems nearly impossible when your newborn is in her first month to get yourself up and ready before lunchtime (even if dropping your eldest at school in your dressing gown has you cringing with embarrassment), and there is no simple solution, only the harsh reality that you must try to make time. Even if it means getting up that extra ten minutes early, taking the Moses basket into the bathroom with you so you can sing 'Twinkle, Twinkle' if the baby awakes, or shoving on a story CD to entertain your older brood while they eat their bagels, do try to make the time to shower, dress and apply even a dab of fragrance/blusher/body cream. These are all tiny, minute-long dents in your day, but they're so crucial to ensuring you feel as special as you should when you have a newborn around. I promise.

Mother knows best

'After I gave birth the second time round, I was ready to burn all my maternity clothes. The sight of dungarees made me go cold. At exactly this time, my best (and identikit clothes-size) friend Susie was reaching the end of her fourth month of pregnancy. We decided to do a straight swap. She exchanged her 'slightly bigger than normal' items for my maternity clothes. After six months or so, we swapped back. It perfectly bridged that awkward gap of being a different size, plus it saved us cash. Brilliant!'

Ruth Auberbach, full-time mother to Jacob (four) and Noah (two)

All Change

OK, so you've done the pregnancy look to the best of your ability (bearing in mind you'd acquired extra flesh in places that you never knew existed) and you've earned the invisible medal for giving birth over thirty-six hours. You've just about worked out a half-decent wardrobe to carry you through the first month post-childbirth, and best of all, you've cooed, cried, laughed and stared in disbelief at your new bundle of joy. It doesn't matter if you're forty (reading this three months after your first baby) or twenty (and devouring this chapter three years after your second); whoever you are, at whatever stage in the mothering game, you can't deny that your world has been turned upside down. Not only has your life been rocked by the new or changing role of motherhood, but your wardrobe has probably been given a good bashing too. Chances are while your life has changed beyond all recognition, your wardrobe is roughly the same and will be struggling to keep up with the changing times. In my experience, new mums with children often make the following mistakes and end up falling into one (or possibly even more) of these categories:

- Wearing impractically glam clothes for the school run.
- Suiting and booting it, like a boardroom mother.
- Wearing tent-like innovations to hide all sins.
- Slobbing out, *à la* downtrodden Britney Spears.
- Reverting to the dress age of their eldest child.
- Slinging on whatever is handy at 6 a.m. (i.e. ripped jeans and your partner's sweatshirt).

All of these come with their own problems of impracticality and confused identity. The slacks-and-sneaker brigade end up feeling like their son's football coach; the glamour puss may make us fellow mums drool at the school gates, but, really, how practical are Jimmy Choo stiletto boots, cashmere roll-necks and sheepskin coats for a muddy walk home from nursery and a baby waiting to puke up carrot purée in the buggy? Equally as unrealistic are those mums who take motherhood as an excuse to dress like the sixth-formers at the local college: miniskirts, padded bras, logo T-shirts (like 'Man-eater', or 'Mean Mother Machine'), jingle-jangle jewellery and all. Poor old boardroom executive can't quite draw the line between bidding for shares and doing her middle child's arithmetic, so treats her home style like a Monday-morning meeting, while the downtrodden mum has to resort to anything baggy and big to hide the fact she hates what's underneath. Last but not least, there's the mum we can all relate to, who throws on the nearest and easiest thing at dawn (yes, those jeans again), just so she can get on with breakfast, the school run and the washing-up before 8.33 a.m. Categories aside, while our identities, careers, families, homes, body size and close relationships have changed and evolved, our wardrobes have stagnated. We just don't know how to dress for our new life.

I have a vivid memory, which is actually not a memory, as I relive it every morning. It goes something like this: open wardrobe, see endless wafty tops and tight jeans, sky-high stilettos and skimpy slip dresses. What the hell am I going to wear to drop my daughter off at pre-school in comfort, ease and style? My 'working uniform' at *Elle* included anything glam, kooky, *über*-stylish and ultra-impractical. It was totally normal for us to head to work in the morning dressed as if we were going to a smart dinner at a Michelin-starred restaurant and not uncommon to change into strappy three-inch stilettos in the office lift, or wear Matthew Williamson tops and Manolo thong sandals 'just because'. I realise this must sound a tad extreme, but I know that wherever you work – as a music teacher, taxi driver, lawyer or pop star – everyone has a wardrobe with an array of staple day-to-day choices that fitted your lifestyle pre-pregnancy and probably don't fit now.

For me, the answer was to aim for outfits that were functional as well as stylish. There's no point in going for the super-cool or ultra-expensive, because you'll always end up cursing when you get baby sick on your latest 'cult' handbag or down your break-the-bank silk blouson top. We need clothes we can wear to run around like tigers (obligatory morning entertainment for my son), feel proud at parents' meetings, hang out at a friend's for Sunday lunch, and bump into our boss at the local shopping centre, not to mention items that hide any lumps and bumps we've given up all hope of getting rid of. The first step is to learn to shop again, then, my friends, we'll tackle the wardrobe!

Mother knows best

'I realised my wardrobe sanity had gone to pot one day on the way to work. My daughter was a year old. I looked down on the bus and realised I had odd shoes on. I'd got dressed in the dark, in such a rush I just hadn't noticed. My quick dash home made me almost

Shopping Hell

My most recent (and for the record, last ever) shopping trip *en famille* is marked in my memory for ever. The idea was that we would saunter up to the West End, browse around the shops (my husband needed new jeans and I needed, well, whatever took my fancy!), go somewhere nice for a late lunch and potter on home for tea. Sounds like a perfect Saturday? More like toddler hell on earth. The shopping trip began OK; we were browsing on the third floor of a leading department store. Four-year-old in sight? Check. Two-year-old strapped to buggy? Check. Within seconds, all hell broke loose. My son (who had been 100 per cent potty-trained for six months) had an 'ickle accident' in the shoe department and embarked on a bucking fit (taking on the appearance of a child-size Incredible Hulk). My daughter then proceeded to smear a chewed-up gunky cereal bar down a £2,000 Nicole Farhi coat that was being tried on by a fellow shopper. Heeeeeeeeeeeeeeelp!

We charged out of the store and into the nearest waiting

cab (the children in tears, my husband cursing) as quickly as you could say, 'We're billing you for that.' Once the beetroot colour had faded from my face, I tried to remember a time when shopping had actually been a pleasure. Who can say they haven't at some point shopped until they dropped? For a moment, wipe from your mind the reluctant toddler being dragged around the brightly lit superstore (yes, and the hot sweats that accompany this 'relaxed shopping experience'). Erase for a second that haunting feeling of dread as you enter a fitting room with no cubicles, knowing that you are three sizes bigger than you were pre-pregnancy. Go back to a time when your pay cheque had cleared and a shopping trip offered endless possibilities of a new wardrobe (or a fake-fur gilet and a new lipstick at least). On top of that, you got the bonus of a pit-stop lunch with a gal pal and a cocktail at the end of a weary shopping day to gloat over your new purchases and try out your new shade of pink gloss. A quick glimpse at your local high street on Saturday lunchtime and you're sure to have a shiver of remembrance at those carefree days gone by.

It's no wonder, then, that we mums decide that it's just not worth the hassle. Until our favourite women's wear store installs a crèche with entertainers, kid-friendly snacks and an endless array of shiny new toys to keep them happy, we'd really rather stick with our old wardrobe (never mind it's a decade old). If the experience of shopping isn't enough to put us off, we're far too busy rushing from the children's party to the supermarket to Grandma's on a Saturday to give 'us' time a second thought. The easy option is never to go shopping with the family again. This, however, is an unrealistic solution and one that will do you, and the kids, no favours in the long run.

Occasionally shopping for kids' clothes and the odd basic with children in tow should be no big deal. It teaches them to behave in public spots (and enhances control over their choices about what they like). It also shows them that life isn't all about indoor play areas and being spoilt by their grandparents. Just remember, don't be too ambitious. Expect little and you may even get a morsel more than you bargained for. Ensure you have toys and snacks to keep them happy, select three essential shop spots and allocate just the amount of time you expect their concentration to last. The next piece of advice is simple: keep calm and hope for the best!

Though kids may be a feature on most shopping trips, it's also essential to make time to shop alone, even if it's only once or twice a year. One of my biggest feats after my first was born happened when she was about eight weeks old. I expressed enough milk for two feeds; I left sheets of A4 instructions on every subject imaginable (from feeding technique to what to do if in those three hours she developed hives or a temperature of 104). Armed with my mobile phone and some breast pads, I left for the shops, waving goodbye to my husband and daughter at the front door. Although at first I quivered at the thought of it (and drove my husband mad with the incessant phone calls), it eventually gave me a perfect window to select strong pieces to tide me through the following six months of breastfeeding and returning to my normal weight. Don't imagine that I instantly chose a complete and perfect wardrobe; far from it. What I did do, though, was to invest in a few basic tops and a cheap pair of well-fitting jeans, as well as some body cream and fragrance (well, it was on special offer!).

This was an experience that I vowed I would try to repeat a couple of times a year. It gave me the opportunity to refocus, to think about what I might need for the coming months. It also gave me a window to invest in myself and give myself a tiny treat to warm the soul. My friend Lyn followed suit after the birth of her son. She called me from the accessories department of Top Shop. 'Oh my God, I've just spent all my overdraft on shoes and tights,' she squealed. 'But it's heaven not to be breastfeeding in front of *This Morning* for once,' she added, and hung up to try on some silver flat pumps in the sale. Even if (unlike the lovely Lyn) you don't buy much, or go armed with nothing more than a tenner, it's the feel-good factor of being free for a moment. It could also be an impulse for forgotten or discarded items in your wardrobe to be given new life. (I saw the best embroidered and sequinned skirt, which would have blown the bank, had I bought it. It reminded me that I'd stuffed a very similar one into the loft a year ago. With an elastic waist, it was perfect and it saved me a fortune!)

There are many obstacles that stand in your way. Prior to children, I knew exactly which designers and brands suited me and what type of dress/bag/top/lingerie would make me feel a million dollars once I'd bought it. And I'd also know which role or function I was buying for: a dress for your best friend's wedding, a sparkly top for the work Christmas party, some undies to treat your Valentine, or just some trainers for bumming around at home. But as a mum, you suddenly find yourself questioning whether it is really worth splashing out on that beaded camisole when you may only wear it once and then it has no place in your mothering life. I've certainly pondered endlessly on whether to pay out for a pair of nice jeans when they will get ruined in five minutes flat once I scrub the floor in them, or whether to dish out for some Chantilly lace knickers in the hope they'll get noticed. Instead, you find yourself veering towards the kids' department and going home with a pack of five basic school knickers for your eldest and nothing for you!

Even if you do manage to find a selection of good items, more often than not, once you reach the fitting room and see all those naked bodies sweating and wriggling, you head straight for Starbucks instead. Changing-room etiquette can be challenging at the best of times, but if you're still conscious of those stretch marks or don't fancy sharing that extra bulge with complete strangers, it can put you off for good. Best to select shops that you know have separate cubicles. (More and more high-street chains are installing them for just this reason.) Alternatively, check out the returns policy on stores so you can edit your selection, buy the items you think are for you and then try them on once the children are in bed. It may be a hassle to return goods that don't fit, but at least you'll be 100 per cent sure about those that do. (You can even try them on at home with different tops/bottoms and different heel heights, which could save you many a fashion faux pas.)

Please, please, please don't give up all hope of shopping yet! The trick is to change your expectations and force yourself to indulge in a little retail treat every so often. It may be true that instead of heading to the extravagant shoe department for a sexy knee-high boot, you feel money would be better spent on a couple of flattering dresses (a print wraparound dress for the evening and a kaftan, to be worn over jeans or belted with bare legs). This is merely a sign of the changing times. Do let yourself indulge in the odd daring item, one that you may only wear out on your birthday, or a bra that makes your bust feel like that of Cindy Crawford and does wonders for your self-esteem. Just because you don't have an endless array of social occasions lined up for every night of the week (or maybe you do, and good for you!), that's no excuse to put your needs and desires for a little treat here and there on the back burner.

What to remember:

- Take time out to shop alone (even if this means begging and bribing the kids' granny for all you're worth).
- Invest in functional, stylish and 'feel-good' clothes for everyday wear. Just because you're not brunching with friends or heading to a boardroom conference doesn't mean you shouldn't look and feel great.
- If you find a basic item you love and will wear and wear, buy two or a variety in different colours. It sounds boring, but it makes for easy morning dressing, and that works for me.
- Buy items that can be returned. It helps to try them on in the comfort of your own home.
- Make sure your purchases can be washed. Who needs the cost and hassle of dry-cleaning once a week (on top of emptying the washing machine daily)?
- Make three key stores your 'friends'. Work out which shops/designers/labels stock things that flatter you, fit into your price range and offer a pleasurable shopping experience. It will save hours of trawling around the 'wrong' shops feeling inadequate and ending up with a ra-ra skirt in a fuchsia pink!

- Buy the occasional 'special' purchase. Just because the family always seems to come first and your baby has outgrown his romper suit doesn't mean you shouldn't allow yourself a lipstick or a pair of nice knickers to lift your mood.

If all else fails, there is always catalogue or Internet shopping or eBay. More and more top brands are making their designs accessible from home (ideal for when the children nap or on your way to work in the morning), and we all know a mum or two who has snatched up a great bargain designer bag on eBay. Still, it shouldn't be an excuse to hide away and never visit the high street again. The social experience of shopping and the feeling of being child-free (even for a split second in a whole year) are good for rekindling feelings of the old you. It also helps with increasing sensory pleasure: feeling the fabrics and seeing the colour tones and prints available is part of learning what suits you and your appearance – lessons for life, really! Living in that mummy bubble (where it is easier to lift the phone and order clothes without leaving our role as mother) can give you a warped sense of what is available and decreases your chances of making informed fashion choices.

Mother knows best

'Once I gave birth to triplets, I thought I'd never shop again. When they reached their first birthday, I opted to return to work part-time (for sanity if nothing else).

It was then that I realised late-night shopping would be the perfect opportunity for a calm retail experience. (Plus, it would mean taking a fashion-savvy workmate along for advice.) Between my partner (God bless him) and mother-in-law, I worked out what we call 'shopping cover'. Once every few months, they put the children to bed alone and I go straight from work to hit the Thursday-evening shops. I always get some good bits and occasionally sneak in an early supper and a glass of wine with my work pals. It certainly keeps me on the right fashion track, even if I am exhausted and run ragged by my three little ones!'

Natalie Mottershead, IT consultant and mother to Lily, Maisy and Alfie (all five)

Wardrobe Success

I have a confession to make. For a while, after my first child was born (and before I had sussed my fashion identity as a new mum), I got it totally wrong. For some reason, even though I was still a working mum and maintaining a busy and active social life, I felt now that I was a mother I should dress like a 1950s housewife. To me, being mummy somehow meant being mumsy. I shed my funky print tops and acquired twinsets in various pearly shades. I bought some hideous flat black ankle boots and prided myself on their 'safe' heel. With my huge feeding bra poking out at every occasion and my large floral nappy bag at my side, I was rapidly becoming a far less stylish version of my mother.

It took me a while to realise why I felt so unlike myself. As I breastfed my daughter in Pizza Express or sipped cappuccinos in Starbucks while spoonfeeding her baby rice, I couldn't work out what was so different. Sure, my life had transformed beyond belief, but my core remained the same. Suddenly it struck me: it wasn't my daughter that made me feel different, she made me feel whole; it was my clothes. I lost my style identity, which had always been a huge part of me, and my wardrobe was in a state of chaos.

That day, while my daughter napped, I opted not to settle down for a session of daytime TV and a digestive, but to attack my wardrobe with military precision. This is now a ritual I undertake every year, new baby or not. It helps me retain a sense of myself. My first job was taking everything out of my wardrobe. (And before you ask, that does include the scrunched-up drawstring trousers hidden beneath your moth-eaten roll-necks.) The idea is to be truly ruthless and separate items into ten piles. (Your bedroom will look like a bomb site, but go beyond this, girls!) Below are the ten different piles:

- I haven't worn it in the last three years.
- Too small to consider getting back into in the next six months.
- Too small for now, but I'm working on it. (This only applies to items one size below your current size.)
- Too tatty to be acceptable. (Yes, even for around the house!)
- Looks far too young for my lifestyle now.

- For winter wear.
- For summer wear.
- Daytime mummy wear.
- For work wear (if applicable).
- For evening wear.

Once this mean feat was accomplished, I put the 'I haven't worn this in the last three years', the 'tatty' and the 'too young' in a bin bag marked 'OUT'. The clothes that were way too small but were a possibility for the future (now, be truthful, ladies!) I put into a separate large zip-up bag marked 'SMALL' with the date and put away in the loft. (A cupboard under the stairs or on top of the wardrobe will do.) I did the same with the clothes for the opposing season and marked them 'WINTER/SUMMER'. It feels like receiving a new wardrobe each time the weather changes. (If you can make that little bit more time, give all your 'loft' clothes a quick wash first. Storing them with a lavender bag, mothball or few drops of cedarwood oil on a handkerchief will deter moths, too.) Finally, I was left with five neat piles and my wardrobe began to give off some hope of salvation.

Inspired by my conquest, I began to sort my clothes for work, home and play into order and hang them up in sections. The clothes I hoped to get into soon I hung to one side, waiting for that great day! I began to see that my evening wear was in plentiful supply (yes, yes, those years on a fashion magazine paying off again), and my work wear was still in pretty good order. I then began to see what was missing. Surprise, surprise, my daytime mummy wear was the category in short supply. Once I'd repeated this ritual with all my shoes and undies (oh my gosh, had I really kept hold of those granny post-labour pants and that ill-fitting Ann Summers thong bodice – bin, bin, bin!), I began to get a sense again of what I wanted to look like and what clothes I needed to feel good in. There was no reason why, with a little imaginative styling, I couldn't build a wardrobe that would help my personality shine.

I found that with my 'out' bag of clothes I could offer a little to the local charity shop and use the rest to earn some extra cash. Both eBay and local second-hand boutiques offer good avenues for selling off new and used designer and high-street items. Even if I only manage £20 twice a year, it goes towards a great new pair of shoes to update my look every season. The trick is to be ruthless and keep reassessing whether specific items are still useful. Less is more, and it makes it so much easier to keep order and clarity and, the ultimate goal, to dress successfully.

Once your wardrobe has some logic to it, you can focus on the essential items you need in order to bounce back with confidence. If what you lack is sequinned pedal-pushers, then great, but I can bet that what you crave more is a set of basic vest tops and the ultimate pair of jeans. Doing a straw poll of my core girlfriends, we came up with what we consider a list of the fundamentals you need in your wardrobe to groove as a mamma. Don't get me wrong, the last thing we want to be is an invisible mass of Stepford wives, wearing the same and doing the same, the very thought gives me goosebumps. However, it's important to feel there are some basics in your closet that you can build on and fall back on should all else fail. Multitasking is hard enough as it is without being stuck in a clothes rut as well.

Wear good underwear

Women constantly underestimate the value of good underwear. We're all guilty of it. Before my first wardrobe-edit session, I had over thirty bras, only five of which fitted properly; now that is madness! Make an appointment at your local lingerie department and get sized professionally. However much you love the bras that don't match your size, be ruthless and honest with yourself; they don't fit, they don't flatter, they're for someone else! Make sure you have good bras for day use (two in black and two in white is ample) and some for special steamy moments (even if they are only few and far between), and if you're planning more babies, best to keep those growing maternity and feeding bras as long as they are in good enough shape!

Keep a good stock of basic T-shirts and vest tops

For both summer and winter, a great selection of well-fitting T-shirts (short, three-quarter and long sleeve) and vest tops is key. They are ideal to wear under things. (I have even started to wear a plain long-sleeved T-shirt under a dressier top. It's a perfect way to dress down an item and get more use out of some of your glitzy tops gathering dust in the closet.) These basics are also great with jeans, smart trousers, cool tracksuits or gypsy skirts. I find white never lasts a day with the kids, and black always gets snot smeared on it somewhere, but keep them anyway because neutral shades always add chic (and there will be moments without sticky chops around). Vest tops are brilliant for summer, layered or worn alone. They're perfect as well under cardigans or see-through tops. Go for a lace edge or daring colour if you feel brave.

Make sure you have a couple of nice sweaters

I'm a big fan of the roll-neck and low-V-neck sweaters. Cashmere is the biggest luxury (and many of the high-street chains are doing it for a reasonable price), but lambswool is equally as good. Even with a puffy, baby-weight face, a roll-neck always felt chic and elegant to me. (I even wore my tighter black roll-necks under fluid chiffon tops in winter to give jeans a lift and help me feel a little special.) If you find a cut that suits you, you're on to a winner. Don't go for mega-tight (unless you are a size eight with abs to drool at) and stay away from oversized men's cuts. Anything snug that lets you breathe, eat and move is ideal. Have a basic selection of other shapes that suit you. Ribbed knits and striped knits should be reserved for the leaner ladies, and round necks are for those blessed with a pert B-cup bosom.

Never say no to a gorgeous top

I admit it, I'm a sucker for the special top (hence 75 per cent of my wardrobe is made up of wafty, floaty, silky numbers). Go for anything that makes you feel gorgeous but isn't covered with sequins, beads and transparent patches. (This will look too glitzy, plus it will shed and your toddler will end up choking on a discarded bead!) The great thing about a good floaty top, kaftan or snug print number in a super-luxurious fabric is that you can save it for a romantic dinner, wear it with jeans in the day, team with a pair of floaty linen trousers in summer, belt it to accentuate your waist or simply wear it with a vest over your favourite skinny denims. Even if you only have one gorgeous top, it's worth it.

Don't ignore your bottom half

For all the multitasking expected of us mums, a good pair of well-fitting, smart jeans is ideal. Versatile, comfortable and sexy, they are a great all-rounder. My friend Lyn has exactly twelve pairs of jeans (and has been seen in nothing else in the two years since the birth of her son). I too love mine and find wearing a slim-leg jean with a small round-toe or kitten-heel boot on 'fat' days seems to give me a little extra height and make my legs look far slimmer than they really are. They are also great to roll up in summer with a pair of flats, flip-flops or sandals, and once the bottoms wear out, cut them off for a spring three-quarter-length. If you venture into skirts, a denim A-line skirt cut off at the knee, a quirky peasant skirt, a sharp pencil skirt and long floaty number all offer versatility and variety. These can all be adapted to relevant trends (by adding a different belt or heel height) and can be dressed up and down accordingly, making them a great bridge between your working and going-out items.

Coats and jackets are important too

Please, please chuck away now any big sports coats handed down from your partner that may be lurking in your wardrobe. They are just another excuse to hide that fabulous person beneath. Seeing as we spend half our lives outdoors with our children (picking them up from school, wheeling them around the freezing-cold park or accompanying them to their first '15' rated film), it's a surprise that so many of us have worn the same coat for the last five years. When choosing your beloved coat, try to make sure you have one good style for summer, the other for winter. For warmer weather, a denim jacket is perfect. (They come in a huge variety of styles and can be relatively cheap.) If you feel flush, go for a spring coat as well; a belted trench coat is ideal and readily available at high street and designer levels. It's versatile enough that you can wear it with flats, heels, jeans or a knee-length skirt and it still looks chic. For cold winters, go for a warm sheepskin or faux-sheepskin coat; it will always be fashionable and practical (well, to a point). Freeze or shine, the above are all ideal, stylish and spirited mum wear.

Shoes to work, rest and play

Shoes are a minefield, and for many women (myself included), there is no logic in their purchase. Of course, you need your dressy sets and your mucking-out sneakers, but do save these for the right occasion. A good ballet pump, a pair of thong sandals (or Birkenstocks), a Converse baseball boot and a leather boot (black kitten heel or warm winter number) are great alternatives. All or some of these provide a solid basis for a good shoe collection.

Don't forget your individual pieces

Within these fundamentals, there must be room for your own flair and experimentation to shine. If dresses are your thing, get some you know you'll love and wear year in, year out. I always feel that in a floaty knee-length dress with flat sandals I've nailed that summer dilemma. (You know the one: the hot sweaty race from school playing field to the local deli and back in 98 degrees!) However, if you feel super-happy in a chinos and polo-shirt combo, then make sure they are there as well.

Important, too, is a good selection of the accessories you love and that will instantly change a look: thick belts, a sequin scarf, a corsage to add to a denim jacket or a great hold-all bag that doesn't scream, 'I am a practical nanny.' Even the odd gypsy earring – for those with an inner hippie (and with older children past the grabbing phase) – or sleek imitation diamond line bracelet – for the princess in us all – are perfect for updating a basic day look.

You'll probably find that in some shape or form, a lot of these already exist in your wardrobe. You may, on the other hand, hate the idea of wearing a ballet pump or a belted mac and would rather stick to the 1980s punk theme that has always worked for you. The idea is not to devise a one-fits-all structure, but to outline some general items that work for the superhuman role expected of today's mum. The aim is to give guidelines and choices. If you can take away from this chapter three fabulous complete outfits (which you can even rotate for ease), then you'll have all the more time for you to do the things you love. You can't expect a complete wardrobe overhaul overnight, but I'll be happy with a little closet spring-clean to start with.

It makes such a difference to your confidence if you've got your clothes sussed. Once you have a wardrobe that reflects your life, it is far easier to take five minutes out before you go to bed to plan a rough outline of what your outfit will be for the next day. I always find that by bedtime I know essentially what the next day will entail (bar a snowstorm or a surprise trip to casualty!). This really helps me to focus on my needs for that day and sort out the 'look' to go with it. In turn, you're not caught short first thing in the morning (with your toddler needing the potty and the rain lashing against the window) with the age-old saying 'I have nothing to wear'. So, come on, girls, ditch one episode of your favourite show and invest some time in your clothes. You'll be surprised at how therapeutic it can be.

Mother knows best

'My biggest investments every season are a fabulous wrap dress for spring and a fitted cashmere roll-neck for winter (plus some killer round-toe boots if I'm feeling flush). A great bag for all occasions is also something I just can't live without. No amount of mayhem will get in the way of these looking great. True lifesavers!'

Paula Whiteman, fashion booker and mother to Toby (five) and Phoebe and Daisy (both two)

Clothes and Confidence

It doesn't take a genius to work out that feeling good about what you wear makes you feel confident about who you are. I own one truly special item that illustrates this perfectly (a peacock-print chiffon number designed by Matthew

Williamson, if you must know!). It is one of those one-in-a-million items that you put on and instantly feel transformed. Although I save it for special evenings out (my wedding anniversary, my best friend's hen night, my sister's thirtieth), it hangs in my wardrobe to remind me of how truly lovely I can sometimes feel.

Admit it, we've all got an item like it. My friend Paula has a vintage Chanel dress that does it for her, and my totally anti-fashion pal Kate even admits to having a 'feel-good-factor' skirt that she's owned for seven years. Even if it's only a pair of plain black wool trousers or a thick-knit cream sweater, we all own something that when we slip it on gives us the power to step out into the world with a strut, feel like Superwoman – sexy and clever and special all in the same breath. In all honesty, tell me the last time you wore something as an on-duty mum and felt this way? Once? Twice (if you're lucky)? Never? It's that same old 'leave Mum until last' trap. We think, Well, if I'm mucking about with the children and multitasking at a million other jobs, I just can't be bothered.

This rut so many of us are stuck in is counter-productive. We don't have the time or energy to make an effort and we end up feeling low in confidence and down about our appearance. I remember when I was working a four-day week in an office. My working days, I felt great. My outfits were stylish and clean (I made sure I had no baby sick or Mini Milk smeared here) and my attitude and confidence reflected this. In contrast, I turned up to the local parish playgroup on a Friday kitted out in ill-fitting jeans (bought just after giving birth and not yet renewed) and a sweatshirt (that I realised only too late was covered in red paint handprints at the back!). When I saw a fellow mum come towards me to discuss our toddlers and share a custard cream, I ducked behind a curtain and hoped I would disappear.

By the time my husband came home from his day at work, my outfit had battled with a peanut-butter-and-jam fest and a wrestle in the local sandpit. Not only this, but my hair had reached maximum bouffant stage (after having been caught in a school-run rainstorm). In short, I felt about as attractive as a bag lady pulled through a hedge backwards. As my weary husband leant over to give me a kiss, I realised that if I wasn't careful, he might start to think these soiled clothes were actually part of my skin, not just overalls to get me through the day. Where had the sexy, stylish, imaginative, funny Grace gone? Even if I felt as exhausted as a long-haul pilot, surely I could look half decent? Time to change my approach.

I needed to stop prioritising my 'good' outfits for the office or that occasional night out at the local Indian. We mums deserve to get dressed in the morning and think 'Hey, I look OK'. Good enough to confront your child's teacher about your child's fears, good enough to ask a fellow mum over for tea and good enough to share a lazy Sunday with your partner or girlfriends and not feel like something the cat dragged in. Trust me, once you get your wardrobe and style back in shape, and start valuing what you wear again, you'll feel great about yourself in every one of those diverse roles you now take on. Come on, fabulous mums, it's time to chuck out that pair of stained joggers and formulate simple, cheap and easy outfits in which you can shine!

Mother knows best

'I was so fed up of being the worst-dressed mum at school I just wanted to curl up in a ball and hide. I was convinced I was still three sizes bigger than I was pre-children and I wore sacks to hide it all. It was my sister who gave me a good talking-to and persuaded me to rethink my clothes. She lent me some lovely items to start me off, and I began to believe I could show off my true shape a little more. I slowly began to feel more sociable because of it and ended up with a sharper wardrobe than my sister, not to mention the other mums at school.'

Deirdre Stephens, full-time mother to Sam (eight) Luke (five) Poppy (three) and Tom (nine months)

Top ten clothes tips

1. Allow yourself time to clarify the old you and the new you, and how your style has evolved.
2. Never wear maternity clothes once you've given birth, but organise your wardrobe to contain bigger clothes for those first few months.
3. At least once a year, take some time to shop alone.
4. Work out key shops for your style that offer a shopping experience that suits your needs.

5. Buy items that can be returned easily if need be. Stay away from dry-cleaning only wherever you can.
6. Explore catalogues, the Internet and eBay for buying and selling clothes.
7. Have a wardrobe overhaul twice a year.
8. Make a list of the fundamental basics you need for day-to-day parenting and build on that. Three full outfits you can rotate is always a simple solution.
9. Don't be afraid to get inspiration from role models.
10. Value your home-life wardrobe. Stylish you = confident, happy you.

Grace's Guru: Gayle Rinkoff

Gayle is a freelance stylist whose résumé lists work as varied as *Vogue*, *Tatler*, *Soap Star Superstar* and a handful of London Fashion Week catwalk shows. She has styled and consulted for celebrity mums such as Ulrika Jonsson, Zoe Ball and Nicole Appleton. Gayle is equally as devoted to frocks as she is to her twin girls, two-year-olds Sienna and Marni.

What are your main fashion and style tips for mums?

A pregnant mum Avoid tent-like designs (such as big T-shirts and shapeless dresses) and stripes; these always pile on extra pounds. Initially, go for floaty, knee-length skirts or very low-slung jeans that will sit neatly under the bump; you may find your pre-pregnancy unstructured tops will still work with a long vest or long-sleeved white T-shirt underneath. Once you've outgrown these, invest in a pair of well-fitting maternity jeans and/or work trousers and a wrap dress; I find they always flatter the leg and give room for the bump to grow. This really is a time to experiment with stretchy tops – show off that bump while you can! Don't rule out a colourful or printed coat on top; they can be worn open throughout and will offset black underneath (a 'safe' colour that has a slimming effect).

On the feet, go for flats, flats and more flats; high shoes will leave you crippled, especially once your feet start to swell. Accessorise with low-slung belts, great jewellery and an interesting bag – these will draw the eye away from parts of the body you want to hide.

A breastfeeding mum No matter how much you love a frock, the majority of dresses are out (apart from a wrap dress). Others may look great but leave no access to your bust when you need it. Separates are the other option, and a top half that isn't so tight and restricting that there is no room for expansion and movement. Cardigans, button-down blouses or a pretty shirt are ideal. Avoid bold prints and patterns as they are guaranteed to add an extra cup size to the look of your bust. Equally as important, don't go for white or light-cream shades – both breast pads and leakages will show through immediately and leave you uncomfortable. Underneath your buttoned top, wear a camisole or a vest and finish off with a lacy feeding bra (Elle Macpherson does the best); you will achieve ease, comfort and femininity. Remember to carry a spare muslin square, so you can cover any exposed breast and the baby's head, should you both want some privacy!

A mum still carrying most of her baby weight
Anything tight around the tummy, garishly printed or cropped
is a big no-no, so go for fluid tops and layer up. There may
be areas (like the neck, shoulder blades, lower arms or hips)
that have slimmed down, so highlight these with a top or
low-slung belt that gives them good mileage. If you opt for
a printed top, go for a plain bottom, or better still, go for
the same colour top and bottom; this will make you look
taller and slimmer. I would always say a great skinny jean
(even if it's three sizes bigger than normal) worn with a small
kitten-heel shoe (round-toe or pointed, whichever you prefer)
and a pretty chiffon top or blouse is elegant without hugging
the areas you're not so proud of. Three-quarter-length sleeves
are also a winner, as are black cords or trousers.

A mum on a budget Don't make the mistake of opting
for synthetic fabrics because they are inexpensive; they will
always look cheap and unflattering. It's much better to invest
in cotton basics that may not be so adventurous in design
but will make you look chic and will be easier to care for.
Try to work out which items you think you'll wear and
enjoy each season and invest in these; it's far better to have
five great, functional pieces than twenty bargain buys that
you'll never wear. It's far easier than you think to copy mum-
friendly trends without breaking the bank. For winter, a
skinny jean tucked in or out of leather or sheepskin boots,
a wool roll-neck sweater and fake-fur gilet/coat, or for
summer, a floral cotton T-dress and flip-flops with a wicker
basket are looks that can be bought easily and cheaply in
both markets and high-street stores nationwide.

A mum wanting to keep clothes fresh and clean throughout the day I've found that wearing layers is perfect for avoiding an accumulation of stains throughout the day. The minute one top gets covered with baby puke, peel it off to reveal a fitted long-sleeve T-shirt and, if need be, wear a short-sleeve one underneath (for that second round of bolognese-throwing). Stashing outdoors shoes (or wellingtons) and a mac in the boot of your car is ideal for keeping clothes and shoes muck- and wet-free on outdoor excursions. You'll feel far more comfortable running around the muddy park if you're not ruining a pair of special shoes. (Note: if you love your shoes, shoe bags and shoeboxes are essential. They will make them last twice as long, so economically, it's worth it too. Remember to clean them as much as you can; even rubbing with the shoe bag every time you wear them is a good second best.) Believe it or not, the best stain-remover I've ever found is Fairy Liquid. If you wet a stain immediately and rub in some Fairy Liquid, you'll never need to bother with Stain Devil again – genius! Both baby wipes and Napisan are also good stain-fixers and are worth having within easy reach, in the event of an accident.

What are your top five accessories for a fashion-savvy mum?

1. a bag with lots of pockets
2. fabulous flat shoes
3. a great pair of sunglasses (to hide those tired eyes)
4. chunky belts
5. well-fitting underwear.

What are the key hot and not-so-hot fabrics, textures, colours and shapes for ultimate grooving?

Dos

- Wear wool, machine-washable cashmere, silk, jersey, cotton and velour – all are comfy, easy to wash and look great.
- Go for shades of chocolate, cream, grey, navy and turquoise, as these flatter most skin tones.
- Verge towards high necks, very low V-necks and three-quarter-length sleeves.
- Accessorise well.
- Buy great jeans and knitwear.
- Invest in great undies; a well-fitting sexy pair is worth a million pounds.
- Think carefully about what clothes to wear whilst breast-feeding.
- Spend money on flats, flats and more flats.
- Look at swapping clothes or selling them second-hand.
- Invest in lots of different-length-sleeve T-shirts – wonderful for wearing under tops.
- Treat yourself to a cult new bag (even if it's a copy!).
- Look after your clothes and remove stains immediately.
- Plan ahead and put energy into your wardrobe and style.

Don'ts

- Never go for anything synthetic, linen or shiny satin.
- Don't opt for fabrics that stain, induce static and are unflattering to lumps and bumps.
- Try not to wear clothes in neon colours, bubblegum pink or anything with horizontal stripes.

- Don't buy into catwalk trends like puffball skirts, high-waisted jeans, low-cut tops, cropped tops and bias-cut dresses and skirts.
- Avoid wearing maternity clothes for months after the birth.
- Try not to wear massive-print or bold designs if you're still carrying most of your baby weight.

> **Gayle's fabulous mum's style mantra:**
> **'"Mummy" needn't mean "mumsy".'**

Desperately Seeking a Tranquil Space

Nursery Dreams

At last you've read the positive blue line on the home pregnancy test. You've given up on booze and stocked up on Zita West's first-trimester vitamins. Check. You've undone the top button of your Levi's and invested in three stretchy T-shirts at £5.99 each. Check. You've told the boss and started counting down the weeks until maternity leave (even if there's still twenty-six left to go). Check. Now it's time for that first ever trip to a leading department store (just to look, mind you, not to spend, of course!). I remember our initial trip well. My husband had worked all weekend and I was owed a morning off by my employers, so we decided to go fresh and perky on a hot July Monday morning. (Tip number one: avoid Saturdays at all costs. After returning later that year on a Saturday, I discovered the place was crammed and heaving with sweaty, round, expectant mums – most on the warpath for *that* buggy, the last one in stock. If you can wangle a few hours on a weekday to shop for the baby, you will find the experience far less stressful.) Greeted by a warm sales assistant (who after having had seven children and sixteen grandchildren, certainly seemed to know her stuff), we were then escorted around the nursery department with a 'nursery checklist'.

After two hours and six minutes, I was about to faint. It seemed absolutely essential for the well-being of child, mother, family and mankind that our tiny flat in North London was kitted out with a mahogany changing station, matching feeding chair (*with* footstool and fitted gingham padded cushions), steriliser, Sanibin, Baby Mozart mobile, Bugaboo buggy, jungle wall border and Babygros in a variety of pastel colours for every day of the week (and did I mention the selection of organic bath, massage oil and washing detergents?), all for the mere fortune of £2,324.62 exactly. After sitting down on the mahogany feeding chair to recover for a moment, we fled down the escalator before the little old sales lady had time to say, 'And the lot comes with a free stuffed teddy and a lilac muslin square!'

In an instant, all my dreams of white French antique wardrobes, hand-crafted sleigh cots and cashmere blankets (that seemed so accessible in *Junior* magazine) came crashing down around me. I have found a good compromise for my nursery dreams. My children do have their own rooms (even if my shoe collection takes up half of my son's). My daughter does have a musty old rocking horse (not from a French antique dealer in Fulham, but one picked up at Portobello Market), and my son does have a patchwork quilt (but instead of one by Cath Kidston, this one was made by his great-grandmother). So, you see, despite all the initial ambition, it's advisable to get the essentials and then wait and see what other goodies you need.

In our cosy-couple flat in busy West Hampstead, we had

to eat seated on Japanese-style floor cushions if we wanted to entertain more than four people, so forget a light, airy and spacious room for our newborn. And the fact that all the kit to go with a fully designed and up-to-date nursery would cost more than a new car just seemed obscene. Our answer? Our new motto, 'Small is beautiful.' Much to the disdain of relatives who came round asking to view the nursery (all hoping for a fifteen-foot room decorated in pastel shades with a lullaby mobile playing softly in the background), we opted for minimalism (well, for the first year at least). We had already decided that our daughter was to sleep in the bed with us at first, then graduate to a Moses basket beside the bed (and then eventually into a cot-bed in our tiny spare room). Moses basket in place, I proceeded to empty the top two drawers of my clothes chest and exchange knickers with basic white Babygros and itsy-bitsy white socks. I then removed the vase of lilies that stood on top of the chest of drawers and replaced it with a simple changing mat and hanging basket filled with nappies, sacks and cotton wool. In the tiny understairs cupboard, I put the basic buggy and papoose, hung the snowsuit, hat and mittens on a hook and closed the door. *Voilà*, we were now ready for our new arrival (and with a saving of £1,568!).

Don't get me wrong, I'm not saying one simple drawer and the bosom is enough to greet the birth of your baby. But I couldn't see that they needed all this stuff – the hand-made cots and cradles, the big changing station, the elaborately stencilled and crafted wardrobes – we wanted to find out, in all the hype, what we actually needed. Things like a nappy bin, a changing station and a newborn cradle might seem 'essential', but in actual fact, I discovered a nappy bin stank (my friend Jennie chucked hers out after three weeks), changing stations were a waste of space (my friend Kate is still cursing hers) and give me a Moses basket instead of an oak embossed rocking crib any day! Plus you'll get so many gifts as new parents I feel it's best to see what you're left with.

I was fed up with visiting new mummy friends and not getting in the door for six-part, three-wheeler buggies, self-assembly baby wardrobes and multicoloured plastic storage solutions (only to find the mum in question in tears and unable to assemble the breast pump). I think a list of 'baby must-haves for the savvy new mum (and the junk we don't need)' is well overdue. Let's face it, how can we honestly get our baby up and out the door, get our buggy into Starbucks (to meet three other mums with similar tanks in tow) and start to get our lives back on track if we've spent all our energy and cash on redundant equipment? Acquiring and putting together all this paraphernalia (often advertised as 'essential', cashing in on a new mum's vulnerability as she embarks on the unknown) can do nothing more than clutter your home (not to mention your brain!).

Baby Must-haves for the Savvy New Mum

Moses basket, mattress and sheets. If you have a pushchair that comes with a detachable carrycot, you can use this instead of a Moses basket to make sure the baby can sleep close to you at all times. Often this is a perfect thing to borrow from friends (especially as you will really only need it for three months, max.). Most mums have one or were given one, and once you change the mattress and sheets, it should be as good as new.

Car seat. This may well come as part of your chosen buggy. If not, invest in a good one separately. Lots of hospitals won't let you leave by car unless you have one. A good tip is to practise with it first; they are a nightmare to work out in the beginning! (My husband and I stood cursing in the snow, both trying to fit the thing into the car correctly. Me: 'You idiot, can't you even fit a car seat?' Him: 'Well, you bloody do it, then!' Our daughter: 'Wa, wa, wa, waaaaaaaaaaaaaaaa.' You get the picture!) I'd suggest getting a new one, but if you opt for a used one, make sure it comes from a reliable source. They withstand one accident and need to be discarded.

Pushchair. Work out your budget and try out a selection. Just because Kate Hudson has a certain one doesn't necessarily mean that it will work for you in terms of size, shape, height and practicality. I made the mistake of getting a heavy three-wheeler, which was impossible to lug in and out of my tiny three-door car – big mistake! And the buggy needs to be suitable for the baby from birth upwards.

Baby monitor. You may not need one of these at first (especially if the baby sleeps in your room), but they are essential for naptimes or holidays when the baby may sleep out of earshot. I know mums who've avoided them saying, 'I will know if my baby cries,' but it's more stressful to constantly listen for baby noises.

Breast pump. Although midwives recommend waiting six weeks before expressing milk with a pump, it's good to familiarise yourself with it early. (It can feel like you need a degree in mechanics to assemble it, especially after just three hours' sleep!) You may also need to express tiny amounts from the breast when the milk first comes in if your breasts are particularly engorged or you need to increase milk supply.

If you are bottlefeeding, you'll need bottles, steriliser, newborn teats and the formula of your choice.

Cot-bed. Look around for the best one in your budget. Although it's slightly more expensive, a cot-bed that will last well into childhood is a great option. Who wants to replace it when the child is only just walking?

Bouncy chair. Once babies are a few weeks old, they often love to sit up and watch the world go by. You can use your car seat or invest in a bouncy chair, which will keep them entertained. Don't put them in it for ages, but it's a lifesaver for a couple of hours, anyway.

Mobile. I have a whole handful of girlfriends who swear on their mobile or else they'd never have a chance to shower or go to the toilet.

Papoose. A papoose that is fitted well, supports the baby's weight evenly and is comfortable to wear is perfect for new-mum ease and mobility. My daughter lived in hers initially (to and from the supermarket/park/health visitor/in-laws), and it proved invaluable once I had my second and was still pushing an eighteen-month-old in the buggy. I also found when my newborn son was fractious pre-bath time, I'd carry him around in it while I did the household chores and feed my daughter supper. It totally calmed him down and gave me the freedom to run around. Again, this is a perfect thing to borrow from friends, as you only need it for the first six months or so. If your child is anything like mine, they will be way too heavy for it by twenty weeks!

Changing mat. Soft, waterproof and raised at the edges,

any will do (well, maybe not neon yellow and covered with images of dummies with an electronic singing head cushion – yes, they do exist!). Buy a portable one as well; it can slip inside your nappy bag. Or choose a square metre of a lovely printed waterproof fabric. (Cath Kidston does great ones.) This can easily fold up and be used as a versatile changing mat while you're on the move.

Blanket. I am a big fan of the cotton cellular blankets with holes in them. They let the newborn breathe, are great for swaddling, and you can layer them to vary the temperature.

Muslin. Great for puke, dribble, breast coverage while feeding and general essential mum stuff; buy a multi-pack of ten, they won't go to waste.

Sleeping bag. Tight, secure, no restless sleep or cold limbs; there are tons of models for summer, winter, etc. Worth its weight in gold.

Changing bag. Now I've never been a big fan of the conventional changing bags. For some reason, many designers assume that women lose all their sense of style once they give birth and therefore make changing bags in dull colours, 'practical shapes' and hideous prints. I've always opted for a spacious 'normal bag' and put inside it a zip-up waterproof washbag kitted out with nappies, nappy sacks, snacks, change of baby vest and Valium (only joking!). Since my last child was born, I've seen several really stylish nappy bags that could even entice me to fall pregnant again! When researching, ask yourself this: would I have been seen dead with this prior to childbirth? If the answer is 'no', then for goodness' sake, don't buy it!

Clothes. This would get you started: cotton sleepsuits with feet, a snowsuit (for a baby born in winter), a sunhat and sleeveless Babygros (for a summer baby), small cotton hat, short-sleeved vests (which have poppers between the legs and can be worn as extra insulation in winter or alone in summer), socks. All other velvet party dresses, newborn waistcoats, designer logo knitwear and baby patent shoes in ruby red are optional and can wait until the newborn is a little older (if at all!).

(And the Junk We Don't Need)

Changing stations. It is far more practical to use the top of a chest of drawers (holding the child safely at all times) or a changing mat on the bed or floor. By the time your child is one, he won't lie still for a nappy change, making high up more hazardous.

Baby wardrobes. Mini-wardrobes are an extravagance. It makes much more sense to invest in a grown-up wardrobe that will last a child for ever. Get shelves fitted at the bottom so it can double up as a chest of drawers or be used as storage for shoes and wellies.

Feeding chair. It's so pricey that although I inherited my sister-in-law's feeding chair (and love it), I wouldn't list it as an essential. A comfy chair (preferably wipe-clean) with good support in which to feed the baby is just as good.

A small cot. Opt for a Moses basket and then move on to a cot-bed instead. A baby will only use a basic cot for a maximum of two years and then it's redundant.

A baby bath. Big, bulbous, bold and used for three weeks and two days until you realise it is far easier to a) bathe with the baby or b) use a towelling bath-stand or baby-shaped sponge (both of which sit in the bottom of the bath and support the baby's weight). These are also far more space-saving.

Electric, whirring, spaceship-type paraphernalia. We were given at least five of these state-of-the-art contraptions (by people promising they would get our baby to sleep in seconds). A rocking chair that rocked so fast it induced vomit, a whirring seat that felt like it was about to take off and an electric bouncer that had flashing lights and gave the effect of being a washing machine on fast spin. Forget it! They will give your child six seconds of comfort (if that), fry your brain and are unlikely to give you any peace and quiet for the next six months.

Mini-me outfits. Satin pink three-tiered party dresses, Matthew Williamson cashmere for the newborn and Ugg boots for a three-month-old might be OK for those ultra-trendy yummy mummies (and I will admit I have on occasion bought the odd Oilily or Rachel Riley dress for my daughter), but keeping your newborn up to date with the latest trends is not necessary or practical. We all love our babies to look cute, but when they grow out of things in less than twenty-four hours (or that's what it feels like), it's madness to kit them out in head-to-toe Burberry from birth. (My daughter lived in white and pale-pink sleepsuits for the first six weeks and never seemed happier.) Better spend the money on a new post-birth outfit for yourself!

Because I was the first of my girlfriends to have a baby, I did have to buy most of the baby paraphernalia brand new. (This was another reason for assessing each item's usefulness before splashing out on it.) The benefit for my gal pals was the cast-offs they received when their time came. The trick is to pass on anything that's still in good nick. I think the Bill Amberg sheepskin baby papoose (given to us by my daughter's most lavish godparent) is on to friend number six and I haven't seen or heard from it for at least three and a half years. (God knows what state it will be in if I eventually get round to having number three!) The thing is, unless you have a loft the size of a golf course, once you've had your baby and she's grown out of her play-gym/hanging bouncer/car seat, you can't wait to see the back of it. There are always clothes with special memories, or a nearly new Tripp Trapp chair you can guarantee you'll use again, but most of the baby stuff you're more than happy to loan out. And if you're an expectant or new mum, don't be proud, it's totally acceptable to share and reuse. OK, buy the new baby sleepsuits and invest in a state-of-the-art pushchair, but really and truly, babies grow out of things in a nanosecond and it's pointless spending hundreds of pounds when you can borrow the same item from a neighbour and pass it on when your one-year-old is sick to death of it.

Chat with friends, family and fellow mums about what they suggest you need and what they can loan. Work out your own personal 'hit list' of what needs buying. Once you have the kit, store it well and don't let it overrun the home. (Under the stairs, accessible loft space or built-in storage under the bed are all good options.) If you can afford to kit out a nursery, think clearly about what style suits your home, the sugar-pink Barbie effect might look OK in the catalogue, but will it drive you to despair once it's wall to wall in your home? How about compromising on one Barbie wall, the rest white? (Likewise, if you have fallen in love with expensive wallpaper, you could do the same.) Kids need to be kids, but opting for suitable colours and shades (I chose pale pinks, whites and antique effects for my daughter; pale blue, dark oak and reds for my son) and making a room a baby can grow in seems so much better than going jungle-theme mad. A baby is only a baby for a blink of an eye, so my tip would be to start off with the least and work up.

Mother knows best

'I had waited years to be a mum so I admit when the time came I went berserk decorating a nursery. We knew we were having a girl, so pink was the order of the day. Once Sophie was born, she grew so fast and by the age of eighteen months, there was no denying her tomboy streak. Her pink room drove us all mad and we ended up redoing it using whites, pale blues and lilacs, and replacing all the fairies with books and a doll's house *with* garage and cars. In the end, we wasted silly amounts of money and energy. I wish I'd started off with a plain white canvas and built it up as Sophie's personality developed.'

Karena Larkin, full-time mother to Sophie (three)

Toddler Toy Overload

Can I just share a question with you, and it's a question asked by a million mums all over the country? *What the hell happened to my home?*

It's something all baby bibles forget to address. However chic and minimal it has been in former life, three years into parenthood your home will resemble something of a rainbow-coloured plastic indoor play area. Toddlers know no boundaries when it comes to mess, destruction and chaos. The same living room that had welcomed friends to visit my newborn – scented candles wafting, fire burning, uncluttered surfaces, whiter-than-white sofas – had become something from a Disney Channel set. If I'd known all this before, I would have started on this journey called motherhood covering my living space in clingfilm. How is it possible to clearly define one's identity when overwhelmed with kids' junk? I asked myself this again and again as I cleared up yet another Spot book/wooden brick/felt-tip pen/leaking beaker/Pooh Bear sticker from my floors.

The thing is, it creeps up on you slowly and then, almost overnight, it's too much. One minute you are discussing whether to opt for the Maclaren lightweight traveller or the three-wheeler cross-country rambler (and we're talking buggies, not cars here), the next you are knee-deep in toddler toys. No sooner has the soft pink paint dried on the nursery walls than your toddler is saying, 'No like it pink, Mamma, me like Sleeping Beauty' (and she means 100 per cent coverage). And as if to purposely destroy your minimal approach to the pre-baby years, every relative, friend and neighbour will come armed with the most plastic, red, flashing 'developmental toy' on the market for your child's first birthday (and don't even get me started on the rainforests cut down just to package the darn things!).

I know I risk sounding like a minimal freak (with a tight black bob and wearing a white apron), but is it really necessary for children to have sooooo much plastic junk with obligatory high-pitched noises and in a range of startling neon colours? Oh, come on, I'm sure you must share the sneaky feeling that this consumer toy market is having the last laugh (at the expense of us parents). Well, in my ideal world, I would have a home totally clutter-free where my children run around in a rambling garden and are happy with one book and one wooden block each. (Chance would be a fine thing.) Sure, they have their fair share of plastic fun and are never denied the opportunity to get friendly with a walking, talking, bleeping, times-table-teaching robot, but I've had to set a limit to this. It's important to balance the kiddy world with the adult world, but how can you have space to think and carve out a niche for you grown-ups when toddler-chaos overruns our lives?

My friends Elaine and Bob are classic examples of this. (And I know they won't mind being used as examples; they are the first to admit they couldn't see straight for kids' mess.) Their first Christmas as parents was a big knees-up. (With an extended family of over thirty, it was bound to be.) Their daughter, Ella, received no less than forty-eight toys, all of which were pink plastic and huge (bar a teddy, which although it was brown, was bigger than Ella). Now, Elaine and Bob live in a humble two-up, two-down house, Bob writes scripts from a tiny shoebox-sized study, and their daughter has a small room at the back of the house. By the time all the Christmas goodies were unpacked and added to Ella's existing stash of bricks, Brio, dolls, tea sets, farm animals, play-food and a collection of thirteen soft toys, no one could fit through the front door. Elaine even popped over to see me one evening armed with a bottle of wine. 'I can't face going home,' she said, reaching for the bottle-opener. 'If I see one more Barbie castle or fluorescent-pink dressing table with rings, necklaces and crowns, I think I will throw up.' She proceeded to drink a large glass of Pinot Noir, headed home to face the mess and ended up in casualty after tripping over a stash of My Little Ponies, which had been left on the doormat to greet her. I'm not joking.

I shouldn't put all the emphasis on Elaine; we are all guilty of letting toddler toys get out of hand, myself included. It was only six weeks ago that I finished writing a long feature for a parenting magazine. I opened my study door and was confronted with surprise toys everywhere. Although I'd done a pre-school sweep, my babysitter had shoved a lot into the toy chest before going home and my kids had taken part in the six o'clock 'tidy-up time', the place looked like a bomb site. On my way downstairs, I picked up six felt-tip pens, a Play-Doh snowman, three odd fairy slippers, two wands and a pink necklace that had been attacked by my son and scattered into a hundred pieces across the kitchen floor. Time for action. If you've ever felt the same, here are some good pointers to keep the volume of toddler junk under control (we'll deal with storing and tidying them up later!):

Three-monthly toy reassessment

I find that if I put aside an hour or two every twelve weeks to work out what toys are still used, still in good nick and still working, I can make a big difference. Take the last time I did a 'toy sweep', for example. I went through the kids' rooms and the play area downstairs and realised my two-year-old son was still hoarding six teething rings, my daughter had claimed two toys that had totally fallen apart, and their bookshelves contained at least ten torn or worn-out books. I put broken toys beyond repair in a sack for the rubbish (bar the much-loved falling-apart teddies that my daughter would be heartbroken without). I then sorted all the toys far too young for my toddlers in a bag for storage (or to loan to friends) and toys that hadn't been used for months in a carrier bag to take to the local playgroup (which is always thrilled to receive extra toys). I then worked out what toys were 'in favour' at the moment (you know, the doctor's kit in daily use and the tractor that is joined to your son's hip) and put the less favoured toys away in clear boxes under the stairs. In six weeks, when the doctor's kit was discarded and the truck was dropped in favour of a forklift truck, I exchanged the toys that had been in hiding under the stairs. A brilliant way to keep the children entertained with novel toys without over-saturating them with choice (plus saving you a few pounds on endless trips to the toy shop for new models!).

Research before you buy

So little Olivia wants the Barbie kingdom with twenty-three rooms (and attached Jeep and helipad), Eddie insists on a BMX, equipped with radioactive lights and 3D helmet, and baby Susie won't put down the neon spinning top at her Thursday-afternoon crèche? Before you head straight for the local shopping centre and splash out £100 on the lot, ask yourself how much use each toy will get and how long the lifespan is. Not all toys can be fully interactive and highly educational, but if you could opt for one that is (and you're sure it will interest your child for more than a split second), then surely it's worth it? Read the packaging, work out what functions a toy has and weigh up whether it's going to be a one-hit wonder. Of course, my kids have plastic drums, talking telephones and red flashing cars (and I can see that peer pressure plays into choices too), but sometimes I steer them towards the book and creative section (and away from the aisle stuffed full of walking, talking, crying, pooing dolls) and they are none the wiser. A handful of glitter and some stickers go a long way and take up a hell of a lot less space than a three-wheeler doll's buggy with pink flowers (which my daughter already has two of in the first place!).

Utilise the elements

Isn't it amazing how when you take your children on holiday, they thrive on sun, sea, sand and a bucket and spade for two whole weeks? Get them home and suddenly DVDs, drum kits, alphabet slot machines, Action Men and Barbie hairdressing salons are essential to their everyday life. Could this be telling us something? You'd be stunned at how much fun can be had using non-toy activities. Ever seen how much a toddler loves a set of saucepans and a wooden spoon? Ever given a three-year-old an old frock, a pair of kitten heels, a hat and a tie and seen them disappear in dress-up world for an hour? More to the point, ever let the kids loose in a garden with a child's spade and a watering can? My point? Minimal toy input, maximum fun. Combine toy fun with unstructured free play, let their imaginations grow and you'll be amazed at their ability to forget requests for a walkie-talkie (for an afternoon at least).

Gift list

I know that the odd grandparent and great-aunt will insist on buying endless plastic gendered toys whatever you say. (This is of course the advantage of being a grandparent.) This doesn't mean, however, that you can't advise friends and family about what toys and gifts are suitable for your child's birthday and Christmas. If your daughter already owns four My Little Ponies (as mine does), then before her fourth birthday, let people know that what she really needs is a dressing-up outfit or some paints. If you feel the toy situation is getting out of hand and you have already chosen a pirate ship for your son's third birthday, then subtly hint at pirates to go in it from well-wishers. A combined effort can work a treat. Kids love pretty much anything (within plastic reason); it's you who knows what you can fit in your home and whether your child will benefit from it – is a sixth pair of plastic high heels really necessary? Advising friends and relatives (and dropping heavy hints) works wonders; however, if you still feel overwhelmed by kids' presents at Christmas (forty new books, thirty-two new toy sports cars, eighteen pots of Play-Doh, seven crying dolls and six of exactly the same pet-shop models ring any bells?), a trick I use year in, year out is to sneak some of the presents away and stash them in my wardrobe for later in the year.

Use alternative rewards

If your answer to good behaviour/a clean plate/successful potty training/a new sibling or just a way to spend a Saturday afternoon is the toy shop, then you may be your own worst enemy. A trip to the theatre, an afternoon at the zoo, a bunch of stickers or afternoon tea out followed by an indulgent ice cream work equally well, and using other rewards for your children and making the toy shop the exception, not the rule is a good way forward in decluttering your house.

Toy swap shop

Since most mums you know are at the same toy saturation point, why not help each other out? My girlfriends and I often have tea dates and request a 'swap shop' at the same time. We ask our toddlers to take along one toy and they trade this (for a week or so) with a toy from another friend of a similar age. It doesn't always work (my daughter once left in floods when she realised her Coco-Bear had been given to Minnie in exchange for a Monty Monkey), but most of the time, it's pretty successful. The kids go home with a new top toy that keeps them happy for a few days and you've got no more teddies/cars/dolls/skipping ropes/swords/trains to add to your already-packed playroom.

I'm endlessly surprised at the number of free or low-cost libraries, playgroups and community schemes that offer toy solutions (not to mention a cup of tea and a little inter-action for us mums). In our area, there are at least eight playgroups and one 'toy library' operating once a week. Heaps of local mums use the toy library (at a cost of £10 per year) to meet other mums, engage their kids in story time and crafts with the added bonus of borrowing toys, books, CDs and videos for the week ahead. My friend Kym, who lives in the village of Frome, Somerset, assures me this isn't just a London phenomenon. Her one-year-old has taken full advantage of their toy-library loans and has expe-rienced everything from a walking, talking, singing Bambie (which thankfully had to be returned after a week) to a brand-new wooden trolley with shiny red bricks (that had her walking within four days).

Mums, enjoy your children, spoil them (as we all do from time to time), but don't let all their paraphernalia take over from free, toy-less play and make sure you bring parental order to their chaos.

Mother knows best

'When we moved to the country, I thought toys would increase tenfold. With more space, I was sure we'd fill it. In fact, the opposite happened. The move meant we chucked away a lot of stuff; we really had hoarded all

Creating Boundaries

I now remember one of the reasons I wanted to wait to have children. I was in my early twenties and was invited to supper by some old friends who had recently come back to the social scene after having two sons in close succession. My husband and I turned up at their home armed with good red wine and some handmade chocolates. (The last time they'd come to us for lunch, they'd brought twenty lilies and homemade bread, so I felt I needed something to match!) As the front door opened, the smell of roasting lamb filled the air and I expected blissful white sofas, open fires and French linen to greet us. (Remember, I was childless at the time!) Boy, was I in for a shock. The once airy, light and minimalist Edwardian household was knee-deep in Action Men, Power Rangers, Lego and guns, not a rose petal in sight. Not only that, but the kitchen had been divided into two parts, 20 per cent cooker, kitchen table and cupboards, 80 per cent slide, indoor climbing frame, mini trampoline (yes, you read it right) and Wendy house kitted out with its own sink, fridge and microwave. I sat down on their new 'kid-friendly' brown wipe-clean sofa (removing at least fifteen pirate figures from the Thomas the Tank Engine cushions) and gave a sympathetic smile to my haggard, worn-out-looking friend (kitted out in trousers covered in kids' paint and baby sick). As I took a sip of wine from a plastic glass beaker ('Sorry, wine glasses are too much of a hazard in this house'), I vowed to put off having children until my mid-thirties at the very least.

Of course, love, an overactive biological clock and the sight of endless newborns snuggled in buggies on the High Street eventually got the better of me, but I wanted to get the hang of the kids' chaos. Toys would be put away at the end of each night, and out would come the clean jeans (or unstained tracksuit bottoms at least), the wine glasses, the scented candles, and an adult world would resume. Sure, I want friends to arrive for drinks and see kids' pictures on the wall and princess party invites stuck to the fridge, and I'm not about to hide all the toys under a huge blanket, but I don't want old pals to be removing kids' glitter glue from their shoe during the starter and to fight their way through a trail of plastic knights and dragons on their way to the toilet. Creating boundaries, teaching the importance of tidying up after oneself and devising useful storage solutions are a lifesaver for mums, dads and kids alike (especially those looking to regain a sense of grown-up identity). Not only will you feel the benefits of a clutter-free home, but children actually like boundaries and you can turn clearing up after themselves into a game – ever seen a kid smile from ear to ear when you clap at their efforts at packing up bricks?

In my home, we have a set of simple rules, which I've managed to keep pretty much since my first was a baby. Of course, there are days when there can be no order to the chaos, when the children have play-dates or on a rainy half-term when there are more toys in my kitchen than in the whole of Toys 'R' Us. The only way to manage this is to relax and just let this happen, and by the end of the day, all the mess can be cleared efficiently.

Make it safe

You should know by now that I'm not one for a total blanket approach to child-safe, kid-friendly interiors. I believe it's crucial to make play safe and to invest in some key safety aspects, but I also think it's important not to cover every sharp corner, soften every hard surface and generally make your home one soft-play area. I would suggest getting child-locks for cupboards with china, glass and cleaning products (leaving one 'safe' cupboard free for your child to access is a good tip; it can be used as a distraction from the others!), a stair-gate until your child has been taught to go up and down independently (I think the roll-gates are much more compact and nicer to look at than the metal versions) and a toilet lock (if you have a particularly inquisitive child). Use your common sense and keep sharp knives and important documents you value out of reach, but no need to completely sterilise your home. Children need to learn from being given reasonable limitations. My son actually worked out how to open most child locks. In the end, a firm 'no' and a distraction served us much better and saved my husband days of reattaching fiddly cupboard locks!

Keep a creative cupboard

Creative toys (puzzles, paints, sticking materiel, Play-Doh, chalks, etc.) are an essential part of a child's play. My kids love Play-Doh and find it even more enticing than the offer of a gingerbread man. I have a small cupboard in our kitchen where I keep all this stuff and the children have learnt to ask before they start messy play. That way, I (or another adult) can always participate and the glitter and neon felt-tips don't end up all over the walls!

Invest in one large, sturdy toy chest

The second thing I invested in after the Moses basket was a wicker toy chest. (Choose one with holes in it so if your child climbs in, which believe me, they do, they can still breathe.) The chest has pride of place in our kitchen (which is the main family room), and I try to live by the motto 'If it doesn't fit, it isn't coming in!' By this I mean that if the toy chest is full and a new toy arrives, something has to be moved elsewhere or given away before it joins the toys. Now it sounds cruel, but really, this toy box is massive and it means that I can contain all the kid's paraphernalia easily and practically. The minute you allow overflow, you'll find the whole room becomes a kids' free-for-all and not even a toddler can make sense of it. By ensuring that all the toys are put away in there at the end of the day, it means grown-up supper-time is Pooh Bear-free! Obviously, if you have the space to delegate a whole playroom to toys, the chest policy need not apply. But for those mums whose 'playroom' is their living area, it can be an essential clutter-saver.

Box things up

This is a little tip I learnt from one of my children's baby-sitters, Gillian. It takes four simple steps and ensures you can store and locate toys with ease:

1. Buy a heap of cheap see-through plastic boxes (with lids) from your local supermarket or hardware store. (Alternatively, try old ice-cream tubs.)
2. Delegate a box to the related toys – e.g. separate trains in one, dolls in another, puzzle pieces in the third. Label the boxes clearly.
3. Stack the boxes within the toy box/creative cupboard/ children's under-bed drawer. Kids can find toys without fuss, and the boxes make it easier to put things away at the end of a game. (You can even make a learning game of it – e.g. box some toys according to colours or letters of the alphabet.)
4. Once the kids are in bed and the toys boxed up, sit down with a glass of chilled wine (not a toy in sight) and congratulate yourself on your organisational skills!

Keep as much as you can in kids' bedrooms

Apart from the creative cupboard, the toy chest, a small wooden table and chairs (where the kids often do puzzles and eat their snacks) and the handful of super-bulky toys (play kitchen, wooden trike and pink princess doll's buggy), all other toys are assigned to my children's bedrooms. Of course, half of the bedroom junk comes down at breakfast (especially since my daughter has begun bringing down a backpack, which is attached to her at all times!), but the trick is to monitor it and try to return most of the toys at bedtime.

Don't ignore bedroom chaos

I try to organise the kids' bedrooms as I do the rest of the house. A lot of my friends have siblings sharing rooms, so they live even more by the 'organisation is key' rule to prevent the bedrooms from descending into a black hole of toys. See-through crates, open wicker baskets or pretty, self-assemble cardboard boxes (which your child could even decorate, paint or put stickers on) are ideal for under-bed storage.

Bookshelves, wall hooks (to hang bags, aprons, dressing gowns, ballet kits, etc.) and a grown-up chest of drawers and wardrobe (with shelves or drawers for toys) are also brilliant ways of clearing clutter. Remember to make these accessible to kids and at a good height for toddlers; this gives them independence to play freely. (A good idea is to squat down on their level and see what they can and can't reach.) My kids have free-standing furniture (all of which I chose on the basis that it will see them through to their teenage years), but my sister-in-law Jo, for example, swears by fitted cupboards. Enter her kids' rooms and all you see is stream-lined white cupboards, which once opened, reveal beautifully organised winter coats, wellington boots, pirate ships, fairy costumes and soft toys. How she finds time to organise this lot and cook her own bread I'll never know.

Limit the toy fest

While storage is crucial, restricting toy mania is also key. Recently, when my daughter had three little girlfriends for tea, pink princess madness reached its peak. When they all traipsed down the stairs on their third round trip of collecting everything and anything pink and fluffy, I had to be a little firm. 'Come on, girls,' I said, 'three toys each and a dressing-up outfit to wear – the rest needs to be cleared up.' When this fell on deaf ears, I admit I resorted to bribery. 'OK, ladies, the first one upstairs to help me put the Barbies back gets a pink iced-gem biscuit.' You've never seen three pairs of little feet (clad in plastic high heels, I should add) move so fast in your life!

Don't succumb to 'plastic equals fantastic'

With a little imagination you can create play spaces and storage solutions that are chic and not entirely plastic. Ever thought of covering large storage boxes with pretty floral paper for your daughter's room instead of opting for pink neon storage crates? Have you tried stencilling boats against a white background for the walls of your toddler's playroom rather than going for *Jungle Book* wallpaper? Or why not go for fairy lights over a mirror in your twins' shared box room instead of emphasising the cluttered bookshelf and lack of space with bright lighting? Being creative and innovative with fabrics, lighting and storage can make the difference between a kid's space that looks overcrowded and overpowering and one that exudes calm and openness.

Involve the kids

I am absolutely convinced that by involving your kids in organising and tidying (and offering heaps of praise when they do it well), you are encouraging independence and good social skills. A fellow mum at my children's school, Rachel, has three sons who have always been encouraged to clear the table, tidy up toys and help around the house. My children went to her youngest's birthday party at the weekend and I almost fainted at the polite, helpful and accommodating manner in which her boys conducted themselves. Not only did her seven-year-old fetch all the mums a glass of wine (with a smile that melted hearts), but her five-year-old helped to clear the cake plates away and stack them in the dishwasher. Her secret? A little insistence, a lot of inclusion and heaps of congratulations at a job well done. (If this seems a world away from your terrible toddler, try a sticker chart for helpful behaviour or assign one job that only she can do. It's amazing how two-year-olds love to own tasks, it makes them feel important.)

In my house, we have 'tidy-up time' at the end of a game and all hands are expected to be on deck. My son, especially, can't wait to help clear up and bask in the glory of all the praise it rewards him with. Sometimes we make it a race, or reward it with a treat, or for my daughter, who hoards absolutely everything, I encourage her to collect the stones, shells, beads, crowns and general princess accessories and arrange them on her 'treasure shelf' – well out of her brother's reach and ready to retrieve in the morning. Generally, they now know the form and are at least willing to put half the jungle puzzle pieces back in the box. (Yes, I said 'half';

no mum should aim for more than that without operating some sort of mini boot camp!) If this helps to make your home tidy and your toddlers self-sufficient young adults, it's worth it, I think!

Always tidy up and organise once the kids go to bed

I know we're all knackered and would much rather flop on the sofa in front of the soaps, but a fifteen-minute sweep of all kids' stuff is essential to a mum's and dad's sanity. Sure, don't beat yourself up when you've come in late from work and, frankly, just can't be bothered, or you have six emails and a basket of ironing that, let's face it, are more of a priority, but if you can give a little time and energy to reclaiming some adult space, you'll feel heaps more in control. I'm not saying seek perfection here (come on, I'm no dream house-wife − I don't even know how to iron a collar convincingly), I just think mums need a viable way of kicking back after a long day without being overrun by children's paraphernalia.

A speedy collection of all stray toys, a quick round-up of school letters, party invites and kids' paintings (to stick on a pinboard later or file in an easy-access drawer) and a removal of all kids' coats, shoes, odd socks and dirty football kits (to bung on coat hooks, in the washing basket or under the stairs) will make you feel so much more relaxed, not to mention grown-up. If you eat supper surrounded by muddy wellies, crumpled PTA letters and still-flashing shape-sorters, you'll go to bed feeling that you've literally not turned off all day.

★

Just remember, children don't need to equal constant chaos all of the time. Of course, a lot of the time they can't help it, but don't give up hope of having any order whatsoever. You can insist on a toy-controlled living space, you can request that your toddlers help tidy up before bath time and you can have input (or a discussion at least) into a seven-year-old's choice of wallpaper. This is your shared home, after all, and you must find an interior balance that suits you all (for work, rest and play).

Mother knows best

'My husband was useless around the house, and when he came home from work, he always insisted on getting out *all* the boys' toys and playing with them until late into the night. When they eventually went to bed, I was left to pick up the pieces. When we split up, I decided to reclaim the home a little. I managed somehow to build a cheap self-assembly wooden house for our tiny garden and put a lot of their bulky toys out there. In summer, they play in it for hours, and in winter, it's great storage. I also implemented sticker charts to encourage the boys to help me clear up before school and before bed. They are now my little helpers and I feel they reap the benefits of having a mum with a tidy, adult space in which to relax in the evening.'

Tracey Lewis, dinner lady and mother to Rory (eight), Sean (six) and Brooklyn (two)

Sacred Space

I'm sure I'm not alone in envying those families who have more space than they know what to do with. Forget the Porche four-by-four, forget the housekeeper and gardener and forget about the limitless M&S food account (OK, I suppose the last one would come in handy), it's the abundance of household space that really makes me green with envy. Just imagine how nice it would be to pack the kids off to a garden with a tree house, state-of-the-art climbing frame and a shed stuffed full of toys. Just picture Sunday lunch while the children played happily in an enormous playroom (leaving you to read the papers by an open fire). For a moment there, I was that woman calling her children in from the 200-foot garden – what bliss! Sadly, for most of us, child's play must fit into a more confined space. For me, it's a four-bedroom house; for my friend Jennie, it's an itsy-bitsy two-up, two-down; and for my friend Esme, it's a one-bedroom flat in inner-city London.

While all my fellow mums have found storage solutions and answers to the toy chaos important, the mantra we now recite is 'Sacred space, sacred space, sacred space'. Like a mass of tranquillity-deprived monks, we all met one afternoon at a local playgroup. The conversation went something like this:

Amy: Bloody hell, since when is it OK for my nine-year-old to play PlayStation in my bed like he owned it?
Rainbow: You think that's bad? My boys have decorated the whole downstairs with warrior paint and Indian masks.
Gayle: Tell me about it, there is so much of my daughter's

pink paraphernalia in the living room that my husband is scared to come home from work.

Me: Last night I returned home to find my son raiding my wardrobe and trashing my favourite pair of heels. He ran around screaming like a hyena wearing nothing but my three-inch snake-skin stilettos – what a sight!

Reaching for the digestives and roaring with laughter, we all said in unison, 'We need a sacred space!!!'

It can seem nearly impossible to achieve this when space is in short supply and you're using every inch of the home as it is. The solution we came up with was to delegate one space, however tiny, as a child no-go zone. Now, this doesn't mean plastering it with 'Out of bounds, no access' tape and forbidding your children ever to cross the invisible divide, but it does mean mentally saving a morsel of space for grown-up time. I am lucky enough to have a kitchen that is a good family space and a living room, which we have made a pretty much exclusive adult area. The kitchen is child-friendly and child-safe; it's decorated with kids' paintings and consists of their toy chest, kids' table and chairs and wooden tricycles. In contrast, our living room has cream sofas, a coffee table, my laptop, a huge stash of *Vogues* (dating back to the 1980s) and the TV. The kids come into the living room to watch TV, but this is really the only time they come in – we've made it clear this is not a playroom! (This rule has also helped us control and monitor the amount of TV they watch. It is our only television, and if it goes on, it's to watch a specific children's show or DVD. I desperately wanted to avoid TV as general household background noise.)

The lovely thing is, in the evening, when the children are

asleep, my husband and I can relax in the living room, watch a movie, listen to some records, read the paper or a book and generally unwind from the day. This 'sacred space' is an integral part of feeling adult at the end of the day and turning off from the hubbub of kids painting, Tumble Tots CDs, singing Noddy cars and primary colours. My old friend Sophie doesn't have the luxury of a living-room space, but she delegated her bedroom as the 'sacred space'. She keeps a crate of her children's toys under her bed so they can play there while she dresses in the morning, but beyond that it is a grown-up space. She covered a lamp in a Victorian lace shawl, invested in a second-hand trunk (which she stencilled in flowers), arranged her shoes in clear boxes and made a tiny side table into a miniature dressing table. (Over the years, she's collected antique atomisers and compacts, which she's arranged beautifully on a pearly crocheted table mat.) Being a single mum, she felt it gave her licence to indulge in her girlie side, and it made it even more crucial to carve a space where she could feel like a woman, not just a lawyer, a mum and Jeremy's ex!

Having a sacred space doesn't give you an excuse to let the rest of the home descend into primary-colour mayhem! In fact, I found investing in a grown-up sphere made me focus even harder on making the rest of the home more a sanctuary and less a pre-school. At the beginning of last summer, the children's eight-week holidays fast approaching, I decided to rejig the home to give it a fresh, inspiring feel, not least to brace myself for eight weeks of kids-at-home chaos! By changing a few heavy curtains to those made of vintage lace, bunging some fresh summer flowers in vases or jam jars and covering the kitchen table with a clean, floral tablecloth, I had in no time at all given the house a little lift (not to mention my sprits!).

It was only a week after the initial playgroup moan and we mums met once again. Amy had banned PlayStation from her bedroom (and borrowed a second-hand BMX for her nine-year-old instead); Rainbow had made a 'warrior wall' for her boys and cleared out her tiny storage room, making it a mum-only zone (filling one and a half skips while she was at it); Gayle had invested in a toy chest for all the pink paraphernalia (and once again reclaimed her living room, to the relief of her husband); and I'd blitzed the home with flowers, aired the living room and sorted my shoes into boxes out of my son's toddler reach. We all felt we deserved a medal and agreed that having prioritised an inch of mum space, we felt a little more sane and a lot more empowered (so much so Gayle invited all three of us over for drinks, nibbles and the new Brad Pitt movie in her very own grown-up living room, no pink in sight!).

Mother knows best

'I have the smallest house on the planet, and with four children it often feels like we live in a phone box! I was at my wits' end with constant dirty laundry, indoor ball games and children's toys everywhere! For my fortieth birthday, my partner, Eddie, invested in a tiny conservatory at the back of the house. It's just big enough for an armchair, a little desk, a bookshelf, some potted plants and a CD player. I can't tell you how I treasure this place; it has become my safe haven. Whenever the yelling, the pop dancing and the demands for more ice cream become too much, I escape to my mini retreat, pick up my novel and dream of being in a beach hut by the sea. It's prevented any more grey hairs, I can tell you!'

Nancy McDonald, full-time mother to Ailsa (thirteen), Scott (ten), Gregory (six) and Freddie (five)

Benefits All Round

There can't be a woman on the planet who doesn't feel better when her living space is organised. Even my pals who couldn't tidy an empty soft-padded cell (and live by the 'chaos is creative' ethos) found once they have kids, they had to rethink their ways. The thing I discovered was that once I'd had children, I craved (more than ever before) a little order and sanctuary at the end of a long day. Not only that, but I felt my relationship needed it more than ever. How would I ever muster the energy to make love if the house was in such chaos it required an extra hour to sort out in the evening? And how could I possibly entice my husband to bed when once we got there it was filled with Brio? Would it be possible to hold one of my much-treasured supper parties if I'd let go of my flair for interiors and let the house descend into stain-free, child-friendly, red, yellow and blue plastic? And more to the point, what space would

I have to write my book if every inch of the house was taken up with Barbie (with room for little else)?

You can't underestimate the power our living spaces have in shaping our well-being and mood. All the other aspects of regaining your identity post-children (relationships, work, sleep and nutrition) are made easier and more viable with a well-organised home that represents your style, as well as that of your children. Just think how much easier it is to blend up a smoothie when you've not got a toddler opening the utility cupboard and attempting suicide with the blades every five minutes. (A simple child lock should solve that.) How much better to nip out to a girlfriend's for a cup of tea and a gossip one evening, when you haven't got a week's worth of toys to clear up and absolutely nowhere to store them. And think how much better you'll sleep without your toddler in your room because you haven't got round to painting and tidying their bedroom.

Not only do we mums benefit from having a home we can tidy and sort easily, but who can deny the lift we get from waking up in the morning to the sight of a fresh bunch of sweetpeas beside the bed, or the light streaming in the window, making patterns through the new lace curtains? I'm not following a 'how clean is your home?' doctrine, I'm simply saying a little effort goes a long way. Take good old hard-working Sophie; she's the first to admit that when her marriage broke up she completely gave up on housework and the home. By the time the divorce papers came in, her space looked like the 'armpit of London' (her words, not mine). It was her sister, a counsellor, who suggested that one weekend while Jeremy had the children she should spring-clean the home, sort through and chuck out a whole load of books, records and chairs that he'd brought to the marriage and give the flat a lift. She admits now that it was this weekend in late November (and the two bottles of mulled wine she consumed with an old school friend while she did it) that initiated her recovery. It's amazing what a collection of atomisers, a bunch of lilies and a dustbin bag full of his football magazines can do.

I might not be single, but I often take a leaf out of Sophie's book. It can be therapy for the soul to sort out, chuck out, tidy and invest in our homes. The brilliant thing is the children always seem to benefit, too. The amount of times I've found a long-lost dog-eared teddy when I've had a sort-out of my daughter's room, or gained moments of extra quality time with my son because the school run hasn't been fraught with lost lunch boxes, un-findable gym kits and missing PTA letters. These are all worth their weight in gold. Both my children also have a real sense of pride in their bedrooms; they love their private worlds and seem to thrive on knowing everything has a place (even a three-week-old snail's shell, a conker and a button from Grandma's sewing box!). If my children are happy, my husband and I have a little grown-up space and I have the time to invest in other aspects of my life (like my book, a girlfriend, a swim and the preparation of a Sunday roast), then I couldn't really ask for much more. Try it some time; if a little interior creativity and some simple tips on controlling toy volume worked for me (and at least six other mums in the last few weeks), then I'm pretty sure it can work for you, too!

Top ten interior tips

1. Don't buy like mad before the birth; work out what is really necessary and what you can do without.
2. If you do have the luxury of doing up a nursery, think of the space and furniture as a long-term environment for the child, not just a space for a four-month-old.
3. Work out strategies for preventing toy overload: key for your home and the development of your child.
4. Make storage solutions a top priority!
5. Invest in child-safety systems, but don't blanket your home with every harm-free gadget going. You can't live in a totally sharp-edge-free/germ-free/no-stairs environment (and who'd want to?).
6. Make tidying up a family effort. Give toys and children's 'stuff' assigned places; this will help you to get organised and make it easier for children to participate.
7. Make sure you and your partner do a quick clean-up sweep once the kids go to bed. You'll feel better eating your supper in a chaos-free zone.
8. Don't neglect the rest of the home. Utilising natural light, investing in seasonal flowers and keeping the home clutter-free will give your sanity a boost.
9. Reclaim a morsel of child-free space; a living room, your bedroom, a small desk area or even a conservatory can make ideal spaces for maximum grown-up time and minimum toy levels.
10. Once you've implemented interior solutions, make sure you use some of the time it saves for yourself. Fancy a face pack?

Grace's Guru: Amanda Smith

Amanda trained as an architect and interior designer at Chelsea College of Art and Design in London. Moments after she'd graduated, she landed a job on *Elle Decoration*, where she reigns today as style director. She's still found time to rebuild, remodel and transform a derelict bunch of flats in West London into a stylish, modern family home to share with her husband and two sons, Sam, aged three, and Jesse, one.

What are your main interior tips for mums?

A mum who's sharing her bedroom and living space with her children Remember, babies and children actually take up very little room and don't need an awful lot to keep them happy. Try not to over-indulge them and aim to minimise clutter by having only as much as you need and to clear out at least once a year. (Car-boot sales, charity shops and eBay are all useful for this.) Often toys are in bad shape after a year of excess sandpit usage, so it's best to get rid of them! Keep a check on toy levels – in general, a kid can only play with one thing at a time, so resist spoiling them. Turn to toys that will grow with a child. The same applies to furniture. I'd always choose play tables with storage underneath, a tabletop that doubles as a blackboard, easel or train circuit, for example.

For a mum with little space, good ingenious storage is mega important. Banks of floor-to-ceiling storage is ideal, with smaller storage ideas within. (There's no use just chucking it all in unless it's organised in smaller crates, drawers or baskets inside.) Also good, but a little cheaper, are banks of shelves filled with lots of baskets or crates. Or for something a little quirkier, try old school or sports lockers. I love being inventive and often use vintage luggage trunks, which blend well with grown-up interiors; I also try catering companies and suppliers, as they are a good place to find unusual bins and tubs.

The bottom line is to be inventive with space and imaginative with storage. If you have a one-bedroom flat, don't necessarily assume the child must share your bedroom. Have you looked at the space objectively? Have you considered every alcove, quiet corner of the hallway, landing or windowed attic? Simply hanging a curtain, piece of fabric or screen will make the child's space separate and cosy, and help to filter light and noise. If you must share your bedroom, have you thought about hanging the Moses basket or baby hammock from a ceiling joist? This is ideal to free up floor space. If you choose a stand-alone cot, go for something simple and space-saving, and avoid brazen bed linen if you can. A child will sleep just as well on white cotton as she will on Barbie, and it will help your bedroom space feel less like a playschool! (Dimmer lights are also a good way to make the space feel calmer and warmer; a bright room always feels more cluttered in my view.)

A mum with children of varying ages The only way to organise the clutter of a large family is storage, storage and more storage. Make sure your storage systems are easy and child-friendly; remember, if kids can tidy away their own clobber, it will help you. Don't adopt complex systems with clothes hooks and shelves out of reach. Use big storage baskets, dustbins, trunks and crates wherever clutter accumulates around the home, and teach your children the importance of tidying up after themselves. (Another good idea is to adopt playful, fun storage solutions. Pull-down springy baskets, suspended fishing nets and systems with holes instead of lids are all novel ideas.)

Let me take you through two rooms that people tend to find hard to declutter and you'll see how storage solutions can work for you, whatever the age range of your children.

- **Hallway.** For outdoor hats, shoes, balls, bats, buckets and spades, etc. invest in child-height hooks that will encourage children not to throw their coats on the floor. Make it fun by giving each child their own coat hook and identify it with their name, a colour or picture they love. The Eames 'hang it all' coat rack, for example, is good-looking, fun and perfect for colour coding.
- **Bathroom.** Place a storage basket or bin in here for all bath toys, just ensure it has a watertight lining or place a binliner inside. These solutions are so much better than those horrid bath nets, especially if you share the bathroom and want a relaxing toy-free bath!

If you find you also get stuck for ideas in the main family room or kitchen, why not try storing toys in type – one red box for trains, a pink one for tea sets and a beige one for bricks – this way tidying up will become easier, for both you and the kids. I like to stick a Polaroid on the box – i.e. a drum for music stuff, a ballet shoe for dance kits, etc. – it helps keep the home organised and looks cool, too. Whatever storage you choose, remember the ideal is to blend it with the rest of the home. Aim for boxes or crates that will look good in or out of a cupboard.

A mum wanting a stylish yet functional nursery
When thinking about a nursery space, don't make the classic mistake of arranging it solely for the under-threes. You'll find you spend an awful lot of time in there as well, so make sure there is comfortable seating for you to feed, sit, watch and play with your child. For novel storage, I love coat hooks because they are instant decoration and a great way of displaying your baby's prettiest garments. I think baby booties look lovely hung up like a pair of ballet shoes; you could even choose a lovely ribbon to hang them from to really make a feature of them.

As I've said before, a baby doesn't need much, but a nursery should aim to be both tranquil and stimulating. Young babies have poor eyesight, so try and see the room through their eyes. Simplicity is the key, so don't overcrowd it with too much going on in terms of colour and pattern. I adore off-beat muted shades, even plums and greys, as opposed to the classic pale pink. In general, I'd opt for a white colour scheme accented with more colourful accessories.

I find simple things are best, and ones that catch the light or breeze and move are even better. Babies spend the majority of their time on their backs, so string a mobile or Chinese lantern from the ceiling, stick up some dayglo stars, too, or how about some fairy lights? Babies also love looking at pictures of babies and children, including themselves, so you could create an informal family pinboard of Polaroids or blow up a favourite picture and get it mounted on canvas. You could even get it digitally printed Warhol style!

At all times, try and anticipate a child or toddler's growing needs. You don't want her tripping on trailing wires or knocking over table lamps when she's up and about, so position lights and sockets carefully. Two things that I find ageless in terms of a baby's nursery or child's room are sheepskin rugs and beanbags. A baby of six months will love either and so will a child of twelve, so they are good investments, even if you make a rug out of fake fur yourself!

A mum wanting to keep boundaries on adult space
Keeping boundaries on adult space shouldn't mean segregating your children. For most of us, time is at a premium today, especially if you're a working parent, so when you are together, *be* together, rather than locked behind different doors. Young children especially don't feel comfortable playing alone in a separate area, so unless you have a warehouse flat or bungalow, you need to be ingenious with blending space. You can integrate a child's play area into your home without having to give up on adult style and glamour, I promise!

The idea is to create areas where kids can play alongside you. Large wall-mounted blackboards or walls painted in blackboard paint are fab and *über*-stylish, I think. Not only are they good for kids to scribble on, but they also make handy impromptu notepads or shopping lists. Don't just restrict these to the kitchen; hallways and cupboard doors are great too. All kids I know love to play 'house', so invest in a pop-up tent or little wooden home, which can be space-saving as they can be pushed into a corner and also provide great storage for other toys. If you are redesigning your home, think about cool new ideas such as a sunken cushion area for kids' quiet play or a hammock to hang from internal joints. Ideas like that can be striking, contemporary and ideal for providing kids with little pockets of their own space.

Whatever the size of your house, if you want to create firm boundaries, you need to set some house rules from day one. Compromise is the key here: for example, you can't jump on the new suede sofa, but you can jump on your own bed. Educate them from very young to respect furniture, both yours and theirs.

A mum wanting ideas for creating a fun and modern living environment I always think choosing one eye-catching prop and placing it against a neutral background (such as a giant wooden aeroplane hung from the ceiling) gives a great modern twist to a room. I've also used fairy lights or large vintage letters to spell a name across a room or to liven up a wall in a child's bedroom. Don't be scared to be creative (or to rope someone in who's gifted with a paintbrush). Try a single image painted graphically on a wall – i.e. a train, car, guitar, dog, cat or flower – use stencils to paint a tree in blossom on a girl's bedroom wall, or even paint a road map on the floor of a boy's room so he can play cars from morning to night.

Children love secret hideaways, and these can be both fun and modern. Floaty canopies and mosquito nets sewn with fake flowers for girls, or camouflage nets for boys, hung over a bed create instant dens. In the same way, you could use a curtain or sari over any nook and cranny to make a dead space come to life. As much as hiding away, kids also love to be on show. Designating one wall for the artwork and giving them an old school desk and chair for cutting and sticking will make any child very happy!

A mum wanting to prevent her home getting tatty from overuse Even the best-behaved children will get up to some mischief, get overexcited and test the boundaries occasionally. With the best will in the world, you don't have eyes in the back of your head, so try to choose a home you don't need to police round the clock to minimise the effect of damage. Where possible, choose practical, hardwearing, easy-to-clean surfaces. As a rule, hard flooring is better than soft, as it is easier to keep clean and great for pushing and riding toys. Wood is ideal as it is not too hard for knocks and tumbles; it's a little softer and warmer than concrete, tiles or rubber. Whatever hard flooring you choose, though, ensure that it has a sealed finish or is at least waxed (or limed in the case of wood), otherwise it will stain too easily. Top the floor off with rugs for glamour and warmth. (If you do prefer carpets, go for coir, jute or sisal as these are very hard-wearing.)

For camouflaging a multitude of sins, pattern is better than plain. No need to go down the swirly-whirly pub fitted-carpet route – there are so many great ethnic and vintage rugs out there that will work well with today's modern eclectic interiors. Similarly, painted walls are great for hiding dirty handprints and graffiti, and can be wiped away or painted over if severely marked. This is much easier and more cost-effective than repapering an entire wall or recreating a specialist plaster finish.

In terms of safety, be careful with glass. If your interior style demands large expanses of glass, ensure that it is safety glass even on your coffee table. If this isn't an option, you can obtain special films that will hold the glass in place, should it shatter. Corner cushions are so unattractive, and I would try and avoid sharp corners and furniture made from fragile materials – for example glass-topped coffee tables – why not opt for acrylic or Perspex instead? You don't have to banish all fragile things, but do bear in mind that they may well get knocked about, so if it's priceless or irreplaceable, it may be a good idea to put it out of harm's way. You may even want to consider the huge selection of antique and vintage furniture around. Not only does it look stylish, you may not worry so much about the occasional bump or scratch as it will just add to the overall charm of a piece!

Another safety issue that is crucial to keep in mind is an open working fireplace. If it is in a room where the kids are likely to hang out without adult supervision, think carefully about a fireguard. Depending on your style of fireplace, there is a huge variety of styles available, from traditional to modern and minimal plain glass.

What are your top five must-haves for a mum in search of a stylish family home?

1. Make sure you have one space at home you can call your own.
2. Opt for wooden toys, not the plastic type in primary colours.
3. Be imaginative; paint, stencil, suspend and invent!
4. Go for wooden floors, easy to clean surfaces and open spaces.
5. Use vintage drapes, dim lights, black and white photos or an antique mirror to create a tranquil mood and add an element of glamour.

What are the key dos and don'ts for creating a stylish yet child-friendly home?

Dos

- Prioritise space in your kitchen; you will spend a lot of time there, so invest in it!
- Try to keep things open-plan if possible. You will feel less crowded and overwhelmed with clutter.
- Store, store, store! There are so many useful storage ideas out there, it can be easy to declutter and stay chic.
- Get the kids to help clean up and instil respect for furniture and fixtures.
- Use lighting to create a mood. (Bright lights are a big 'no'.)
- Invest in a sheepskin and chuck it on your favourite armchair to curl up on.
- Keep one set of bed linen for 'best'. Every so often, get it pressed and starched at the dry-cleaner's, light some scented candles, play some subtle music and create a 'hotel-style' feeling at home.

Don'ts

- No need to go for the obvious in kids' nursery furniture and toys. Don't be scared to be individual.
- Try to avoid plastic toys; wooden toys are gorgeous to look at and are just as fun.
- Be careful not to let kids rule your home! Set boundaries and rules, but be realistic at the same time.
- Don't expect a stark, child-free home with everything in its place come 8 p.m. But make storage fun, and create systems that can declutter without banishing all sense of your children.

Amanda's fabulous mum's interior mantra: 'Creating a child-friendly house doesn't mean you have to give up on style and glamour.'

Work-life Balance

The Bubble

Thirty-seven weeks pregnant. December. Rain, rain and more rain. I step off the 6.23 p.m. Underground train from my office in Central London for the last time before my baby is born. Even if I didn't know it at the time, what I really step into is a bubble. The world outside consists of sweaty carriages commuting to and from work (where men in suits bury their heads in the *Financial Times* so as not to be obliged to give up their seat), deadlines that don't ease because of your horrendous sciatica pain and issues of *Junior Pregnancy and Baby* that peep out from under your desk, dying to be read. Inside, all is fluffy and white. It is a world of anticipation, longing and excitement. It is also a world that can now contain afternoons drinking hot chocolate in bed with your Sheila Kitzinger birthing book, lunchtimes with your mother-in-law checking out mobiles in Mothercare and evenings fantasising about the 'meeting' with your baby. The bubble is yours and your newborn's (with a little space for your partner if required), and work seems a million miles away.

My friend Kara (who happens to be a super-sleek fashion

press officer) was the last person I expected to get all mushy at bubble time. She worked all the hours that God sent, spent most nights in Milan, Paris or New York seeing work clients, and I'd never seen her miss a champagne launch or boutique opening in all my eight years in fashion. However, once she crept into thirty-eight weeks of pregnancy, the only place to find her was on the sofa practising breathing exercises and embroidering a patchwork quilt for the arrival of her daughter. Forget work schedules and smoked-salmon vol-au-vents, she was nesting big time!

Bar my girlfriends who run their own companies (and even my friend Liza was known to kip under the main table of her restaurant, her birth plan at her side, in week thirty-nine), nearly all the new mums I know who have left work for maternity leave talk about the bubble. Even though many of us expect to be constantly attached to the email, on the phone all morning to our boss or worrying manically about whether the shipment from Hong Kong has arrived safely, most of us are pleasantly surprised at how easy it is to let it all go. I had a two-week overlap with my replacement (a sweet girl called Cassie, who despite being drop-dead gorgeous and single, didn't make me resent my maternity leave one bit). By the time I left the office for my six months 'off', I felt confident I could nest to my heart's content while Cassie sought out the next exclusive fashion scoop, or got drunk next to John Galliano.

Once my beautiful daughter arrived, the last thing on my mind was the October issue of *Elle* and what fashion features we should pack it with. Many mums I know – and their career has been a pivotal part of their life – enjoyed the break from the speed of working life. Of course, dirty nappies, leaky boobs and a lack of grown-up conversation will at times make you pine for a business meeting or a catch-up in the ladies' with a colleague, but personally, I found these moments fleeting and instead relished the chance to bond with my baby and take a step back from the power suit.

My great friend Lyn has always been successful at work. She's a true example of the modern working woman. She's ambitious, she sets her sights high, and she (nearly) always gets what she wants. She's the only woman I know who can create jobs in companies where the title has never existed before. You need an events co-ordinator with flair and origin-ality? Of course you do. You need a whiz woman to rebrand, remarket, repitch and relaunch your beauty range? Why not. You need to up your offer by £10,000? Hell yes! But once Lyn stepped off the fast track and gave birth to her son, she found herself needing nothing more than an afternoon strolling with him in the park or sharing half a Guinness with a fellow mum while he shook a rattle on her knee for all he was worth. It's no surprise that she calls those six months of maternity leave 'the wonder months'.

I already anticipate the odd voice of protest. 'But it's sooo boring,' I can hear one or two of you cry. 'I couldn't wait to get back on the train and in the boardroom.' This may be true for some of you, and believe me, after seven months of maternity leave, there was part of me that secretly yearned for a power lunch, an interview with a top model and an excuse to dress up for work. Generally, though, I adored my maternity leave, wept at the mere thought of leaving my tiny baby and tried my hardest to savour every second we had together. Every fresh spring walk in the park, every evening massage, every breastfeed, when she patted my chest with a

twinkle in her eye, all this would soon be gone . . . replaced
by harassed editors, deadlines that loom and the thought that
someone else would be sharing magic moments with *my*
daughter. My bubble was soon to burst.

Mother knows best

'I so desperately wanted to have the maximum time
possible with my newborn that I worked right up to
the wire before the birth. Millie was four days early and
I'd literally just finished work that day. The birth was
very traumatic and I felt very sad that I hadn't given
myself a few days, a week even, to wind down and
prepare. In the end, I took an extra three months' maternity leave, but I advise all my mum-to-be friends to put
aside a week or two prior to the birth to nest and
pamper themselves. I think having a relaxed mum is
crucial to raising a relaxed baby; how is this possible if
you've stepped straight from the boardroom to the labour
room?'

Jok Tandoi, City accountant and mother to Skyla (one)

Guilt and Sacrifices

I can hardly even say the words 'guilt' and 'sacrifice' without
being awash with feelings of remorse about at least a million
and one parenting issues. Never is this more true than with

246

the topic of striking the work–life balance. From my experience, it doesn't matter whether you're the breadwinner, the equal earner, the part-time contributor or the single parent, the feelings of guilt, confusion and heart-wrenching dismay are the same. After giving birth to my daughter, I knew I really had no option but to return to work. I had a fabulous job (that after years of working up the ladder as an assistant had become my 'dream job'). It not only made up a huge part of my identity, it also made up a large part of the bill-paying.

Yes, magazine journalists are paid a pittance (I suppose the 'glamour' of the job is supposed to compensate for the lack of funds), and it seems unlikely I'll ever be the one to fork out for a three-storey house in a plush area of London, but I've always paid my way. We enjoy holidays, two cars, nice meals out and a pretty good standard of living. Without two incomes, all that would change. We would say 'goodbye' to our four-bedroom house, our annual holidays in Ibiza and our preference for organic food. I'd have to address my fetish for shoes, my weakness for monthly glossy magazines and my desire for the kids to have extra-curricular activities like the odd Monkey Music class. I'm sure we'd manage, but I'm the first to admit that as a family we've got used to a lifestyle dependent on two incomes. Lots of my friends' households depend even more significantly on a second salary.

Take my friend Jennie, who busts a gut in her job for a local arts depot so she can pay the mortgage and have food on the table. Whilst her super-creative husband launches his art gallery, her income will continue to be the backbone of the family. Sophie is a single mother of three pre-school children. Her husband buggered off with a Greek dancer (yes, really) and has not been seen since. Forget maintenance, forget a contribution to childcare, this woman has to work or her family will fall apart. She may weep at night about what milestones she misses, but without her monthly pay cheque, she would lose her house and everything in it. (Try sleeping rough with three under-fives!)

When Jennie, Sophie and I meet with the children on a Saturday afternoon (once we've vented our frustrations about respective client/boss/magazine editor in question), much of what overshadows the discussions are feelings of guilt and sacrifice. My son is hanging on to me like clingfilm because I've been writing for the bulk of the week, Jennie's daughter isn't talking to her because she's worked late for the last two nights, and Sophie, well, she's wracked with remorse at skidding into the school play with four minutes to go before curtain call. We beat ourselves up, we console each other, and then we all jump into the sandpit with extra enthusiasm, lapping up the weekend moments that give us the freedom to play with our children.

I was incredibly lucky that I could scale down to four (and then three) days per week after having my children. I feel blessed further with the fact that I was able to leave my office job and earn similar amounts of cash by writing freelance. It is a job I love and that gives me more time with my children (compared with the old days when I worked twelve-hour days and never got home before dark). This doesn't mean, however, I make no sacrifices and feel 100 per cent right about the work choices I've made. Only in my wildest dreams would I wake up and feel confident day in, day out that my work commitments were the right priorities to make and that my children weren't suffering as a consequence.

It was only yesterday that I sat down with my husband

(when we should have been safely tucked up in bed or in front of a good Woody Allen movie at least) to discuss making some 'mummy' time for my daughter. Since my son was born, just eighteen months after her, it has been very difficult to carve out 'special' time for either of them, and over the last few months, work has been coming in thick and fast. It wasn't until my daughter started to show signs of insecurity (lots of 'Mummy, are you going out again?' and 'Mum, will you be here in the morning?') that her anxiety was brought to my attention. There was no denying after the third refusal of supper that she needed some real one-on-one from me. I could have drowned in the guilt. How could I have prioritised Chapter Three over an hour of doll's house play with my daughter? How could I have failed to take her to school the last three days because nine o'clock in the morning was the only time that the designer Alice Temperley could be interviewed? And how could I possibly have forgotten my promise to bake muffins on Thursday afternoon and instead be found researching maternity fashion for a parenting magazine on the Internet? Bad mother, bad mother, bad mother!!! I remembered with a pang the moment I'd held my daughter to me at seven months old, weeping into her soft blonde locks. The thought that tomorrow I'd be at the office and the sweet baby smell I'd cherished would be replaced with the aroma of lip gloss and strong coffee drove me to despair. Would I miss her first words? Would I miss her first steps? And would she ever, ever, ever forgive me for wanting to be a writer as well as a mother?

Talk to my friend Danni, a businesswoman and a mother of two children who are almost teenagers, and she'll tell you this guilt never goes away. Talk to my friend Sara, a super-successful fashion designer and a mother of one, and she'll tell you that even if you're earning a fortune and flying first-class around the world, the sound of your little one saying, 'Goodnight, Mummy,' over the phone breaks your heart. Talk to any working mum, in fact, and they will all sing from the same song sheet: working with children means guilt, sacrifices and a damn fine balancing act. Surely there must be a way to get it right without your children suffering? (Or for that matter, without letting your career go down the plughole while you're doing a three-day week!) Should my friend Sophie feel like the evil witch because her career as a lawyer keeps the family afloat? Should my friend Rainbow feel shame because she runs her boutique part-time to keep part of her identity alive? Should I feel guilty because I love to write, just in a different way from loving my children? I think not. What I think is needed, by all these mums (myself included), is to put down the wooden spoon we beat ourselves up with and replace it with a less punishing attitude and a voice that says, 'As mums, we do the best we can.' The trick is to make your choice, make it work for you, your partner and your child, and when the guilt creeps up on you, use that wooden spoon to shoo it away. (Well, until you fail to make a homemade flapjack for the school fête when the guilt will inevitably return again!)

Mother knows best

'I had no idea going back to work would fill me with such intense guilt and fear. I was always such a confident worker and no one made me feel wrong about

Work Choices

You've worked throughout your pregnancy. You've found outfits that are bump-friendly while being smart, conquered sickness during a conference call to New York and fought off colleagues suddenly very interested in your job now they know you're pregnant and may consider reassessing your career. If you thought this was the hard part, then you're in for a shock. My friend Elaine swears that throwing up for every day of her pregnancy didn't come close to the discomfort she felt at having to decide if and when to return to work. I know my head was a fuzz of hormones, nerves, emotion and confusion; questions whirred around my brain like a tumble-dryer on maximum speed. Should I try to give up work and make ends meet as a stay-at-home mum? How about I attempt a job-share with the glamorous Cassie (knowing full well she would be the one still in the office, while I left at six o'clock to scrape through the door for bath time)? Maybe I could go part-time and make the extra cash by freelancing and writing up articles in the evenings? Would my employers even consider a different job title and one that involved less travel and more five o'clock home times? What with breastfeeding, lack of sleep and the thought of researching childcare options, I felt ready to collapse in a heap and cry.

I know I'm not alone in this. I bored my single girlfriends to death with the pros and cons of every working option under the sun. I'm sure my mother had a tape recording of sympathetic responses that she played automatically every time the phone rang at seven thirty on a weekday evening. Once my girlfriends had been through their first labours, they too became the quivering, questioning new mum I'd been three years previously. I remember talking to my friend Lyn as she walked to work six months after the birth of her son. As she wept down the phone, asking me how I thought her boss would react to the thought of her working two of her five days from home, it felt like déjà vu. Hadn't this been me (and a million other working mums) only a few years previously?

Even if you are the type of mum who is gagging to get back to work after only a few weeks (and have left a sleepy six-week-old in order to catch up on emails before the ten o'clock feed), you're still sure to feel the pressure of being a hands-on mum. I've got a handful of girlfriends who went back to work very early on after giving birth. Many of them run their own companies or work for themselves – if they took too long out, the company would suffer, others loved their senior position and didn't want children to dent their opportunities or career prospects. From the outside, they may have seemed like swans swimming perfectly across the water, but I know from fraught conversations at midnight and teary confessions over a Friday-night drink that they were anything but. They may have been juggling client phone calls with a hungry baby under the desk, but trying to make everyone happy in those precious first few months ended up running them ragged. Sara even remembers having to leave a key meeting with buyers so she could express milk; the wet patches on her blouse were a dead give-away. (Luckily for her, the buyers in question were both mothers so it actually served as a form of camaraderie and she secured the deal because of it!)

As a whole in Britain, we are offered a pretty generous maternity entitlement. (Just think, in the US, the average maternity leave is six weeks!) The average time British women can take is anywhere between three and twelve months. (For my contemporaries, it was around the six-month mark, because that is usually when full pay becomes half pay, or half becomes statutory pay.) For most of us, this period was a time of pure indulgence for both the child and ourselves. Bonding was a top priority. Baby massage, lazy days at the local duck pond/café, feeding, weaning and pulling funny faces all replaced the hubbub of office politics and emails. What separates us mums is what we did after this point. The only way to make an informed choice about what working option is best for you, your partner, your child and your bank manager is to know what is out there.

There's no going back

However much you prepare for your return to work, for some women, there is just no going back. Every second mum I meet at the pre-school gates has a similar story. 'I went back for a week and I just couldn't carry on', 'Working was just torture – after my second, I felt there was no option but to become a stay-at-home mum.' For my friend Amy, there was never any question of her returning to work after her second. Her City job had forced her to miss so much of her firstborn's early years, that she was adamant not to let that happen again. The questions you must ask yourself if you feel you can't return to work are the following:

- Can you financially afford not to work?
- Are you rejecting work because once you've paid for childcare there isn't enough money left to make it worth your while? If so, have you considered all forms of child-care? (Often nanny-shares, childminders and live-in helpers are more economical than sole-charge nannies and nurseries.)
- Have you considered scaling down or looking into alter-native, less high-pressured careers?
- Have you considered the effects leaving work may have on your self-confidence? (Losing one's identity to follow the stay-at-home dream is a classic problem amongst my fellow mums.)

- Have you thought about extending your maternity leave to a year, or possibly even two years, to maximise those nurturing years while keeping a job to return to?

If you answer 'yes' to the above, and know that the working world is not for you, then go for it! Looking after your kids full-time is a full-time job in and of itself, and if the family won't suffer financially, and you won't suffer emotionally, then it's an incredibly lucky position to be in. Make sure you keep up with work friends, your own interests and hobbies as much as you can. Giving up your career (or putting it on hold) can make a huge dent in your self-worth and sense of independence. My strong-minded pal (and new-mum) Elaine ended up chucking in her managerial job in a bank after her daughter was born. She loved spending time with her, but hadn't bargained on how demoralising it would be to have to ask her fiancé for every penny she needed. Her face fell when she saw a pair of new shoes and realised she couldn't buy them and then hide them from Bob, but had to ring him to ask him if £69.99 was OK in that month's budget! It's wise to work out finances before you quit your day job.

All or nothing

The complete antithesis of the stay-at-home mum is the mother who returns to work full-time. The working world is full of ambitious, bright and career-orientated high-flyers who would rather stick needles in their eyes than stay at home and look after a dribbling baby. My friend Carol made this choice because her husband was happy to stay at home working on occasional scripts while she edited a newspaper. My friend Paula, on the other hand, opted for full-time work purely because the state schools in her London borough were so terrible that she felt educating them privately would be the only fail-safe route. Sending three kids through the private school system requires her to put in some serious graft!

If you are hell-bent on returning to work full-time, bear in mind the following:

- How much of your income will be spent on childcare? Does this leave a good proportion to survive on? Consider childcare wisely.

- Can your job be relied on to release you for bath time and bedtime most nights? If not, can you work on maximising a fully engaging weekend relationship with the kids? (Paula, who works a full five-day week, swears the only way she makes this work is by giving her three kids 100 per cent on Saturday afternoons and all day Sunday, leaving Saturday mornings for herself.)

- Is there any way you could work one day from home or leave early once a week to pick the children up from school?

- Do you have a partner or family member who could share the childcare burden and give the children extra 'key-carer' time? (Don't overestimate the heartache induced by hearing that your babysitter was the first one to be called 'Mummy'!)

- Does a five-day week leave any time for you? Can you weave exercise, a little shopping, seeing a girlfriend or the reading of a good novel into your working week?

You may find it impossible to squeeze this into week-ends.

• Have you considered the following as an alternative ... ?

Part-time girl

Until the birth of my second child, working a four-day week suited me (and my daughter) very well. Although I'm sure she would have said (if she spoke at the time) that she would have preferred me around all the time, at twenty-six, with a fledging journalism career and the mortgage on a new house to pay, working any less than that wasn't an option. However, I also knew that I was never going to be the type of power-suited working mum who left her babies with a nanny whilst she completed an eighty-hour week. From that first-ever scan, I knew I'd have to find a part-time balance. Even the thought of returning to work (and I hadn't even reached thirteen weeks of pregnancy!) made my heart ache, so I knew a compromise had to be made.

I very cunningly worked super-hard throughout my pregnancy, all the time acquiring brownie points from my editor. (Sorry, Sarah Bailey, it was partly for the good of the magazine, too!) Just before I departed with my roly-poly tum on maternity leave, I vied (and got) a promotion. The job in question was one I knew I could do in four days, and one that would enable me to leave at six o'clock on the dot. Now, I'm not suggesting all you new mums should be as cunning as that, but if you have an idea about what part-time basis you'd like to work, sow the seed with your employer. Although you don't want to commit to any new changes when you're in the flush of pregnancy hormones, it's ideal to establish the possibility of a new working format while still in the office. When you're around, people will remember your good points, your skills and just how much they want to accommodate you! Companies are obliged to consider proposals for part-time and flexi-time, so as soon as you have a clear head after the birth (and have established what your ideal scenario would be), write up a red-hot proposal of how it would work, how much pay cut you would consider and make the offer too good to refuse. I'd say 85 per cent of my mum friends now work part-time, so you won't be alone. I think we'd all agree that in the end you do five days' work in whatever time you have (so the company wins by getting the same output for less money), but really, you and your child win hands down. Extra time in those early years especially is worth its weight in gold.

Flexi-time

If financially part-time work isn't an option, flexi-time might be a good alternative. At some of the women's magazines I've worked for, there wouldn't be a mum's bum left on their seat after six o'clock. So much was the trend for a five-thirty finish that there would always be a crush for the lift as the clock chimed half past. That's not to say this happens every-where, but I certainly see from friends and colleagues that it is becoming more popular. What with commuting and the demands of nursery and childminder pick-up times, having a set time to leave work is crucial. (My friend Kate's children attend a nursery where they charge you a £5 fine for every five minutes late you are in picking the kids up. She leaves her office every day as if her knickers are on fire!) It's definitely worth negotiating an earlier start and earlier finish. (Hey, the kids are up at six o'clock every morning, anyway.) Even cutting your lunch break to half an hour (and opting for a salad in a local park) can give you an extra hour with the children at bedtime.

Share it out

Several fellow mums I know have found job-shares to be the ideal solution to the working-mum dilemma. My friend Carolina actually worked out a three-day-a-week job-share with the woman who had covered her maternity leave. Before she returned to work, she took her out for a drink, discussed her proposal and spent several similar meetings getting to know her better. They clicked well, shared the same work ethos, and both considered kids and a little 'me' time to be top priorities. By overlapping for one day a week, they developed a good 'handover' period, and because they both valued family time, there was little interruption on either of their days off. It can be a nightmare if one of the sharers is more ambitious than the other. My pal Luella has a horror story about her job-share planting incriminating websites on her computer. Boobs, porn and 'hot sex' didn't go down too well when she showed them as part of her slide show to chief executives! However, Luella is the first to confess she didn't vet her partner well enough and has since gone on to share with someone who complements her well. (She is a secretary, and both women have very different organisational skills. Almost by accident the job has become higher-powered and the position has been elevated beyond its original one-woman level.)

Freelance

In some jobs, working under a freelance contract offers a good downscaling of a full-time position. I was thrilled to have freelance writing as an option after the birth of my second child. Although initially it seemed I would leave *Elle* and write mainly for them (keeping my wage constant), it really served as a much-needed excuse to spread my wings. Once I'd left the company where I'd grown up, I found my ideas were often better suited elsewhere – somehow fashion features were replaced by emotional features and those that involved bumps, babies and families – not ideally suited to a magazine aimed at the early twenties!

If you have an opportunity to use your trade to work freelance, and you think you can take the insecurity of it, then go for it! (Any freelancer will tell you of the recurring paranoia that their most recent pay cheque will be their last, and don't even get us on to chasing the goddamn cheque in the first place!) If you can be disciplined about your work and when you do it (not during bath time), it can be the perfect way of seeing a lot more of your kids. I employ child-care three days a week and all my work must fit into these days; the other four are sacred kids' times. My friend Fiona is a self-employed fitness trainer (see Chapter 3). She makes sure all her work is done in the five mornings her daughter is at nursery or in the evening, when her husband can babysit. This way, she gets the best of all worlds: an income, a slice of her own life and a child who feel she's around most of the time.

My friend Kym knew her high-flying designer job was never going to accommodate a decrease in her responsibilities. The moment she was pregnant with Martha, she actively sought out a job that would offer her stability, an income that her family could live on and hours that would give her time to be a mum. In the end, she surprised us all by getting a brilliant low-key maternity-wear line going. At first she found it an adjustment to say the least, but she took the time to refocus on family life and think about her ambitions for the future. I know it sounds romantic, but really she's never been happier. Her new job represented so much more of her passions as a mother, and although money is tight, she has become a whiz at doing the weekly shop for under £100! Downsizing her career not only gave her more time with her family, but without the change her own needs would have drowned. As she swung from top fashion designer to mother and back again, there would have been zero time for her own identity to breathe. It isn't the right thing for everyone, but if your working life doesn't gel with your mothering life, hasn't it got to be worth a thought?

Mother knows best

'After Carla was born, I knew I had to go back to work for four days at least. My aim was to work my arse off in those days, save up some cash and give up work when I had my second child. Although my commitment to my job was 100 per cent, I couldn't bear the thought that if I left work with my colleagues at 8 p.m., I'd miss Carla's bedtime. My solution was to get Carla to the childminder at seven thirty in the morning, be at my desk by eight and work like billy-o throughout the day (grabbing sushi for fifteen minutes at lunch). My boss agreed that this way I could leave at five thirty in the evening. We stretched Carla's bedtime out to eight o'clock and I'd get a good two hours with her every night. I've just had my second baby, and yes, I have given up work and we're moving to the country next month!'

Arabella Steinberg, full-time mother to Carla (two) and Theo (two days)

The Biggest Balancing Act of All

Think of being a working mother as a little like a seesaw. On one end of the seesaw is your job (your boss with her deadlines, the trip to Glasgow in the autumn and the fax machine that has broken again!); on the other end is your child (sucking her thumb, clasping her comforter, her Elmer book and her juice, waiting to go to her 'working mum's' nursery). Somewhere in the middle is you. Black pencil skirts and trainers, a satin blouse with mashed-up banana on the collar, a briefcase with baby wipes peeping out of the top. Being a mother, a partner, a worker and a woman is the biggest balancing act of all.

Once you've established in exactly what form you will be returning to employment, the seriously hard trick to master is how to make the choice work for you. One of my old colleagues, Esme, felt delighted that she had sussed the working-mum rhythm. Her boyfriend would do two days of childcare, a nursery would do the remainder, and her boss had agreed she could leave at three o'clock every Wednesday afternoon. Perfect, she thought. Well, that was until her boyfriend found himself a great job in the music industry (there goes childcare for Monday and Tuesday), Esme *and* her daughter cried at nursery drop-off, and every time she attempted to leave the office on a Wednesday, she would get evil glances from her child-free co-workers! It's a year on and she's now solved her nightmare (cue a great childminder and a different role in the company that allows her a four-day week), but I can tell you, she's lost half her hair in the last year through worry alone!

No one can ever claim that this working-mother lark is easy. Even girlfriends who seem to have it all nicely organised are the first to admit that actually there's a lot more to it. My sister-in-law Jo had fifteen dud au pairs before they stumbled on the perfect Manira, and Jo's sister, Sue, says that she's only just got over the trauma of selecting her own 'near-perfect' live-in help (after interviewing more than thirty interested parties). So, you see, even when the seesaw seems to be balancing just about OK, you scratch beneath the surface and remember this is actually bloody hard work. Finding the perfect working-mum scenario is a constant work in progress. Being a mum who's done the four-day, three-day and then freelance option with periods of being a full-time mum, taking tips from my business-owning fellow mums, my full-time working mums and my one-day-a-week working mums, I think I've managed to construct something like a working mum's essential hit list. Here's what you need to know to get it right . . .

Look after yourself

Easy, huh? That's a joke. When you're dashing from the nursery to the Tube to the office via Starbucks, all before eight o'clock in the morning, you could be forgiven for wearing your pyjamas by mistake. (Good old Esme, she actually did arrive wearing her nightdress over her jeans. This wasn't intended as boudoir chic, but a symbol of her highly stressed departure from home that morning.) Making sure you have at least five minutes to shower, select a good outfit (or better yet, put it together the night before) and comb your hair is essential, as is keeping up your nutritional needs and eating an energising, balanced diet (even if that's a fruit salad and a slice of rye bread on the Tube). Mental, physical and emotional well-being are key to being in control of the balancing act. I made an extra effort to look good at work after the birth of my children. You want to show your employer that you can have children, contribute to your job and still look fabulous. No one wants to see a harassed, bedraggled new mum drowning under the pressures, least of all you!

Pick childcare you are 100 per cent confident with

I will discuss childcare options and support systems in the next section, but the crucial thing to ensure your working life is successful is to have good, trustworthy care for your child. The only way I flourished at work was by knowing that my children were getting the best care (bar myself or their father) that I could give them. Although it cost an arm and a leg (and I had to secure endless freelance commissions on top of my day job to fund it), a good carer was a top priority for me. Getting it right for you and your children gives you the confidence to focus on work throughout the day. I'll never forget my fellow *Elle* mum Paula and the day she got her new au pair. She got over thirteen calls within her first hour with questions like 'Does Daisy normally cry so much?' and 'Is it three ounces or thirteen ounces of milk for Phoebe's feed?' In the end, she left work early (fearing that her twins may have been fed chicken for breakfast and left to sleep all afternoon in an overheated room). Of course, her babies were fine, but the anxiety had made her lose a day's work and it took her a while to feel confident about leaving her children again.

Be professional

Plan the ideal working structure for you and your family and don't be scared to ask for it. If you are serious about working part-time for example, write up the proposal citing every detail. If you think your boss won't go for four days a week, ask for three days and she may choose four as a compromise (cunning or what?). If you think they may want you to start work earlier, second-guess this and offer a time that you can stick to. The worst thing you can do is to fit the stereotype of the working mother – all wild hair and baby sick on her roll-neck (without a clue about what she's doing). Instead, be professional, organised and show you mean business (even if inside you are fading after only three hours' sleep, and your breasts are still leaking from a missed feed!).

Also good to remember in creating a professional illusion is your work interiors set-up. If you want a photo of your child at work, keep a small image on your computer or in your locker. I made the mistake of decorating my whole desk with a vast montage of intimate pictures. My editor actually got her clothes caught on a hand-painted, hand-sequinned collage (given to me earlier in the week by my toddler) that I had pinned to my computer. I should add here that her Chanel skirt never regained its shape. You can have too much family company at work. One or two cheeky snaps to make you smile are ideal.

Handbag overhaul

I know this sounds silly, but clearing out your handbag before a Monday morning at work (or having a separate bag) can be important in distinguishing your working self from your mummy self. There's nothing worse than turning up to a meeting and while you're taking your notepad from your bag, out falls a half-eaten rusk, a dummy and a crumpled-up nappy sack. Make a pact to clear out your handbag of all baby paraphernalia before the working week begins.

Be prepared for jealousy and resentment

However nice your job is and however friendly your co-workers are, you can bet there will be at least one who resents that now you have children you are getting 'special treatment'. My friend Sophie found her fellow male lawyers total pigs once she'd had children. When they were constantly referring to her occasional calls from the nanny or the stain from the Heinz baby jar that appeared on her file for a Hong Kong client, it was a real effort to stay focused and keep her head held high. Working on a fashion magazine with heaps of fellow mums, my experience was far better, but some women without children can give you a hard time when you exit at six o'clock, leaving them to work until midnight. 'Off already?' (said with a wry smile) was a common goodbye from a writer on a neighbouring desk. Standing in her shoes, I'm sure it was hard seeing us mums granted part-time positions or flexi-hours. The trick is to work hard, show you are totally committed and can still be relied upon as a member of the team.

Learn to say 'yes' and a firm 'no'

Sounds simple, but if you're anything like me, it can be much harder than it first seems. The trick is to say 'yes' to anything that will ease the burden and help you balance all your eggs in the one basket. 'Yes' to a partner who wants to cook so you can read to your son whom you've missed all day, 'yes' to your mother-in-law, who wants to help with a few days' childcare (even if she's interfering at times), and 'yes' to a helpful assistant who's offering to do a heap of photocopying for you. Being a control freak about doing everything yourself can cripple the working mum.

Saying 'no' is also crucial to staying afloat. 'No' to your boss when he asks if there is any way of taking on double the workload within your three-day week, 'no' to the chief executive who begs you to return to work four weeks after giving birth and 'no' to fellow mums who make you feel guilty for working and not taking part in the PTA.

Sacred weekends

However many days per week you work, one of the best tips I can give is to make weekends sacred. I felt fortunate to have Fridays 'off' (although, with a screaming toddler who hated me for leaving her the previous four days that week, it hardly felt like 'time off'!). I would use Fridays to do the weekly food shop, some exercise for myself, pay my phone bill, call Lily's mum about a tea date, meet a friend and her kids for lunch and make roast chicken for supper. By using Friday for the chores, 'me' time and social time, it meant I could totally indulge the children at the weekend. A museum, a day trip, the theatre and a picnic in the park – all things to make them feel I was prioritising them, something children with working parents often need. Of course, I'd make the odd girlie phone call, and sometimes sneak off for a swim or for coffee with a neighbour, but largely weekends were family time and for the children to be close to me.

My friend Jennie does the same. She does exercise on two week nights (leaving her husband to put Minnie to bed, something father and daughter love), sees girlfriends on a Friday night and saves the weekends for 'Minnie and me' time. Although she often does family lunches at the weekend, 'Minnie and me' time just means she won't spend the whole weekend traipsing the buggy around Selfridges or leaving Minnie with her mother so she can catch up on work at home. I know they both start Mondays rebonded and with precious memories to keep them going throughout the week.

Talk, talk, talk

Last, but by no means least talk with fellow working mums about the employment choices you make. Share tips on childcare, pleasing the boss, getting home from work in thirty minutes flat and the best ways to stay afloat when everything seems to be sinking. Sharing hopes, fears and solutions with mums in the same boat can offer up endless wisdom (not to mention unique tricks on achieving the impossible multitasking working-mum feats). I learnt some of my best working-mum habits from the likes of Danni and Paula; talking may have cost me a fortune in phone bills, but it saved my sanity.

It's impossible to get the seesaw balancing act perfect all the time. All you can do is to try your best to make a success of your job, your family and yourself. If one is sliding at the expense of another, take a little time out to try to redress the scales. When my daughter needed me to settle her into a new nursery, I made it absolutely clear at work that I needed to be the person to do this. I also proposed exactly where I would make up the hours and I followed through with my promise. Similarly, when a feature came back with red pen all over it, I knew I'd been slacking due to my son's chickenpox. My babysitter put in a few extra hours, my partner came home early a couple of days, and I invested time making my second draft sparkle.

Fellow mums, just do the best you can and don't beat yourselves up if at times you feel you're failing everyone (including yourself). As we know by now, this is a classic symptom of mother's guilt and is shared with every mum on the planet. (Yes, that includes full-time mums and jet-setting executive mums alike!)

Mother knows best

'I desperately wanted family time at the weekends, but I knew I couldn't afford childcare for a full week. I managed to change my shifts in retail to two weekdays and the whole weekend. My husband cares for the kids at weekends, but I get them for a large chunk of the week, which I treasure as they're not yet in school. The perfect balance would be a whole weekend as a family, but at the moment we pay for only two days' childcare and Mum and Dad are around heaps. This is as near to perfect as we're going to get!'

Sally Hope, shop manager and mother to Billy (three), Cassie (two) and Pippa (six months)

Support Systems

I admit I can become a green-eyed monster when I witness close friends with huge support systems. My friend Jennie, for example, has a mother-in-law made in heaven. She looks after Jennie's daughter three days a week while she works and also at the drop of a hat if Jennie needs a break or a lie-in. Similarly, my friend Danielle is often away at one glamorous mini-break or another, her two children in the safe hands of her parents (fully equipped with their own bedrooms at Grandma and Grandpa's house). While my parents and in-laws are a source of endless parenting wisdom (both of mine work in education) and are the perfect grandparents for the occasional Sunday lunch, regular childcare support has never been an option. Every ounce of babysitting (be that to work, rest or play) comes with a bill, and anyone who's paid London prices for a babysitter will know this can be crippling.

Top dollar or given with love, one of the crucial elements for a successful working life is a support system. One of my first vows to my newborn daughter (as well as to love, hold, honour and protect her) was to make sure she had a loving, professional, warm and nurturing carer when I went back to work. I even started researching the options way before she was born. I'd seen enough of my girlfriends in a panic six weeks before returning to employment to know that planning would open up my options and make me feel confident about my choices. Before you even start to look, think long and hard about what budget you can stretch to and what specific care you want for your child. I realised after visiting three local nurseries for babies aged three months and up that nursery care was never going to satisfy my beliefs about childcare. Maybe it was the nurseries I saw, maybe it was because it was a bleak, rainy day at the time or maybe it was just bad luck, but I really couldn't imagine leaving my six-month-old daughter in such a formal environment.

Lucky in some ways that I discovered this early on, as it gave me extra time to plough through the alternative options.

Before tackling the list of childcare below, take half an hour out with your partner or a relative or friend you can trust and write down the 'must-have' criteria for childcare. If things like 'flexible hours', 'one-on-one care' and 'household chores' are on the top of your list, you know not to spend hours exploring nurseries. If 'social interaction', a '7 a.m. start' and a 'twenty-year solid reputation' are hot on your agenda, then a young, bright nanny may not be for you. A list like this is sure to help you when it comes to the endless task of choosing the right care scheme for you and your child.

Once you know your needs, research, research, research. Ask around until you've spoken to every mum in the neighbourhood. Look at the nurseries close to home or work. Visit the nanny and au pair agencies, and conduct an informal tea with the respective childminders. Before you visit or interview, work out questions you want to ask and things you need to know – you'll forget when you're put on the spot. Queries like 'What are your views on discipline and routine?' and 'How flexible are your hours?' are useful in working out whether you are on the same path. When you visit the nursery, childminder or existing post, look out for children in their care showing signs of happiness and affection or, equally, distress and over-stimulation. Inspect levels of hygiene and the amount of good-quality stimulus. Ask for a list of references and (if it's a nursery or childminder) an OFSTED report. Check these thoroughly. Lastly, ask yourself this: do you feel confident about this care? Could you see your child thriving here? Do you get on with the carer/s? Do they share your opinions on child-rearing? You need to answer 'yes' to all of these to make it a choice you are happy with.

So, what are the options for us mums wanting to balance work and life?

Nurseries

Many of my girlfriends have found nurturing nurseries that they and their little ones love. My old editor, Lorraine, had such bad experiences with live-in au pairs (bulimics, smokers, eat-you-out-of-house-and-homers) that she chose a good nursery between her home and the office. She adores it and her daughters are thriving (far more than they ever would watching CBeebies while the live-in smoked out of the back door!). Although for many mums, leaving a baby in a nursery at three months just seems too heartbreaking, many women find they work well with office hours, offer reliable care you can check up on at any time and give babies and children a ready-made network of mini-me friends. They can also be less expensive than a nanny, which for a lot of families is a deal-clincher.

Nannies and nanny-shares

Sole-charge, live-out nannies are the most expensive child-care option (in London, it can be anything from £20,000 upwards), but if you find the right one, they can be a gift from God. Going through a nanny agency costs an extra whack (a percentage of the nanny's monthly wage), but if you find a reputable agency, you can be pretty confident of

finding someone to suit you. (Agencies will offer fully qualified girls, with full CVs and a hit list of reliable references.)
We practically remortgaged our house to pay for our
wonderful nanny, Helen, but with her creative skills, love of
the children, endless energy, culinary expertise and absolute
devotion to the family, she has been worth every penny.
Having two children close together would have meant
double the childcare cost in a nursery, for example; with a
nanny, you can have seven children and her fee is set. (Not
that I'm planning this, mind you!)

My friend Sara and her husband both work all the hours
under the sun, so a good live-in nanny was an essential crite-
rion for starting a family. (Their nanny researches kids' extra-
curricular activities for them, cooks all their daughter's meals
and puts her to bed at the drop of a hat.) With their long
hours and travel, any other form of childcare would have
been impossible. (They can also enjoy the fruits of their
labour – a house big enough for a live-in nanny, who actually costs less than a live-out one.)

If the wage of a nanny sends you into a hot sweat (and
believe me, my husband and I still shake our heads in disbelief on pay day), then a nanny-share could be a good option
for you. If you can find a fellow working mum near you
(who could work compatible days), sharing the nanny can
be a stroke of genius. Luella drove fellow mums at the local
playgroup/Gymboree/children's theatre mad trying to find
a share, until she stumbled across Ruby. Like Luella, Ruby
wanted to work full-time and had a daughter of a similar
age. When approaching the nanny agencies, they specifically
requested a share and ended up splitting the cost down the
middle. Although they've had the odd heated discussion

about whether the food is all organic and whether the girls should attend ballet or karate on a Thursday, things have gone pretty smoothly. Equally, this option could work if you want to work part-time and can find a family who needs care the days you don't work. (Some nannies will happily work three days for one family and two for another, for example.) Whether you choose a live-in, live-out, nanny-share or part-time nanny, make sure you have a clear contract written up of all the things you expect from your employee (even down to teaching the kids to tie their shoelaces or to ride a bike, if these are important to you).

Au pairs

If you have enough space for live-in help, this can be a less expensive form of childcare. If it works well (as it has done for my friend Gayle and her twins), it can be ideal. You get cooking, cleaning and childcare and all for a lot less money than a nanny. If it fails (cue my sister-in-law Jo), it can be hell on earth. Jo entertains us on a weekly basis (and I know we shouldn't laugh) with stories of ten-ton Tessies who sit on the sofa all day eating Nutella with a spoon and Slovakian girls getting lost on arrival at King's Cross and ending up in brothels at midnight. Hardly conducive to a trustworthy support system! In my experience, au pairs are ideal as a mother's help, for mums with schoolchildren who need assistance with the three o'clock pick-up or for women with flexible working schedules (part-time work, for example). If you intend to go out to work five days a week leaving your toddlers in sole charge of an au pair, you either need a huge amount of time to vet and train the girls or a massive pot of good luck.

Childminders

Like a good nanny, a top childminder can be a miracle for us working mums. As long as you get a list of state-registered childminders, you vet them carefully and thoroughly first (looking closely at the home environment, the number of children in their care, the structure of the day and the ethos of the carer), you can strike it very lucky. We have the most wonderful evening babysitter, Gillian, who is a childminder locally. After our recommendation, she now looks after my good friend Lyn's son, Riley. Along with two other children, they paint, they bake, they visit the zoo, and they receive endless cuddles, love and encouragement, so much so I sometimes wonder how the children ever want to go home. Good, highly skilled and qualified childminders do exist, even if you have to see ten before you stumble on a Gillian.

Family help

Although many of my girlfriends can rely on a family member to chip in here and there, it is becoming less of the norm these days for a close relative to offer substantial and regular childcare. (Try asking your aunt Maud, who lives 160 miles away, to watch little Alex two days a week!) If you are one of the lucky ones who can share childcare with a partner or family member, then it could be the most economical and reliable choice. As long as you can establish the rules and boundaries early on (like whether you want your child to eat sweets, even if Grandma thinks the odd Sherbet Dib Dab is OK), it can be a perfect way of investing in a long-term relationship for both the child and family member.

Even if your husband or a close relative isn't the main carer, it's important to have them on board to help out if you need them. If you're running late to pick your child up from nursery, or you know you must work until ten at night on a document, it's crucial to have someone who can cover you at short notice.

I know it seems like a minefield (and in many ways it is), but as soon as you start looking, you'll get a very clear idea of what form of childcare you want and what you definitely don't. My friend Elaine desperately wanted a childminder for her daughter, but three months and thirteen dark, dingy basement flats later, she decided to opt for a nursery three days a week and a nanny-share on the other two days. By researching all the options, she was able to find childcare that came within budget and offered her energetic daughter stability and stimulation. The trick is, once you've chosen your childcare, you must work on gaining trust and respect with the relevant carers; they are doing the most important job in the world, so treat them well! They are not 'friends' (although I sometimes need to remind myself of this as Helen and I discuss the latest *Celebrity Big Brother*), but you do want open and honest channels of communication.

Imperative to success is ensuring your child has a good settling-in process, for which I suggest leaving up to a month. You can't expect to throw your child into a new environment immediately; it takes time for you both to settle. If they have their special toy or teddy with them, this can help familiarise them with a change of scene, also keeping to their existing routine will help them to adjust more easily.

Remember, too, (however young the child is) that constant, calm reassurance that 'Mummy is coming back' and 'Mummy loves you' will help enhance feelings of safety and security. It's so important to put aside time before your return to work to make sure this handover goes smoothly. You will be a nervous wreck if every time you leave your baby she is screaming, you are sobbing, and the phone rings after twenty minutes requesting your return.

The last trick in getting childcare sussed is to write everything down. I know, I know, I know, I'm a journalist, so banging lists out on the laptop gives me a perverse kind of pleasure, but writing a comprehensive list of all the things a carer needs to know about your child and her needs is so valuable. I did a jokey 'Loves and Hates' document for Helen before she began, which I update every few months. It included all sorts; the routine of their day (with sleeptimes, mealtimes and quiet times), what to do if they get upset, what their favourite toys are (and where they are kept), what type of vegetable they reject (forget courgettes, go for broccoli every time), what treats to offer them (never sweets, but chocolate buttons are OK – kept in the far right kitchen cupboard), where the arnica and Calpol live and emergency numbers for everything from a fall down the stairs to friends for play-dates. Although Helen could easily write one herself now, it made me feel confident initially that all their needs would be covered (even down to which position my son liked to sleep in).

Mother knows best

'Not only was I a nervous wreck about going back to work, but I also felt absolutely desolate about what form of childcare was best. In the end, we opted for a live-in nanny, and my two children doubled up their bedroom so she could have her own room. I compiled a huge list of 'nanny questions' before the interviewing process began and made sure the nanny we liked stayed with us for a few nights first before I committed. I needed to see we could all live together and that she didn't have any bad habits that would drive us up the wall (or vice versa!). Initially, we signed a month's contract so we could get out of it if it wasn't working. She's been with us for two years now, so I suppose you could say it worked pretty damn well!'

Angelina Norton, hairdresser and mother to Lilly (five) and Rudy (two)

Children's Needs

My friend Kate recently made a confession. On Tuesday, she'd got herself and her two kids ready for nursery, fed them breakfast and organised herself for a meeting with a TV broadcaster (and all before 7.40 a.m.). She then proceeded to drive to the end of her road, leaving the children behind waiting silently on the landing buttoned up in their duffel coats. Kate felt terrible and was ready to chuck her job in and flee to Cornwall to start growing organic produce and be an obliging mother and wife, until I and two other working mums confessed to similar sins. (I know you'll be wondering, so I'll confess too. Mine consisted of an important copy deadline and the first-ever sports day that accidentally slipped my mind. I still can't look the other egg-and-spoon mums in the eye.)

Any mum trying to juggle work, kids, childcare, extra school activities, a fifth birthday party for thirty and a trip to Thorpe Park could be forgiven for forgetting that at the heart of all this is your child. I'm sure most working mums can identify with Kate and her minor slip-up (OK, mega slip-up) or my failed sports day attendance. It's virtually impossible to do everything for everyone (yes, that includes boss, PA, childminder, form teacher and you). You'd not be far from the truth if you felt that these feats of time management were beyond even Superwoman's capabilities. However, one of the main challenges we face is making sure our children and their needs aren't completely lost in the logistical nightmare that is balancing all 106 roles now expected of us.

When I first found out I was pregnant, I couldn't have been happier with my job. Reaching my mid-twenties, I still had a lot of goals to achieve and certainly had a lot more fashion folk and celebrities on my 'wish list' of interviewees. Deciding after my daughter's birth to work part-time, and in some ways hold back on many of these ambitions, was a hard decision to make (and one which cost me a few pairs of free Manolo Blahniks). However, there really wasn't any contest in order to be able to have a dual-income family but still offer nurturing and regular childcare – someone had to cut back on the workload. There was never any doubt in my mind that it would be me. Although as a family we earned less (and paid for childcare out of this decreased income), making the pinch seemed an inevitable part of making the decision to bring up children. If you'd asked me pre-parenthood to opt for less money and more dirty nappies, I'd have shown you my monthly shoe bill and then the door. Once I'd given birth and fallen in love with my daughter's chuckle, I realised there was someone else's needs I had to consider.

Even if you don't cut down your hours, being around for a set bedtime and bath time each week will make all the difference to your child. Ensuring you turn off your mobile, slip out of your stuffy shirt and high black courts and really focus on your child for that half-hour or more is essential to making them feel number one again. If you get the option of a late morning (your meeting isn't until ten), dedicate twenty minutes extra after breakfast to story time and a cuddle. Likewise, if once in a blue moon you get to slip away from the office early, surprise your babysitter and take your child to Tumble Tots; all that group singing and 'circle time' may feel like another world, but your child won't forget being on Mum's lap in a hurry.

Discussing the importance of those early years in building secure, happy, engaged and loved individuals is another book entirely. I could write reams and reams on the value of making special 'Mummy moments', choosing the absolute best in childcare that you can afford and ensuring the time you have with the kids is quality time. All this can seem a mean feat when the cupboards are bare, you feel knackered after a huge week at work, and the house is a tip, but at the end of the day, these are your kids and you have a responsibility to consider what's best for them. Making them feel loved and considering their needs (especially in the pre-school years, when you are their main link to the outside world) must make it pretty high up on your priority list, even if a promotion is in the pipeline or you're a struggling single parent. Like you, I am still on the learning curve of those early years. I'm constantly asking myself, Is this the right choice? Am I doing this OK? Will this decision mess up my kids for life? I'm not saying I have all the answers, but I do know that every parent I meet with children over five says the same thing (and either it's a conspiracy or it must be a pearl of wisdom). 'Those early years are so precious,' they say. 'Before you know it, they'll be off to school and won't even turn to wave to you at the school gates. Cherish them while you can.' Bar evoking huge guilt (for the nativity play missed, the maths homework not done and the days you can't possibly meet them from nursery), this familiar phrase always reminds me that at the crux of all those work-life decisions is the child. They may not be able to talk yet (a dribble is more apt), but considering what is best for them must always go hand in hand with what is best for you. Most working mums soon see that having a contented child (whose needs are met as best as humanly possible) only enhances their ability to get their groove back. It's a darn sight easier to look and feel great when your little one is happy and cared for. (Try leaving the house for a job interview when she's having a tantrum at the front door, while the sixteen-year-old babysitter chats on her mobile phone!)

Mother knows best

'My job is very demanding and I was back to work eight weeks after giving birth to Billy. I knew in my heart that the nursery I settled him into wasn't right for him, but it was close to work, so seemed convenient. He had terrible colic and reflux and was very clingy. I think the staff just couldn't give him the huge amount of care he needed to thrive. After six months, I moved him to another, smaller nursery, but by this point he had terrible separation anxiety and the whole thing was traumatic for us both. I wish now I'd listened to my instinct and not rushed into the childcare that suited me but not Billy. I'll never get that time back and it will always make me sad to think I made ill-informed choices at that time.'

Henrietta Hill, barrister and mother to Billy (two)

Finding Time for You

It may seem a complete contradiction in terms to suggest you rush home from work for bath time and then still make time for yourself at some point, but bear with me, it is possible! However stretched you are with deadlines, manic with strategy meetings and frantic you feel paying all the bills (with childcare on top), spare a thought for the stay-at-home mum, who in actual fact has even less opportunity for 'me' time than you. For someone who has resided in both camps at various times, I can vouch for the fact that as a worker I had a lot more time (if you call one hour twelve minutes a lot) to myself. The forty minutes I had to read *Red* on the Tube to work and the twenty-three minutes I had to share a sandwich with a colleague at noon were far more time 'off' than I ever got as a full-time mum (when even the possibility of brushing your teeth without World War III breaking out in the kitchen seemed an impossibility).

If you're a full-time working mum ready to write to me in disagreement, just stop a minute and think of the moments you have managed a morsel of 'me' time within your working week. A sneaky call to a friend before your boss arrived? A nip into Starbucks for a skinny latte and a muffin prior work (and a naughty flick through *Vogue* while you were at it)? A quick-as-a-flash bikini wax instead of a dash around Prêt at lunchtime? Come on, we've all done at least one of the above! It may feel at times that the demands of being supermum and super-working-woman leave zero time for your own life, but if you look at your week strategically, you may find these little opportunities can be maximised to your own benefit.

The hard part about creating (and then savouring) time for yourself as a working mum is preventing it from eating away at your time with your child. If you spend endless evenings out drinking with girlfriends or in the gym in an attempt to get your life back, it doesn't take a genius to work out that your child will be the one to lose out. On the other hand, if you rush home religiously every night to bathe the baby, you may be at risk of never, ever getting a moment to yourself. It's that balancing act again. It's all about striking a fine balance between 'you' time, 'work' time and 'kids' time.

Some of the little things that I've always capitalised on are the commute to and from the office, the lunch-break allowance and what I call 'quiet' time at work. Over the years, my friends and I have started calling these the 'stolen me minutes' – times in the working day when you can grab opportunities to read a novel, call a gal pal, get some exercise, write down some thoughts or simply eat a salad, your face in the sun, doing nothing but sitting very still! Although much of this is redundant now that I work from home (and the commute consists of four steps to my study, the 'lunch break' is a hectic array of plastic plates, fish fingers and 'Mummy, more juice please', and the 'quiet' time is when the kids finally hit the sack at night), it still serves as a good tip for other working mums I know. My friend Sophie is famous for getting through a novel a week on her commute to the City from South London (and has even navigated a perfect place to stand on the platform that offers her maximum potential for a seat on the 8.06 from Balham). Similarly, my friend Paula religiously meets a non-work-related girlfriend once a fortnight for lunch, something she never gets the chance to do with her three children at the weekend.

Even if 'quiet' times at work are virtually non-existent (I can already hear you scoffing at the thought), there is always an occasional ten-minute slot here or there when you can book an appointment at the hairdresser or for an Indian meal with your partner at the weekend. All these little pockets of time will serve you well in the quest for relaxation and downtime. They enhance the feeling that you have control over your working and mummy life and that you have time to catch up with a good book, old friend or trip to the salon!

Many working mums I know have also found that allocating one night a week of 'free' time makes them heaps fresher for work and their families. When I worked part-time for *Elle* after my first child, I used to do one late night a week. I would try to get my writing done then. (Without the chatter of fellow *Elle* fashionistas and the constant sound of the phone ringing, the words actually began to flow with ease!) As long as I planned the day the week before, my husband would guarantee to be home from work and man the bath/bottle/story/bed fort. It made sense, then, for me to utilise that one evening well. I'd work until around eight thirty in the evening and then grab a light supper and go for a swim and a long, relaxing sauna or catch a movie, a drink and a bite to eat or even a little late-night shopping with a girlfriend. This way, myself, the kids (they love 'Daddy' time, plus he does the best Gruffalo impression on demand of any other father I know!) and work all win. Of course, occasionally that 'night off' would be eaten up by a work event or a child's bronchitis (no mum can happily leave a coughing child to sip Pinot Grigio and catch up on Kate Moss gossip!), but even if I managed it twice a month, I felt I'd done well.

The point about being a fabulous mum is to try to defy obstacles that imply 'having it all is impossible'. OK, having it all may be a slight myth, but there is no reason we can't have a good chunk of what we want. If you aspire to be a great mum, a respected worker and still have regular time to yourself, there is no reason you can't make this happen. Learn to snatch a forty-minute yoga class at lunchtime (instead of getting back to the fifteen emails that really can wait until the afternoon), nip into a local gallery for ten minutes to view your favourite Monet (instead of heading to John Lewis for kids' vests) and ensure that under no circumstances do you feel guilty about this; you are investing in yourself, and there is absolutely nothing wrong with that.

> ## Mother knows best
>
> 'My kids are early risers and my mother-in-law arrives at eight in the morning to look after them. I walk to work, which clears my head and keeps me fit, and still arrive half an hour before anyone else. I resist the temptation to check emails or open my post, but use that time to catch up on quick personal calls, eat a couple of slices of soda bread and read one leading feature in a newspaper. By the time my working day starts, I feel focused, calm and more 'Rachel' than 'Mummy', which is important to me.'
>
> Rachel Fontaine, music teacher and mother to Indigo (four) and Alexia (two)

Top ten work-life balance tips

1. Relish the bubble of maternity leave and don't rush back too early. This is sacred time for and your child.
2. Don't feel guilty about the working decisions you make. Stand firm and be proud of your choices.

3. Consider all the options – being a full-time worker or a full-time mum are just two of many choices available.
4. Try to structure your working week so you can have at least a few evenings or mornings with your child.
5. Make sure the working life you choose gives you a combination of financial security, family time and a sense of identity. Having one without the others means everything will crumble.
6. Learn to say 'yes' to offers of help and 'no' to demands you just can't meet.
7. Create firm and flexible support systems. This includes paid help, help from your friends, family and partner and fellow working women to confide in.
8. Research and select childcare thoroughly. Good care for your child is essential to a successful working life.
9. Consider your child's needs at all times, especially in the early years, when nurturing care and forming key attachments to a specific carer are essential.
10. Don't neglect yourself – carve out 'you' time wherever possible.

Grace's guru: Camilla Palmer

Camilla Palmer started her career as an adviser for Gingerbread (the parent organisation) before studying law. After becoming a consultant solicitor specialising in discrimination, she set up her own firm with partner Joanna Wade. They specialise in discrimination work, mainly in employment, and write, teach and work with families and organisations such as Working Families and the Fawcett Society. She has tried and tested much of her advice first-hand by negotiating flexi-time and part-time work when her children, Jamie (now sixteen) and Robert (now nineteen), were young.

What are your main working, legal and childcare tips for mums?

A breadwinner still wanting to maximise family time
As the top family earner, make it clear to your employer that you will be returning to work and want to come back to the same job. Be friendly, enthusiastic, yet professional and make sure they realise your loyalty to them as a company. Whatever your job, senior or junior, you should be able to stress your desire to return in the same capacity and your aim to contribute to working life with the same passion and vigour.

Even though you are entitled to earn the same salary and be part of a strong team, it doesn't necessarily mean you can't consider doing the job flexibly to suit your childcare needs and help maximise family time. If it fits with the job you do, you could suggest flexi-time, which could include working from home one day a week perhaps. If this is your desire, make sure that structures are in place to make it viable – e.g. a work phone line, email address and possibly a fax are all important in selling the prospect of working from home convincingly. You will also need to ensure that although you are working from home, your child is still cared for by a third party – taking a conference call with a screaming baby in the background will do no good in convincing your employers that you are working productively from home!

Other viable flexi-time possibilities that won't affect your wage could be to adjust your working hours by asking for a flexible starting or leaving time and avoiding overtime and weekend working (or any other antisocial hours such as rotating of shifts).

Depending on your job, if you work part-time, you could make yourself available at the end of the phone on days off, if there is an emergency – this should give you good brownie points if nothing else!

A single mum needing to work and find viable, economical childcare If you want to change your hours, first and foremost you need to work out what hours you would like to return to work, as this might well dictate the sort of childcare you require. If you hope to reduce your hours, plan this well in advance and try to sort it out with your employer first, as it may take some time to find cover for your reduced hours. (Remember, too, that if you are asking for a change in hours, you may have to go through the flexible working procedure, which can take three months.)

Once you've sorted out working hours, sit down with a good friend, family member or someone you can trust who understands your situation as a single parent, and look at all possible avenues for childcare. If you are on a tight budget, you may find that a nursery or childminder will suit your needs better. I would suggest going to visit as many as you can well in advance – good places tend to be snapped up in a nanosecond and you don't want to be left in a panic. If you are confronted with a huge waiting list, put your name down – people move, situations change, and you might just get lucky. Remember, whatever childcare you choose, make sure you take up references and ask probing questions. As a single parent, it is also important you find out what their policies are on parents picking up late. (Say you got stuck in the office one evening without someone else to rush to the nursery for collection time – you don't want to be stung with a big penalty.) Ideally in this situation, you need to get good people on side (colleagues, friends, family and your childcarer or nursery) so they are sympathetic to your needs and can help out or be accommodating.

A mum wanting to propose flexi-time, part-time or a job-share at work Every woman is entitled to return to the same job after maternity leave. If this job cannot be done part-time or as a job-share, you should argue for flexible working in your existing job. Check whether your employer has any set policies covering flexible working hours before you enter into discussions; it's always advisable to know your stuff first! It is then crucial to check out the Equal Opportunities Commission (EOC) website (www.eoc-law.org.uk) to work out how flexi-hours may affect your tax credit. You must always bear in mind that working less than the minimum number of hours may mean you're not eligible for benefits, including tax credit, and this could have a serious effect on your finances. Do your homework and know your rights first!

The next step is to think of the flexible working hours you want to propose. Check out the Working Families website (www.workingfamilies.org.uk) for useful information on how to negotiate the hours you want. Make the prospect of a change in your working life attractive to your employers; they can't legally say a firm 'no' unless they have a strong reason, so really work out a good strategy and give it the hard, yet friendly sell. If, for example, you want to do a job-share, consider if there is anyone in the workplace who may be interested and qualified to job-share with you. Otherwise, how about suggesting your employer advertises for a part-time employee to do the job-share? Another good idea would be to illustrate other workplaces where your suggested flexi-time has worked, highlighting its viability and merits. You could also suggest a trial period to convince your employer that flexibility is workable. (It could also give you peace of mind that the new working regime will work for you and your child.)

I would suggest going armed with this knowledge into any meeting with your employer, but be realistic and consider how your proposal fits in with their business needs. If you cannot negotiate on an informal basis, make a formal application for flexible working hours and go through the procedure. If after negotiations your application is still refused, you may have to consider accepting other work in your preferred hours. Do remember, however, that refusal of flexible hours may be indirect sexual discrimination unless the employer can justify the refusal.

A mum wanting to downscale her career, yet still stay in a senior position First off, you need to think long and hard about whether your existing job can be done on fewer hours or partly from home. Remember, you are entitled to return to the same job and if the job can be done on more child-friendly hours, your employer should agree to this. Don't be fooled or put off by the myth that senior jobs can't accommodate family values. I've seen many women manage incredibly senior roles with child-friendly hours, so don't take no for an answer until you've tried very hard.

If the same job is absolutely impossible to do on the hours you want, consider what job you think you can do. Talk to your employer about whether there is an alternative role within the same company that would allow the flexibility you need. Make sure you take their suggestions away and give them a lot of thought. There's no point in downscaling to a different job that doesn't interest you, leaving you bored and dissatisfied. It is often the case that the employer will offer an alternative, lower-status job to avoid compromising on the more senior job. It is all about negotiating, but remember, try to keep it friendly – you may find you get more of what you want this way!

A mum wanting to extend her maternity leave If you want to take more time, the best way to go about it is to ask your boss frankly and directly. There is no entitlement to longer maternity leave (the standard is fifty-two weeks for those who have worked for their employer for nine months before the birth) but you can of course negotiate anything. My tip would be to do this early on so that the employer can arrange for your locum to stay a bit longer. If you do reach a compromise, it is best to get it in writing so you are clear on what terms have been agreed. You also want to make sure you keep continuous employment with the same employer as this gives you protection from unfair dismissal and other rights.

If your employer is reluctant to extend your maternity leave you could try taking accrued holiday; you accrue contractual holiday during the first twenty-six weeks and statutory holiday (i.e. twenty days per annum) during additional maternity leave (the second twenty-six weeks). This may help you add a few valuable weeks to your time with the baby.

A mum who feels she has been discriminated against at work because of her family responsibilities If you feel you have been discriminated against by your employers, call a meeting and raise this with them directly, asking for an explanation. It is good to keep a record of the discrimination you feel you've suffered, almost like a log so you can bring this up face to face. If it is not resolved on the spot, or you feel it is still going on after the meeting, you must put in a written grievance (generally within three months of the decision) and wait twenty-eight days before bringing a claim for discrimination. If you are unsure what type of discrimination you are experiencing, bear in mind the following: if you have been treated less favourably for a reason related to your pregnancy (including pregnancy-related sickness) or maternity leave, this is sex discrimination. If your employer assumes that you will want less responsibility after having a baby and offers you a less responsible job, this is discrimination.

Just remember, you are not alone – women worldwide are facing similar problems after returning to work as mums and you shouldn't feel isolated or scared to speak up. According to the EOC, of the 400,000 women who are pregnant each year, 50 per cent suffer from discrimination, so this gives you some idea of the extent! As a whole, women's earnings before they become pregnant are 91 per cent of men's; after pregnancy, the gap widens to 67 per cent, so as you can see, discrimination can be expensive. It's a burden that falls on mums, so you shouldn't ignore it if you feel it's affecting you.

What are your top five tips for a mum wanting a successful work-life balance?

1. Don't be scared to prioritise your family by asking for flexi-time; you are entitled to ask for a good balance.
2. Source childcare carefully. Good help with your child is crucial to confidence in returning to the workplace.
3. Negotiate first: litigation is uncertain, expensive, stressful and time-consuming – avoid it if you can!
4. Read up on your rights – the EOC website may help – or seek legal advice. Knowledge is power!
5. In whatever form you return to work, be professional yet friendly and put your all into making flexibility work for you, your employer and your family!

What are the key dos and don'ts for a working mum?

Dos
- Plan ahead – whether for childcare or working hours.
- Consider flexi-time that suits your individual needs.
- Consider if you can afford to work part-time; pay and benefits will be pro rata.
- Negotiate with your employer and put your case for alternative hours in a well-argued but friendly way.
- Get proper legal advice if you think you've been discrim-inated against. (The Citizens Advice Bureau, Law Centre

and Equal Opportunities Commission all offer free advice.)

- Enjoy your maternity leave!

Don'ts

- Don't agree to any form of childcare without checking references thoroughly. It's also advisable to have a trial period before agreeing to a long-term contract.
- Make sure you never accept less favourable treatment on the grounds of your pregnancy or maternity leave. It may be common, but it is unlawful.
- Try not to forget if things start to go wrong, to keep a diary of meetings, discussions and telephone calls. It is easy to forget some weeks later.
- You may think you only need flexible hours once your child is very young. In fact, the juggling often gets harder when children are at school (school holidays, homework to supervise, etc.).
- You don't have to go it alone. Working mums need a good support network of friends, family, neighbours and colleagues.

Camilla's fabulous working mum's mantra: 'Work-life balance benefits everyone – it's your job and your life, and you can have both!'

Grown-up Time

Coupledom

Unless your child was the result of a brief, erotic fling, a holiday romance on Mykonos or a sperm donor, it is likely you and the father experienced some sort of coupledom prior to conception. This could constitute six months of candlelit dinners and the odd bottle of Chanel perfume or, as in my case, ten years of it. Whether it's five weeks or five years, you are sure to have got used to the passing flattery and the un-interrupted Sunday snuggles under the duvet. Each of my girlfriends owns the rights to at least one sacred coupledom memory. For my friend Jennie and her husband, Justin, that treasure-box memory consists of a booth in a musty pub in London's trendy Hoxton. There (prior to children) they'd sit on a Saturday afternoon, a pint of Stella in one hand, the *Guardian* in the other. For my friends Kym and Marc, being just two meant walking to work together (passing a bakery with extra-strong coffees and blueberry muffins en route), sharing a long kiss at the Tube and meeting again most nights for drinks, bar snacks and then supper out (so much so their flat prior to the birth of their daughter had no kitchen or table!). For my husband and me, being a couple meant nothing more complicated than an uninterrupted Sunday morning. We'd leave the phone off the hook, eat fresh smoked-salmon bagels whilst devouring every newspaper on the market and then fall back into bed until well past midday.

I know not all memories prior to children are quite so simple and rose-tinted (hungover rows about who's to pay the gas bill and Sundays when all he wants to do is watch or play football spring to mind), but I'll bet you've got a few nice times stored up too. Your man may not have bought you chocolates on Valentine's and may tend to think a bouquet of flowers on your anniversary consists of carnations from the Esso garage, but I'm pretty sure that before having kids you had a lot more time to indulge in one another and the things that you loved as a couple. You fancy a walk in the countryside, stopping at a pub for lunch? Hey, why not? You feel like an afternoon at the movies followed by cocktails and assorted nuts? Make mine a margarita. You want to decorate the kitchen and then eat a Chinese take-away on cushions? Who needs a table, or cutlery for that matter? More to the point, you fancy sex at four o'clock in the afternoon? I shouldn't think you'd have to ask twice! The issue is, you can! With no teething toddler, delightful but insistent fairy-clad four-year-old ('I need my wand, I need my wand, I need my wand!') or breastfed on demand four-month-old, you really can indulge in being a couple and all the spontaneity and intimacy that this entails.

For us mums with one or more children already under our belt, there's no point harping on about the guilt-free romantic meals or weekend lie-ins free of interruptions (and really and truly, we wouldn't change it for the world). The best thing to do is to stash these lovely memories some-where safe but accessible (call it the treasure trove of memo-ries if you like), draw on them when the going gets tough, and remind yourself that these are the foundations that built your relationship. My mother sent me a Keats poem years ago (incidentally, when I was experiencing a rough time with my then husband-to-be), the gist being that you must treat your relationship like a house. The bricks, mortar and scaf-folding need to be in place for the house to withstand the elements (rain, wind, fire – you name it). Just like a part-nership, a house will take weathering, but one with foun-dations that run deep and strong will stand the test of time.

I remembered this poem as I fed my first daughter in the early hours of the morning, watching my husband snooze peacefully. I was tired, hormonal and run-down, and I couldn't recall the last time we'd shared a long kiss or a fond exchange, let alone a deep embrace wrapped in each other's arms. But I knew the foundations were there to get us through, and I thought of a peaceful moment involving white sandy beach and my husband standing with a Pimm's in each hand and I knew we would be all right.

Bearing this box of magic tricks in mind, I think every new parent-to-be (or couple trying for a baby) should make it their mission to indulge in at least half of the following before giving birth. If you've already given birth (and are cursing yourself for missing out on number three of the list), then don't worry – pass it on to an expectant friend; she will thank you for it later, I promise.

- Enjoy intimacy as much as possible.
- Go on a mini-break with your partner, ditto a sun-filled

holiday (if your budget allows).

- See at least three movies at the cinema or on DVD (you'll be far too knackered to watch one from beginning to end once a newborn arrives!), ditto the theatre.
- Go to a very un-child-friendly restaurant (that means one without a kids' menu) and enjoy a candlelit dinner in peace.
- Lie in or go back to bed as much as possible.
- Tell your partner you love them whenever you can.
- Take a moment to appreciate peace and quiet.
- Read a magazine, newspaper or novel from cover to cover.
- Cook each other a special meal.
- Have breakfast in bed (followed by a long snog).

All of the above become increasingly difficult (not that I'd say impossible, though) once you have children, and it doesn't hurt to make a little time for them prior to your new arrival, relishing those moments shared as a couple before the pitter-patter of tiny feet expands your family unit for ever.

Mother knows best

'Go to an art gallery and follow this with a lunch that lasts longer than fifteen minutes. That would be my tip for any expectant couples. Luxuries like these fall so low on your list of priorities it's good to fit them in while you can!'

Angie Nicholson, full-time mother to Missy (two)

No Longer Number One

About six weeks ago, at 6.55 a.m., my little boy shuffled into our bedroom in his Grobag (I know, he walks around in it, weird or what?), climbed into the bed and snuggled under the covers with 100 per cent body contact to his mummy. Pleased that he was happy and sleepy and not insisting on a 'dinosaur story, pleeeeeeeeeeeeeease' just yet, I closed my eyes again. 'You two and your bloody love affair,' said my husband as he half rolled, half fell from the tiny corner of the bed he'd been left with. 'I'm redundant now, aren't I?' he exclaimed, and with that he sulked off to the bathroom to shave (and, no doubt, curse his neglectful wife).

And there we have it. My man, my wonderful, loved and special man, replaced in an instant by a curly-haired toddler and his older sister. Of course, he was half joking, but the other half is a slightly wounded grown man who, after ten years at the centre of my world, has been left out in the cold. Assigned to a tiny square of the sheet and the back of my head, he's been deserted, while I nestle into the sleepy Grobag of our child. I know it's an old cliché, but most of my girlfriends recall their men feeling a little left out when a new addition arrived. Suddenly it's 'Not now, darling' as opposed to 'Come to bed, sweetie', and although we hate to admit it, there's a little more 'Oh, will you just shut up?' instead of 'Fancy breakfast in bed, honey?'

These feelings of jealousy and resentment may only be fleeting, or half said with humour, nevertheless, as most men would tell you, they are very real. You can't really blame them, can you? One minute they're breathing deeply with you in the labour ward, the next you're shooing them off with your order for pain au chocolat while you stare into your newborn's eyes. As they run around collecting pink baby socks, calling friends and relatives and filling the parking meter (will someone tell me why London hospital parking meters need so much filling?), you're busy 'bonding' with your baby and getting to grips with breastfeeding. When you get home, this division of labour usually continues. While I breastfed my daughter 24/7 and checked on her breathing, my husband got the groceries, entertained my in-laws, searched for a padded pink snowsuit in size three months and eventually started to turn a distinct shade of grey. By the time he returned to work after two weeks' paternity leave, he probably felt delighted for the break. My friend Lyn was no different. She was so intent on figuring out the feeding and sleeping patterns of her little boy, Riley, that she retreated to her mother's house sixty miles away. Her husband came to visit at weekends and was restricted to 'cuddle-Riley' time from Saturday morning to Sunday afternoon. Forget any intimate moments with his wife; expressing and swaddling were top of the agenda, for now at least.

This feeling of taking second place isn't just reserved for the men, of course. It involves you too. As their child grows, many women get a tinge of jealousy when their partner practically ignores them at the front door, so desperate is he for a glimpse of his 'little angel' in her high chair (and you thought you were his little angel?). My friend Elaine vividly remembers coming home from a long day at work to see her husband and daughter sharing a cuddle and story in front of the fire. The green-eyed monster soon replaced her immediate heart-melting reaction. How dare he share these moments while she worked hard to pay the mortgage? How unfair that her daughter was now the centre of his world and she was to sit on a back burner (getting burnt at that!). This thirty-six-year-old career woman was left muttering, 'What about me? What about me? What about me?' like a four-year-old who's been the only one left without an ice cream!

It's very hard (especially in those early months) to make time for your partner in both your life and the baby's life. Making up bottles, filling the fridge and wheeling the pram around the park don't always constitute quality time. Likewise, as your partner tickles your toddler, ignoring all requests from you to pass the jam, it can seem that both of you have been replaced in one another's affections.

Not only are intimacy, endearing words and affection reserved for the kids, conversation about your children dominates. The moment they're in bed, talk about nursery places, whether it's the right time to start potty training and why on earth the youngest has started this obsession with knives take the place of what's on the box, who's coming for supper on Saturday night and whether it's red or white wine to unwind at the end of a long day. Your other half could be forgiven for believing his partner had in fact been abducted by aliens and replaced by a childminder or primary-school teacher, so high up the agenda are discussions of phonics and packed lunches. I mean, when was the last time you spent a whole meal discussing the election or the ins and outs of your partner's new boss? If it's more than a month, then welcome to that parenting feeling that neither of you is number one any longer!

The best thing you can do to ease this transition from two to three is to make time for each other as a family. Even if in the early days that means sharing bath time (or, as we did, all getting in the tub together), reading the children stories together or involving Dad in the feeds, it's the small gestures that count. Going to the park as a family and asking about your partner's week at work while you push the swing, or making an effort to praise each other and your skills as parents and other halves are tiny things you can do to ensure your partner isn't pushed into the background. As mothers, we tend to constantly niggle our partner's family skills ('Do you have to feed her like that?', 'She doesn't wear that coat any more' or 'No rough play before bed. How many times have I told you?'), making us sound more like matrons than spouses. Just consciously thinking about how we integrate our partners and how we talk to them now we're parents can help stave off feelings of neglect and resentment.

Mother knows best

'My boyfriend found the adjustment of a new baby really tough. He hated all the attention I gave Clara and it made him withdrawn and really tricky. The only way to ease it was to give him an hour a day to bond with Clara without me interfering. They'd watch some football together, he'd give her a bath and an evening bottle, all mundane stuff but important nevertheless. By helping them fall in love, it helped him and me fall back in love with one another.'

Sharon Benjamin, full-time mother to Clara (three) and Imogen (one)

I've Got a Headache

Confession time, Mums – how many of you have used the old 'I've got a headache' line to avoid any intimacy that might get in the way of you and your soft, fluffy pillow at 10 p.m.? Come on, be honest! It doesn't take a genius to work out that post-child a quick fumble under the sheets before brunch is out of the question, and any late-night erotic action falls below an early night on our priority list. You're exhausted, only too aware that you'll be up with the lark and that your tummy still resembles the 'before' picture in a liposuction advertisement. Really and truly, the furthest thing from your mind is lighting some candles and slipping into something satin and seductive.

Take my good friend Samantha (which isn't her real name, but I have vowed to protect her modesty), mother of three and also master of every excuse in the book for avoiding sex. After a day shipping her eldest to school, her middle child to nursery and her youngest around the supermarket with her (followed by endless rounds of fish fingers, football and fight-control), the last thing on her mind at bedtime is intimacy. The strange thing is, Samantha was known prior to this mothering lark, as 'sexy Samantha'. Ann Summers parties, weird sex toys called things like 'Tommy Tickle' (and it's not a kids' entertainer), 'Bone' and 'Electric Eddie', and reports of dirty weekends in Dorset (where she and her partner didn't get out of bed for forty-eight hours) were not uncommon for our Sam. Since the birth of her youngest ten months ago, she swears she has only made love twice. Now you may be wondering if her sex-starved partner (let's call him Joe) has either a) run off with a younger child-free woman or b) also lost his libido in the labour room. Neither is actually true, but even Samantha will admit that she is running out of excuses in the bedroom, and if she's starting to feel a little jaded, how is good old Joe (used to sex three times a night) feeling?

Although you may not have been a highly active sex goddess prior to having children, you're sure to have participated enough to start a family in the first place! Even though my friend Elaine wasn't a fiend in the bedroom, she and her husband loved nothing more than to draw the curtains every Saturday night, drink a bottle of red wine and be intimate. Although once a week wasn't going to smash the Guinness World Record, it suited them and kept them connected and happy together. The thing about having children is that the amount of intimate time you can get with your partner becomes quite a challenge. Suddenly even once a week can seem a drain on resources and yet another 'must do' written in red pen on your hand.

My pal Sophie was typical of a lot of women I know. The moment she found out she was pregnant for the first time, she went off sex altogether. Fears about miscarriage, weirdness about having sex with a baby 'in there' and hormones flying around all over the place meant she practically wore a boiler suit in bed. Once she'd given birth, the thirteen stitches, leaky boobs and monthly mastitis meant she fancied making love about as much as riding a horse bareback down the Grand Canyon. In her words, 'Not even for all the shoes in Top Shop!' Even if you feel like a cuddle and some intimacy, midwives recommend waiting at least six weeks for total healing to take place. For many women, it can take much longer before they feel ready to venture into full-blown sexual relations (especially after a thirty-hour labour including forceps – ouch!). You're the only one who will know when you feel ready to start exploring intimacy, and the trick is not to rush it. You'll lose a lot of pleasure if you feel forced back into the bedroom before your body is good and ready.

I found that six to twelve weeks post-birth was a good starting point for trying to re-establish sexual relations. (But really it could be any other time frame – it just depends.) By then my body felt less bruised and battered, I was slowly establishing a breastfeeding pattern (meaning the milk supply and sore nipples were less intense), and I was getting more than six minutes' sleep a night. When the time's right for you, your body and your emotional well-being (not to mention your partner's), there are some key rules to bear in mind. My friends and I call them our 'mums' sex secrets'.

Fall back in love

I know it sounds obvious, but who wants a kiss (let alone anything more) from a man you don't know or share interests with any more? If you spend the week barking at each other, how much will you actually fancy him when it comes to a Saturday night under the covers? Reconnecting with each other is the only way to induce that loving feeling. Take an interest in one another's lives (even if the last thing you want to hear about is his nightmare commute to work), do things together and share parenting as much as is viable. Even watching a movie or reading the same newspaper article can give you something to talk about and make you feel closer. Be nice to the man in your life and prompt him to do the same. A small comment about his cooking or a nice remark about your hair can do wonders in the battle to be noticed.

Stop putting it off and make a date!

Don't make sex a chore. Every mum I know says the same: even though it can take a little bit of planning and some extra energy reserves, once they make the time for intimacy and throw a little bit of their rigid day-to-day routine aside for an evening, they feel tons better about themselves, their partner and their relationship. 'I was dreading it, but, wow, I felt so amazing afterwards. We just lay there talking for hours and felt so much closer,' was a phrase I heard only yesterday from a close girlfriend, who walked into our tea date like the cat who got the cream.

If you can plan ahead, although it seems calculating and unromantic, it can make you prepare yourself emotionally and physically. You don't want to take away spontaneity; on the other hand, if you keep putting it off or waiting for the 'perfect moment', your babies might be teenagers before you get to have sex again! My good friend Lyn has a 'couple night' once a month. They send Riley off to Lyn's mum for the evening, keep their diaries free and spend one whole night indulging one another. Taking it in turns to cook, they have a delicious meal, light tons of candles, play some good music, drink some nice wine, give each other a massage and generally 'reconnect'. Before, they could have done this any night of the week, but as parents, they need to book it well in advance!

Attempt to feel lovely

Tired, ratty and fat, how sexy do you feel? This doesn't, however, mean you should excuse never having sex ever, ever again! Invest a little time in pampering, sling on a nice blouse for supper (or a clean logo T-shirt instead of a tracksuit top at the very least) and run a comb through your hair. I used to think it was hilarious that my mum sprayed on perfume and put her earrings in before my stepdad came home from work (sooooo 1950s!), but now I'm a wife and mum, I understand why she made the effort. It made her feel nice and made him feel like she'd given him a passing thought in the mania of her day. Twenty years on and they're still happily married; it's amazing what Chanel No. 19 can do! If you feel like pushing the boat out, invest in some nice undies that will make you feel special or even some new, fresh, clean sheets and a scented candle. They can make all the difference between having a headache and having a lovely night with the man you love.

Reconnect with your sexuality

It may take more than a nice meal and a pair of frilly M&S undies to get you back in bed. For many women, it's not just about lack of energy, it's about a total loss of libido. I know several women who, now that they've reached the 'one-year-without-sex' mark, have given up all hope of enjoying intercourse again. Combining a long or traumatic birth with confused emotions about your new role as mother/woman/wife/sexual being can be the biggest turn-off going. Another one is somewhere deep in your subconscious – seeing 'mothers' as non-sexual beings.

When I asked my good friend (and champion of 'no sex for two years') for a solution, her answer was simple: 'A series of nights "off", hot baths, glasses of wine and a vibrator.' Really! Now, this may not work for all women, but what it suggests is that rekindling your own sexuality and feelings of being a sexual woman (not just so-and-so's mum) takes time and effort. Maybe you need time alone (or eventually with your partner) to really go back to basics and rebuild your confidence and libido from scratch. After two years eighteen days, my pal is now back in the sack, but as you can see, it can take a lot of patience and a huge dose of willpower!

Remember to laugh

So, you've managed to reignite your sexuality and after a long 'sabbatical' you eventually get that loving feeling. You put the kids to bed, put on a pair of lacy knickers and play a little Marvin Gaye. What now? Taking sex too seriously (especially after giving birth) can be the ruin of a romantic night. The first time my husband and I attempted a cuddle under the covers after my daughter was born, we got more than we'd bargained for. We'd had a few glasses of wine, a lovely meal and the first good chat and laugh in six weeks. We'd talked about something other than the newborn ... great, the first hurdle was out of the way. We lay in bed and a kiss progressed to a cuddle. As I whipped off my feeding bra in the intensity of the moment, out fell two rather soggy breast pads. Second hurdle overcome, my husband braved a touch of the bosom that had once predominantly belonged to him. Whoosh! Out spurted breast milk at the speed of light and hit him straight in the eye. Blinded and in fits of laughter, he toppled on to my other breast, which did the same, except this time it hit the other eye and the moment was well and truly lost. Reason three to laugh? Well, it's that or cry. Needless to say, a week later, a sleepy seven-week-old next door, and armed with a lacy feeding bra that was decent enough to stay on, we succeeded in getting past first base. Thank goodness!

Be prepared for the unexpected

Any mum will tell you that unadulterated, uninterrupted nights of passion are pretty much impossible with a young child in tow. This doesn't mean we can't aspire to a wild night; it just means you have to be prepared for all eventualities. Take my friend Elaine. When she did eventually get round to having a night of romance, she was in mid-strip when her toddler walked in asking for juice and enquiring why she was torturing herself with 'reins'. My friend Luella had a similar experience; every time things got steamy, her daughter seemed to have a sixth sense about it and would roar down the baby monitor. Even if she'd checked on her five minutes beforehand, the moment things began to shape up in the bedroom, she'd suddenly sit bolt upright in her cot, a child possessed, and scream until Mummy came.

I too have had my fair share of awkward disturbances. Take the time my daughter was four months old and still sleeping in our room in a small crib. Sound asleep and dreaming of sheep, we took this opportunity to light a candle, go to bed and have a giggle at times gone by. Just as things were hotting up, we peeped from underneath the duvet to find a little girl arched up on her elbows straining to see more. Horrified that our little cherub (who, incidentally, had done nothing more than lift her head slightly to the right up until now, let alone go up on all fours!) had been corrupted for life, we lay as still as tree trunks for the rest of the night. Needless to say, going forward, we kept her well out of sight on nights like these.

Decoys are acceptable once in a while

If like many of my friends and me, you find that early in the morning is the only reasonable time to even think about sex (let's face it, we are delirious by the evening), then you may need some decoys to keep the kids out of the bedroom and fully entertained. Believe me, you won't be the first mother to let her kids watch twenty minutes of *Noddy* so you can have some intimacy at 7.33 a.m. with your partner. This isn't an excuse for wild S&M while the kids get bored and eat Smarties downstairs, but once in a while a mum should be allowed to exploit TV to get a tiny window alone with her man! I have on several occasions set mine up with *The Lion King* on a Sunday morning just so my husband and I can share a kiss that lasts longer than a peck on the cheek. Sometimes it can make or break the mood for the following week, so, really, twenty-six minutes of a DVD can't constitute a 'bad-mother' label, can it?

For most of us, intimacy takes a little more effort and forward-planning once we're parents. In this house, it's certainly more early nights to sleep than early nights for wild orgies in Agent Provocateur undies. That's not to say it can't happen – you just need to be motivated and realistic. Oh, and did I mention the need for laughter?

Mother knows best

'I hate to admit it, but my husband and I hadn't had sex for seven months after the birth of my firstborn, Clementine. Once I'd healed from the labour, I just couldn't get my libido back and went off the idea totally. It sounds silly, but as a couple, we really had to start from scratch to get our sex life up and running. Jamie really wooed me once again and made an effort to make me feel good about my body and sexuality. We spent weeks just kissing and re-exploring intimacy. When Clem was eight months, we had sex for the first time since her birth. Because Jamie had been patient and was really tender, I felt confident and aroused. I'd forgotten how good it could be!'

Helena Moore, interior designer and mother to Clementine (two)

Girlfriends

I have a confession to make. Although making love with the man I adore can make me feel a million dollars, a good natter, a laugh or two and at least one bottle of wine with my best friend Clare can make me feel a million and one dollars. I know my husband won't mind me saying this (he knows how much I love sex if I'm in the right mood), but he knows only too well how happy I come back after a night with my oldest and truest friend.

The brilliant thing about my friendship with Clare is that although our lives couldn't be more different (she's a hot TV producer, I'm a writer. She's dating and rents a flat with a girlfriend, I'm married with two kids and am stretched to pay the mortgage. At school, she was the swot, I was the rebel. She played the violin, I played the steel drums. She liked peanut M&Ms, I loved Revels), none of these things seem to matter. We've always been poles apart on so many things, and this has just made our friendship stronger. Although M&Ms have been replaced in her affections by TV scripts, and Revels have been taken over by toddler groups, this just gives us even more to talk about when we meet. The fact that she adores my kids and never tires of talk of nursery places, discipline and controlled crying (to a point), and I never tire of descriptions of skydiving, cocktail evenings and romantic weekends away in Berlin means that our friendship is almost a refresher, a breath of fresh air in our different worlds of dating and motherhood.

I bet you have a friend like this, someone who means the world to you and reminds you of who you are and what you value in a friend. And then we have friends for work, rest and play. Those we can call for a cry, those we can call for a gossip and those we can just call for a mundane chat. Even if you only have enough to count on one hand, you're sure to have built them up over the various stages of life (university, your first job, your NCT class and your daughter's primary school).

The thing about starting a family is that many of your friendships will be challenged to the max. Sure, some of them will grow and blossom (but quite a few will crumble under the change), and one of the biggest tasks to keep connected to people, to feel part of a grown-up world is making time for friendships. When you have work deadlines up to your armpits, dirty laundry up to your chin, kids' supper up to your eyes and you're trying hard to find time for your partner, you can see how 'girlfriend' time can become something you just don't get round to. Big mistake! Any new mum who's gone for weeks without a gossip about the latest celebrity break-up, a conversation about how to make kids' lasagne (that isn't interrupted fifteen times with a toddler requesting assistance with Lego) or a night 'off' just to be girls will know how desperate a life without girlfriends can be.

The difficult thing about friendships post-kids (and these don't have to be just with girls; some of my girlfriends have stacks of male friends too) is not only time restrictions but also energy levels, childcare issues and self-esteem. Often if you're exhausted, have no babysitter and still feel ten pounds overweight, the last thing you fancy doing on a Wednesday night is going out to the boozer with a friend. I have a good ally (who would rather remain nameless) who has, after three children in three years, fallen victim to these issues. She has children awake at erratic hours in the night, she has a pretty uncooperative husband who can't be relied on to babysit and her self-esteem is at rock bottom. Over the past three years, she avoided girlie gatherings and evenings out with best friends so much they've now stopped asking. They've lost a friend and she's lost not only friendship but also confidence, conversation and companionship. Not a nice place to be with three demanding kids and a nightmare husband, I can assure you.

It's true that once you have children, the endless girls' nights out and freedom to see friends any time or day diminishes pretty quickly. But it doesn't mean you should make your partner and children the only relationships that matter. We all need another escape, even if that's only once a month. Sure, we see other mums at the school gates, at baby massage and at the checkout at Tesco, but that's not the same as quality time with friends, is it? When an old friend came over with her twins this morning, I counted how many times we'd started a sentence with 'At the weekend, I . . .'. It was seventeen times in total. On the eighteenth attempt, we gave up. We had a lovely morning, but it included face-painting, three dirty nappies, a spilt juice cup and an argument about which child rode the wooden tricycle in the garden, rather than an update on what we'd got up to at the weekend, let alone more pressing issues like who was on the cover of *Vogue* and who'd won the general election.

Making time for friendships without the kids and partner in tow is an essential part of regaining your identity and feeling human again. I've found what works for me is once a week my husband and I hire a babysitter and go out together with mutual friends or as a couple, and once every three to four weeks I go out with my girlfriends alone. (Childcare is provided by my husband, who in turn gets the same favour later in the month.) Even if it's just over to Jennie's for a light supper and a movie, getting out without my other half and my other two quarters makes me feel whole again. If we're feeling flush, we sometimes make it a restaurant or a play, but it's more the act of getting out and doing something that's separate from the humdrum of everyday family life that's important. Admittedly, a good four out of ten times, one of us ladies will cancel ('Teething baby and up all night' or 'Hideous beyond hideous day at work' being our genuine excuses), but more often than not, we make the date and all feel better for it. It's OK if all we end up talking about is the kids, that's totally normal, but the point is we're away from them for all of two and a half hours, and we're investing in something other than the kitchen sink and work figures.

Sometimes (due usually to practicality or finance) it just doesn't work to have a night out every three weeks or so. Last week, for example, my husband couldn't babysit (he was working late all week), I felt too tired to contemplate a night later than nine o'clock (two articles and a whole chapter written that week), and my daughter seemed to be brewing a cold that may have meant she'd wake at night grumpy to find no mum around. Instead of supper at a local Italian, Jennie, Lyn, Clare and I decided (for this month at least) we'd do a Saturday lunch, no partners allowed. This entailed me offering up my kitchen and cooking a large salad, Jennie and Lyn bringing fresh bread and meats, Clare bringing a bottle of wine (and her endless talent with telling stories to the under-fours) and letting the kids run wild in the garden. Even though this wasn't specifically grown-up time, it meant that while our husbands made themselves scarce (something they secretly loved. Tell me, how can a man spend three hours in B&Q and call it pleasure?), we were free to talk parenting tips and drink a sneaky glass of Saturday-lunchtime wine.

As long as you have patience (not all friend dates can happen when you throw teething, chickenpox and tonsillitis into the equation) and determination, you can really make your friendships grow post-children. Believe me when I tell you, you'll need them now more than ever. Who else will listen to you sobbing when you've attempted (and failed) to breastfeed for the tenth time that day? Who else will make you laugh when you're a size eighteen (mostly still from baby weight) and want to be a size ten? And who else will tell you they love you and you are doing a good job, even when you feel a total failure? (And bring chocolate fudge cake while they're at it.) Girlfriends, of course. We may not be living the *Sex and the City* lifestyle any more, but that doesn't mean we don't need the odd night of chatter, Martinis and sex talk, now does it?

Mother knows best

'Just after I gave birth to Martha, we moved to the countryside. Although it was far more space to bring up a child, I was desperately lonely and missed my friends dearly. Instead of wallowing in it, I made sure that I joined a couple of playgroups and also an art class for myself. Through this I made some great friends who ended up being a good source of comfort to me. I also insisted on going back to London once every six weeks and spending the night with my girlfriend Jane. My mum would take Martha, and I'd spend a night talking and drinking red wine at my favourite London local with Jane and a couple of old friends. Without these proactive actions, I'm sure my marriage would have suffered, not to mention my self-esteem.'

Kym Karasick, housewife and mother to Martha (two)

Making Quality Time

Once in a while we all have a '1950s mother moment'. It goes something like this: you're standing at the kitchen sink, elbow-deep in washing-up, wearing ultra-chic yellow plastic washing-up gloves, hoarse from negotiating (not shouting, of course) with your children about sharing the miniature plastic animals, you haven't been out of the house for forty-eight hours and at this moment your partner walks in the door from work/football/the pub/the garden. You are now sick of the third dirty saucepan and the unshiftable bolognese sauce welded to it, you are about to throttle the next under-four who screeches, 'The kangaroo is mine, give it back!' and when your partner looks up from the paper and asks, 'What's for supper?' you drop the saucepans on the floor, spit at least three ★★★★ words at anyone who's within earshot and retreat upstairs ready to do a Shirley Valentine. My girl-friends and I call each other the moment this happens. 'I've had a 1950s mother moment,' we cry, and immediately we know a large glass of wine and some quality time is required. Suddenly you've realised you're the archetypal housewife (even if you work five days a week), knee-deep in house-hold mess and manic children.

It's these moments that make us wonder what the hell has happened to our individuality. You're only too familiar with your role as wife/partner/girlfriend/lover, you know well the ins and outs of your new identity as a mother (and possibly career woman too), and you could list the expectations placed upon you as cleaner/housekeeper/chef/law-enforcer/accountant of the home. Ask yourself to write a list of the things you do outside these roles and you'll be surprised at how stuck you get. Prior to children, in the place of wife, mother, dog-walker and chauffeur, you'd have found best friend, lover, art fanatic, cinema buff, shopaholic and runner. You may possibly have added boozer, shoe fetishist and lie-in-obsessive to the list. Instead of 'brilliant at tying shoelaces with one hand' or 'number one at cooking macaroni cheese while breastfeeding', you would have probably had 'brilliant at discussing the latest five films out at the cinema' or 'number one at cooking roast chicken and apple crumble for a dinner party of eight'. Combine this with the fact you haven't made love in four weeks, you haven't had your hair done in four months, and you definitely haven't had a girlie night out for what feels like four years and it's easy to see how we can lose our identity in the ever-demanding realm of parenthood.

It's not just us mums who can feel rather overwhelmed by the demands of our new role. Dads can feel just as oppressed by the confines of the work-home juxtaposition. I know my husband can look very weary at the end of a long week. The demands of running a company, rushing back to skid in for bath time, giving 100 per cent to the kids before they hit the sack, helping me with supper, calling his grandma and squeezing in an hour of paperwork before he joins me in bed leaves him frazzled. The forty minutes he plays football twice a week are often the only time he has 'off' in a whole week. Sure, if you have a hands-off partner who never touches the washing machine or doesn't know where the kids sleep (and instead can be found on the sofa, a can of beer in one hand, a tabloid in the other), then you've a right to be even more in need of some 'time out'. It seems to me, though, that most modern partners do their fair share of parenting and can also be in desperate need of rediscovering a tiny morsel of their old lives again. There's no question in my mind that the need for a little 'child-out' time is beneficial to both Mum and Dad. If you both get a little space, it will refresh you equally for your relationship and family life.

My friend Molly and her partner, Sam, reached saturation point in typical '1950s-mother-moment' style only last week. They had just moved house, their youngest had been in hospital with a serious chest infection, and they were under a lot of financial strain. The last holiday they'd had was two years previously, Molly was still wearing her early-pregnancy clothes a year after giving birth, neither she nor Sam had been out for even one drink with friends (let alone each other) for over six months, and the last book Molly had read was *Thomas and the Runaway Carriage* (and this was a woman who used to read one of the classic novels once a week). Molly turned up on my doorstep in tears; time for a little rich chocolate brownie and some serious solutions. The first thing we established was that due to all the stress of the past few months, she and Sam hadn't had a conversation about anything other than builders, doctors or bank managers for way too long. Sex? Well, you could forget it; if they hadn't exchanged more than three words all day, how the hell could they feel even remotely intimate? Secondly, Molly had been so stressed she'd given up her fortnightly yoga class ('No time for that'), stopped her weekly coffee morning at home ('No space') and stopped her monthly supper out with her twin sister ('No money'). Combine this with the fact that the last item of clothing she had bought for herself had been a pair of maternity jeans (and even then they were second-hand) and you are left with one very fed-up mum!

Seeing as I had been pretty much in the same position not long before (my downfalls being a husband away on business, a babysitter away on honeymoon, two children with chickenpox, three deadlines for articles and legs left unshaved for two weeks), Molly and I had a lot to discuss. The first thing we agreed for her to do was to write down a list of all the things she liked about herself. Of course, she immediately scribbled down 'good at playing football with my son' and 'OK at maths homework'. This is when we limited the parenting skills to just two. The idea was to find out positive things about her as an individual, not just as Amy and Calum's mum! It took Molly for ever to think of things she liked about herself that weren't defined by her mummy role, but we got there in the end:

- Good friend – has a core of wonderful girlfriends.
- Intelligent – got a first from York.
- Funny – has the mums in stitches at Friday coffee morning.
- Brilliant cook – makes the best moussaka in town.
- Gives the best massage – used to trade one a week with Sam for a weekly head rub.
- Ambitious and successful – now has twenty-six children as private music clients.

From here, we nibbled another slice of brownie, set my kids up in the garden with the paddling pool and I got her to write down five things she loved doing that she hadn't done for a long time:

- Practising yoga.
- Eating Thai meals.
- Reading a book uninterrupted.
- Drinking red wine and eating olives with sister, Sophie, best friend, Rachel, and oldest school friend, Tilda.
- Making love, Frank Sinatra in the background, while burning lavender and chestnut-scented candles.

You won't be surprised to hear that this list took all of five seconds and could have gone on to number eighty-one! The hard thing now was to get Molly to realise some of the things she liked about herself and achieve at least a few of the pursuits she missed. A realistic goal for any stressed-out mum is to do one quality pursuit with the kids, one with a friend, one with your partner and one purely by yourself at least once a month. For Molly, this consisted of the following:

- A weekly mothers' coffee morning. (We agreed that the Friday coffee morning was a brilliant way to see other mums and share a laugh and a moan. Instead of giving herself a hard time about not doing it at her house and therefore scrapping the whole concept, she decided to call the other mums and suggest sharing it out – once a month at her home and the other three at someone else's or, failing that, the local Starbucks.)
- A girls' night out including red wine, olives and an optional open fire. She would suggest to Sam that he look after the kids one Wednesday night a month and she would exchange this with one Friday a month so he could see his friends. I've done this with my husband since my daughter was born and it works brilliantly.

- Either a massage or a Thai meal with Sam. (Depending on their babysitting budget or the kindness of her in-laws, one night a month would be designated to a nice meal out with Sam or a night of Frank Sinatra, scented candles and passion!)
- Either yoga or uninterrupted Jane Austen (to be alternated once a week).

Once Molly and I had consumed a whole chocolate brownie, got drenched by the kids' paddling-pool splashes and decided that some positive action for Molly must be taken to feel good about herself (outside of her role as mum and wife), we agreed it had been a very productive afternoon all in all. I did my good-friend thing and rang Molly later that week to make sure she was a) not distraught and knee-deep in music sheets and builders and b) actively making her 'to-do' list happen. Luckily, she wasn't there to chat: she was out having Thai with Sam, and her sister wasn't expecting them home until after midnight. Go, girl!

Now, not everyone wants to spend their Tuesday mornings doing a salutation to the sun, and some of you may hate the taste of Thai food, but I bet you can all relate to the need for a little of what you love. We all like a walk in the park with the kids, the last goodnight kiss from our toddler and the laughter at seeing your son's Play-Doh interpretation of Spiderman. But what we often forget is how much we love having an adult conversation with our partners, how much we miss a little workout at the end of a long day or how much joy we get from going to a slushy movie with our best friend (accompanied by a scoop of chocolate-chip ice cream, of course).

Even if the things that stop you making quality time for yourself and your partner are money and childcare support, there could be some creative ways round this. OK, if you love shoe shopping and the bank balance says otherwise, it does make it hard, so think of something you like nearly as much that doesn't cost the earth. A long walk, a dinner party at your house (where everyone brings a dish and a bottle) or an hour in a free art gallery can all lift your spirits and rekindle your enthusiasm for life. If you are stuck for what to do with the kids (while you invest in a little 'you' time), there are lots of options that don't cost the earth. Babysitting agencies can be expensive (but if you can afford it, they are a lifesaver for parents in need of a night out), so how about starting a local rota with fellow mums? My girlfriends and I often trade a night of babysitting with one another. Only last night my husband and I saw a film while Jennie came over and read a book when the kids were asleep. (She actually said it got her away from a heap of ironing and a pile of work.) I am going to repay the favour when she goes to a wedding in three weeks. Equally, help your partner to have some 'me' time (mine plays football, poker or grabs a massage) and he can repay you with some of your own. (I swim, drink too much with my girlies or occasionally nip to Space NK for a new body cream and a sniff at all the products that cost the earth.) Making quality time away from family life can sometimes make the difference between a grumpy, stressed-out mum and a fabulous mum with enough energy and enthusiasm to enjoy life.

Mother knows best

'I'd given up going out and getting drunk with my girl–friends, as hangovers weren't conducive to 6 a.m. starts. I really missed the girlie company and it was getting me down. I decided to start a book club where girl–friends and I met once a month at my house and discussed a book we'd all read. I know it sounds boring, but once we'd had one glass of wine and a few nibbles, it was really fun. Half the evening we talk books, the rest we talk the latest jeans or episode of *Supernanny* and potty-training tips. It's just a great excuse to meet up and means I don't have to get a babysitter. I really look forward to the third of every month now; it's been a lifesaver.'

Catherine Stanton, full-time mother to Tom (four) and Alex (two)

Adjusting Your Goalposts

I bet you're sick of hearing me harp on about balance. Well, for this I apologise. I absolutely promise that this is the last time I will utter the B word (in this book at least). The thing is for so many parenting and mums' issues, getting the balance right is imperative to feeling you're doing a good job for you and your family. This has never been more apparent than in making relationships work post-children. The real muddle we mums seem to get into is how to adjust our expectations of friendship and partnership after having a child. There are two extremes . . .

The baby-focused mum

For these women, the moment they read the positive result on the Boots pregnancy test, their whole world becomes fluffy and ga-ga. Drinks out with work pals are replaced by watching the Sky Baby Channel; supper out with another couple is quickly shoved out of the way in favour of playing Mozart to the bump; and all intimate advances are rebuffed, opting instead for a good read of Gina Ford. This attitude goes on well into parenthood, when, after a day of school runs, baby t'ai chi and toddler French, Mum has absolutely no time to phone a friend, let alone contemplate a takeaway (and, God forbid, a non-baby conversation) with her partner. In short, social life, friendships and relationship-building with their partners are out, 100 per cent child-focus is most definitely in.

The 'my life will not change' party mum

These are women who even with a child (or four) in tow will under no circumstances change their friendships and social lives. Wild parties? No problem. Up until 4 a.m. celebrating a friend's birthday? So what? A week's detox in Thailand leaving the kids at home? Have you got an issue with that? Even if you're not a celebrity or supermodel, you can still fit into this category. It basically means you will go out, see your friends, be footloose and fancy-free, and no toddler is going to prevent you from having a good time (and that means good sex, good booze and a good girlie laugh).

Only a fraction of mums come in at either of these ends of the spectrum, and for the rest of us fabulous mums, trying to get the balance between alpha mum and party mum goes something like this . . .

The fabulous mum

A mum that loves her kids, happily spends an afternoon knee-deep in the sandpit and enjoys nothing more than making sunken organic blueberry muffins with her three-year-old. Now, here's the but: she also loves a nice glass of wine with her best friends, relishes grown-up time with her husband (at least once a week) and refuses to miss a fortieth-birthday bash because she's got to be up at 6 a.m. A fabulous mum would confess to missing baby ballet on a Saturday so she could have coffee in the garden with an old friend (while the kids trash the flower beds), but is confident enough to turn down a wild night on the town if it's her eldest's carol service that very same night. She would admit that on the odd occasion she lets her kids watch CBeebies so she can read *Easy Living* and sometimes opts for fish fingers (instead of a freshly made organic kids' stew). The fabulous mum remembers not to beat herself up over these choices; it is, after all, just an attempt to find a middle ground that works for mum and child.

The only way, really, to achieve this kind of balance is to adjust your goalposts and expectations. I'm the first to admit it's pretty much impossible (not to mention financially crippling) to keep up the single social life once you have a child. (And let's face it, who'd want to? Surely one of the reasons we got married and had kids is because the endless blind dates and Mr Wrongs were getting us down?) On the flip side, it is unrealistic to expect to be able to raise children without any social life or grown-up time whatsoever. My friend Amy openly confesses that seven months after the birth of her son, Rafael (with no sign of a night out in the pipeline), she felt like tearing her hair out. How many playgroups could she attend without a night out at a local gastropub to counter-act the custard creams and tantrums? I, too, was absolutely desperate for some grown-up time outside the home after the birth of my first. (When she was four months, I even expressed enough breast milk to feed her for forty-eight hours, so I could have a few glasses of champagne and express the alcohol-contaminated milk afterwards!)

Once children come into the equation, you shouldn't curb your desire to go out or engage in inspiring relationships; you just have to accept that the possibilities for these may shift somewhat. You may not be able to see your girlfriends as much as you'd like, but make sure you call them, or send a quick chatty email, text or card. Weeks can go by and you'll find you haven't caught up with them, so after supper once a week, give yourself half an hour to get in touch. (Remembering birthdays is also crucial. I know it sounds silly, but after the birth of my two in quick succession, I managed to forget Jennie's special day. I felt so terrible I now make sure all my girlfriends' birthdays are written in red pen and underlined at least three times in my diary.) When you do go out, don't feel wracked with remorse if you're the one to fall asleep in the ashtray at midnight; all fellow mums will understand. Equally, if you do stumble in at one o'clock in the morning every so often, hey, the world won't fall apart, and it doesn't mean you love your kids any less!

When changing the goals with your partner, remember to enjoy the small gestures and the morsels of grown-up time you steal in the week. Forty minutes to read the papers together and have a cuddle while the in-laws play hide-and-seek with the kids in the garden, half an hour to listen to music, prepare the supper and talk about the week ahead, a walk to the Tube together before work; these all become stolen moments that you should use wisely. You may miss eating out with your partner three nights a week, as you did when you were dating, so why not try to eat together at home three evenings a week (and more if you can)? Make sitting down for an evening meal an opportunity to share news, show interest in each other's lives and wind down from the day. I'm not saying never eat in front of the TV, but make this an exception, not the rule. My husband reminded me of this last night as we sat down to a roast chicken and a glass of rosé. 'The couple that eats together, stays together,' he said (just before 'Pass the ketchup'), and you know what? I hope more than anything he's right.

Mother knows best

'After trying to conceive for three years, when I eventually did, the pregnancy and baby totally took centre stage. Once Elisa was one, I realised I hadn't gone out more than twice without her and I could tell my husband, Edward, was feeling jaded. I confessed to a good friend that I was feeling guilty about leaving Elisa but also guilty about how little time I'd given Edward. She suggested a monthly dinner party at her house or mine, where Elisa could sleep upstairs and we would still get adult interaction. It worked pretty well and I'm now considering leaving her with a babysitter and attempting to go out somewhere more adventurous. I think Edward has even booked our old favourite French bistro – now wouldn't that be fantastic!'

Carolina Stark, full-time mother to Elisa (one)

Top ten grown-up-time tips

1. During dating and pregnancy, store up those sacred couple memories. Build on these as parents and tap into them when the going gets tough.
2. Make sure you relish time as a couple before the birth – writing a wish list of things to do together is a good idea.
3. Try not to neglect your partner when two becomes three. Involve him wherever possible and help him to bond with the baby.
4. Ensure you still make time to remember what you love about your partner outside of your roles as parents.
5. Take an interest in your partner's life, share hobbies, passions and even small things like the cooking.

6. Make time to make love (but prepare for all eventualities).
7. Invest in your friendships outside the family; the 'once-a-month rule' works wonders.
8. Make the scarce time you have with adults quality time; forward-planning is key.
9. Remind yourself of the social activities you love and miss, and make sure you do at least one regularly in order to boost your identity and self-esteem.
10. Don't expect miracles, but do make an effort. Having loving relationships and grown-up time is possible, it just takes a little more hard work.

Grace's Guru: Paula Hall

Paula is a registered sexual and relationship psychotherapist who works both for Relate and in private practice. Over the past twelve years, she has worked with hundreds of clients helping them to overcome sexual and relationship difficulties. As an expert on relationships and sexuality, she is regularly asked to comment for national press and women's magazines as well as appearing on national radio and television. She has written the BBC's website pages on relationships and sex, and is also a behind-the-scenes consultant for a number of television productions. She is also mother to two 'almost-grown-up' children.

What are your main relationships tips for mums?

A mum in a dual-working household As a working mum, your time is going to be very thinly stretched and there'll be lots of days when you just don't feel that there's enough of you to go around. However, you do have a couple of advantages over some other mums. Although you may feel as though you're always juggling your time, you are still out there in the world meeting people. And when you're with your partner, you can talk about your work lives as well as your home lives.

One of the key things you need to remember is that this time in your life is going to be one of the toughest for *both* of you. You and your partner will need to adjust and adapt so you can be more efficient at running the home. You'll need to ensure that you schedule time for yourselves as individuals, yourselves as couples and time for your friends and extended family. It can feel very unromantic to be putting a date in your diary for each other, but unless you do so, you'll find that time is always taken up by something or someone else.

It really doesn't matter how much time you have as long as you make it quality time. I know it's a cliché, but when it comes to relationships, quality time really is more important than quantity. Grab opportunities when you can, for example when the baby is asleep and, of course, longer chunks of time by getting a babysitter. And make sure you use the time wisely. Don't be tempted to get some chores done – use the time to talk, laugh and get close.

A full-time mum with three under-threes You're going to feel exhausted a lot of the time, and some days it may feel as if you're nothing more than a mother. When you're a full-time mum, it's easy to lose your identity as a woman, so it's important that you remember that no matter how valuable the role is, you're more than just a mum. You might find it helpful to write a list of the other things that you do and roles that you play. You're probably a partner, a lover, a daughter, a friend. And think about your hobbies and interests – are you also a painter or creator, a chef, a rambler, a committee member? You might be a nature-lover, a film buff, a social-affairs-watcher, a fashion-spotter. Take time to broaden your view of yourself and get back in touch with the multilayered and multitalented person that you are.

Remember also that your children are going to grow up and they are going to be less demanding. But in the meantime, focus on what you *can* do, not on what you can't. If you can't spend an hour in the bath, enjoy the fact that you can enjoy ten minutes in the shower. If you can't go out every Friday with the girls, look forward to the monthly lunch that you can do. And when it comes to finding time to be with your partner, try to be as creative as you can. If there's no one who can babysit all three kids, consider babysitting when one of them has already got an invite to a party or is booked into nursery. And make sure you make the most of your evenings. The advantage of under-threes is that they're hopefully all tucked up reasonably early, so you've still got a bit of energy left to have some adult time before you're ready for sleep yourself.

A single mum Single mums have to be particularly resourceful. Without a partner to help share the workload, you're most likely to forget about the importance of taking time for yourself. You need to make sure that you're taking the help and support that's offered by friends and family. If none of your friends have children, then it can be easy to fear that you're taking them for granted if you let them babysit, but remember the time will undoubtedly come in the future when they'll ask you to return the favour. If you haven't already done so, you should think about investigating single mums' clubs in your area. Networking with other single mums will give you a valuable pool of reciprocal babysitters and also help you not to feel isolated in your situation.

A mum going through a divorce There's never a good time to go through a divorce, but if it coincides with becoming a new mum, that's undoubtedly one of the worst times. Whether you're the one that's initiated the separation or it's been forced on you, you'll be going through a hefty emotional ordeal right now. With all the imminent changes, you're bound to feel vulnerable and anxious about the future. It's essential that you take your time and don't let anyone rush you into making any decisions you're not yet ready to make. And make sure you've got the emotional and practical support of people you trust. You may find that one of your friends is going to be particularly good at helping you look at the practical financial, housing and legal things that need to be done, while another friend is the perfect shoulder to cry on. If you can, also find a friend who's good at lifting your spirits and helping you focus on brighter days ahead. Crises are often the times when our friends really show their true strengths, so make full use of them.

A first-time mum who is shy and lacks confidence Becoming a mum is a life-changing experience. It often means saying goodbye to a lifestyle you've become very used to and saying hello to a new one. For a lot of mums, it means making new friends. If you're shy, then this can feel very daunting, but it's actually much easier with a baby than you would think. Baby and toddler groups are often full of women and everyone will have been new at some stage. They are there to help new mums meet other people as well as provide activities for the kids, and on the whole, they are very welcoming indeed. The advantage of all being mums is that you instantly have something in common. If in the past you've struggled to find things to talk about, you can be sure that you won't need to worry any more. New mums can spend hours discussing feeding, sleeping, nappies, first smiles, first crawls, first sleep through the night! The conversations are easy. And as time goes on, you'll find the conversations become more about each other and the invites will start coming in to other mum-and-baby events. What's more, you'll find complete strangers coming up to you to talk about your child. Kids really are the ultimate conversation-opener and it will give you an excellent opportunity to develop social confidence.

A mum who's gone off intimacy For the first few months after childbirth, most women say they're just not in the mood for sex. Or at least, not very often. There are a number of reasons why this is perfectly natural and under-standable. The first is physical. Mother Nature churns out a hormone that helps you bond with your baby but dimin-ishes your sex drive. It's probably her way of making sure that women have fully nursed and reared their first child before producing competitive siblings. The other big reason is exhaus-tion. Exhaustion can make us feel physically ill, mentally drained and emotionally raw, and the last thing you may feel up to at the end of a busy day is having sex with your partner. Becoming a parent is also an anxious time, especially if it's your first child, and anxiety affects both the male and female libido. You need to talk to your partner about your feelings and make sure he knows that you still love him. Even though you may not feel like having sex, there's no reason why the two of you can't still be physically intimate. Make time for being sensual – cuddling on the sofa, a bath together or a massage – but be sure to stress that you don't expect this to lead anywhere. With the expectation of sex taken off you, you can be free to enjoy each other – and who knows, maybe as you're getting close, you'll change your mind, anyway.

What are your top five tips for a mum wanting to promote healthy relationships with her partner, friends and family after having children?

1. Make maintaining relationships a priority – housework can wait, relationships can't.
2. Remember that it is quality time that matters, not quantity, so make sure when you're with people, you give them 100 per cent of your attention.
3. Talk – another cliché, I know – but communication really is the key to maintaining healthy relationships. Talk lots and often.
4. Accept that this is a stressful time. Becoming parents is challenging, and both you and your partner are going to have times when you feel more tense than usual and perhaps overreact to things. When that happens, remember to give each other the benefit of the doubt.

5. Have fun – the great thing about becoming a parent is that it gives you an excuse to play. Laughter is something you can share with your partner, your friends and your family – any time and any place.

What are the key dos and don'ts for a mum wishing to maximise grown-up time?

Dos
- Focus on the opportunities and positives of your current situation.
- Learn to be creative and resourceful with your time.
- Grab every opportunity when the kids are entertained.
- Plan ahead and book time for seeing people.
- Accept people's offers of help.

Don'ts
- Avoid the temptation to become a 'supermum'. You may have to let some of your domestic standards fall so you can find time to be with your partner, friends and family.
- Try not to lose sight of the fact that this is just a phase of your life – no matter how tired you are, things are going to get easier.
- Be careful not to let relationship problems fester – if there's something that needs addressing between the two of you, do it now.

Paula's fabulous mum's relationship mantra: 'Healthy relationships make happy mums and happy mums make healthy children.'

Giving Back

Believe it or not, I am my own worst critic. Like many multi-tasking mums I know (from those in the boardroom and beside the catwalk to those at the under-twos' toddler group and at the pre-school gates), I spend much of my time wracked with guilt, desperately in search of answers to all those knotty parenting questions. Are we right to refuse our kids sweets (especially when we are partial to a mini chocolate muffin ourselves)? Will we really damage them by allowing half an hour of television (because we are desperate to do the ironing)? Is it fair to opt for gendered toys (especially when we vowed in our extreme feminist youth that our daughters would play with cars and wear blue boiler suits!)?

We mums feel guilty about everything. If it's not the lack of quality time we spend with our children, it's the mere thought that we fed them chicken nuggets last week (the fact that the nuggets were accompanied by broccoli, peas and an organic fruit selection is beside the point) or that their snowflake outfit for the school nativity play wasn't nearly as good as supermum-of-four's daughter, Susie's (all hand-crafted sequins, wafting marabou feathers and lovingly appliquéd tinsel).

New mums spend so much time on questions about child-rearing, completely overwhelmed by all the conflicting advice and constantly asking themselves whether they're doing enough as mums (and as partners/lovers/friends/daughters/sisters/employees) that they often get lost along the way. How many of us have attended a supper party a year after giving birth so engrossed in making finger food from butternut squash, organising childcare and fighting off life-altering exhaustion that we can barely string a sentence together?

Eventually, though, there's a point when enough is enough. For me, that was some time last year, when it finally got to me that with the guilt, the pressures of work, home and the million other 'must, must dos' on my list, I had absolutely zero time for myself. The knock-on effect of this was simple: stressed-out, tired and anxious mum equalled ratty, grumpy and miserable mum. I shouted at the kids, I bawled at my husband, I wept to my mother. And forget friends and work colleagues, they didn't even get a look in. (Lucky them, I was like a bear with a sore head – stay well away!) I was fed up of being the mum screaming in the car (as my toddlers tore chunks of each other's hair out) and the partner too tired for conversation, humour, sex and even basic communication, and I was desperate to be more of the woman I knew I could be. I knew the only way to get on top of life as a new mum was to separate all the key areas that I felt triggered this downward spiral and look at ways of changing them.

The brilliant thing about working through problem areas of your life (home, work, intimacy, nutrition, fashion, you name it) is that with some thought, a little hard work and, of course, consistency, we can almost immediately start to feel better about ourselves. Not only are we stronger and happier about all aspects of our lives, but we also have the confidence to give more back. Take this example: my husband was away on business for a week, my kids were on half-term and both had chickenpox. The rain lashed against the window, when I called friends and family it went straight to answer-phone, and, to top things off, my period started. I was in for a weekend of hell (and that would be putting it mildly). After three solid days in this pit of germs, tantrums, Calpol and grumpy under-threes, we turned a corner. Monday came, the first spots scabbed over, and I took this opportu-nity to focus, just for half an hour, on myself. In no less than twenty-nine and a half minutes, I'd showered and washed my hair (with the first nice, smelly shower gel I could grab), whizzed up a banana smoothie for three, called Tanith (who desperately wanted her girls to catch chickenpox before the summer was up) and asked her over for some tea and sympathy, and managed to email a three-line proposal for a feature on 'desperate mums' to a parenting magazine. This tiny, proactive 'me' moment turned me into a completely different person for the afternoon. Sure, I still had black rings under my eyes, no partner to cheer me up and no unbroken night's sleep in sight, but I did feel slightly better in my own skin. Less like hurling myself down the stairs or losing my temper with the kids (and let's face it, they were suffering from a medieval disease at the time!) and more like crawling around on the floor impersonating the Gruffalo to get two poorly toddlers to smile.

We all want to be the best mums we can possibly be, to be inspiring, loving, nurturing, calm and, inevitably, the wonderwoman our children (bless them) thought we were all along. We want to help them with their homework, chase them around the park and possibly even teach them how to make planets from cotton wool or raisin-bran muffins from scratch (should this be your desire). And beyond that, we want to be career women and be taken as seriously as our childless colleagues (who not only have more dosh to spend on power suits, they also have the trump card of working far more late nights), partners who can still be funny and look (on occasion) sexy and unique and we want to do all this without losing our temper at the drop of a hat or feeling so low in self-esteem that we sabotage the lot altogether.

With a little investment in yourself, not just physically but on every level, I promise you, you can turn things round. You'll have more energy, willpower and patience, you'll feel better, healthier, sexier. Fabulous! And in the end, all of that should (I hope) make you feel stronger about your role as mum and help you to achieve all those feats of parenting that often seem impossible.

Good luck, mums. I am in it with you all the way.

Food, Glorious Food

Mums' Muesli

I've never been very adventurous when it comes to breakfast. For as long as I can remember, it's been a good-sized bowl of muesli, porridge or quinoa topped with warm milk (or, as I prefer now, Rice Dream), a sprinkle of cinnamon and a mixture of fresh fruit (ideally blueberries, a chopped apple and half a papaya, but a lonely pear and a half-eaten banana will do!). I honestly think I couldn't get out through the door without it in the morning. (Remember the glowing Ready Brek boy on the advert? Well, that's me!) I have even been known to have a mini bowl at four o'clock in the afternoon just to get me through (or dare I say it, four in the morning whilst breastfeeding a hungry newborn).

Ingredients
Serves four, so double or triple if you fancy storing it in a sealed jar and saving time during the week.

20g unblanched hazelnuts	10g coconut shavings
20g pecan nuts	20g dried apricots

20g dried figs	30g millet flakes
60g rolled oats	40g raisins
30g barley flakes	

Roughly chop your hazelnuts, pecan nuts and coconut, and dice your dried apricots and figs. Mix together the oats, barley and millet, add your other chopped ingredients and chuck in the raisins. Mix it all together and store as required. I guarantee it's best served with yummy fresh fruit (cold in summer, stewed and hot in winter), topped with a sprinkle of cinnamon and accompanied by a cup of piping-hot green tea.

A Girlie Gazpacho

This is an old recipe of my father's that he gave me a few years ago as we sweltered in Ibiza. I suppose I say 'girlie' because in summer when a few mums come for lunch, nothing seems more appetising than a bowl of pinky-red gazpacho with a dollop of crème fraîche.

The best thing about this dish is that you can cook it up in bulk, store it in the freezer and it will save you time on those endless frazzled summer days when you arrive back from the nursery run at lunchtime, hot, sweaty and with eight minutes to spare until under-threes' swimming club! Don't worry too much about proportions; it's enjoyable and economic to experiment with what you've got. Similarly, don't complicate it by making another side dish that will take up double the time; I just dunk in a little wholemeal bread, sprinkle some roasted seeds on top or eat plain and finish off with a bowl of fruit and yoghurt.

Ingredients

Serves six to eight, so increase quantities if you want to freeze it.

2 to 3 eggs
6 to 10 large ripe tomatoes
a chunk of stale bread
3 to 4 large peppers, red and/or green
2 cucumbers

half a red onion (more if you particularly like onion)
plenty of garlic cloves
olive oil
sea salt
black pepper

Put your eggs into a saucepan of water and bring to the boil. Continue to boil for two to three minutes and then remove the eggs and leave them to cool. Keep the water simmering.

Nick the skins of the tomatoes and put them in the boiling water for around half a minute, until the skins start to loosen. Remove the tomatoes and place with the eggs to cool. Once you've done this, soak the stale bread in some of the water you've used for cooking.

Slice open the peppers, get rid of the pith, seeds and any stem, and chop them up. Peel the tomatoes (something my son loves to help with) and dice along with the cucumbers, onion, garlic cloves and shelled eggs. Squeeze the bread (another thing that fascinates my son!) and break into bits.

Mix all the ingredients up in a big bowl.

Put as much of the mixed ingredients into a blender as it will comfortably take, leaving room for a good slug of olive oil and another of cold water. Add salt and pepper. Blend until fairly liquid but not too smooth and then pour it into a big bowl. Repeat the process until you've used up all the ingredients.

Leave it in the fridge for a day or two (I always find it improves over time) and then serve with ice cubes, if it's really hot, or a dollop of low-fat crème fraîche. All you need now are some fellow mums to share it with!

Winter Warmer

So, we've solved the summer-lunchtime dilemma, but who wants ice-cold soup when the rain is pouring and December is fast approaching? Hot soup is the best easy replacement and can be cooked as a batch and eaten as the winter weeks go by. I find this carrot-and-lentil winter warmer the perfect solution for a hectic lunchtime and I love the fact I can cook it at leisure one quiet evening and then reheat while juggling a newborn/toddler/telephone/demands for finger-painting 'Now!' I serve it with several oatcakes and hummus or some rye toast.

Ingredients
Serves four.

1.125 litres of vegetable stock
2 large onions, chopped
2 crushed garlic cloves
1 tbsp cumin

6 large carrots, chopped
2 celery sticks, chopped
125g brown lentils
125ml buttermilk
a handful of fresh coriander

Heat half a cup of stock in a saucepan, add the onions, garlic and cumin, give it a good stir and cook until the onions are soft. Add your carrots and celery, and cook for a further seven minutes. Add the remaining stock and 500ml of water and simmer for around twenty to twenty-five minutes. (When the carrots are nice and soft, you'll know it's time to bring the pan off the heat.) Blend the soup in a blender to your desired consistency. (Like the gazpacho, I like it a little lumpy.)

Return your soup to the pan, add the brown lentils and let it simmer for around twenty to twenty-five minutes (until the lentils are soft). If you want to freeze it, let it cool and then do it at this point. If you're eating it fresh, stir in the buttermilk and sprinkle with the fresh chopped coriander.

Cathy's Classic Butternut Salad

I love butternut squash and find it always satisfies my craving for potato without involving the white starch that I find makes me feel heavy and sluggish. My friend Cathy served this up for lunch at a play-date recently and the mums (not to mention most of our four-year-old fairy-princess daughters) devoured it. When I whipped it up a few days later for supper with my husband (to accompany a chicken breast each), I was surprised at how quick and simple it was. Don't you just love a dish you can prepare in five minutes, bung in the oven for an hour and forget about? And did I mention it's great cold for lunch the next day? Genius!

Ingredients
Serves four.

1 butternut squash   a handful of fresh rosemary
a good glug of olive oil   and oregano

sea salt

black pepper

100g pine nuts

feta cheese

a large bag of watercress, rocket and spinach salad

Preheat your oven to 180°C/350°F/gas mark 5.

Peel your butternut squash; they are buggers to peal, so make sure your knife is sharp. Chop it up and place on a baking tray, dressing it with your olive oil and some chopped rosemary and oregano. Give it a good sprinkle of salt and black pepper and bung it in the oven for an hour.

Get busy with the kids' bath/ironing/work emails/spelling homework.

After about forty-five-minutes, toast your pine nuts in a dry pan, making sure they don't burn – blackened pine nuts can taste very sour.

Once the butternut is nice and soft, remove it from the oven, sprinkle with the pine nuts and feta, and add it to your green salad. Drizzle a little extra olive oil to taste. Yummy!

Lazy Mums' Lamb Kebabs

Now, everyone knows we mums don't have the time to be lazy, but if time is of the essence (and you don't have three full hours on your hands to do a slow lamb marinade), then this dish is perfect for you. Lamb is full of iron, and if you choose lean lamb steaks, then this can be a good low-fat, high-protein dish, ideal for lunch (accompanied by a green salad, some green beans and a little sweet potato) or as a supper with a bowl of couscous and a dollop of plain yoghurt. I even find that it's a great family meal. I bung the meat on cocktail sticks for the kids and am always astonished at how the lack of a knife and fork will make the children try something new!

Ingredients

Serves two.

1 garlic clove	sea salt
1 tbsp olive oil	black pepper
the juice of one lemon	400g lamb cut into 2cm
2 tbsp fresh mint	cubes
1tbsp fresh thyme	

Once you've chopped the garlic (as finely as you have the patience for), mix up all the other ingredients to make a marinade. Add the diced lamb and leave for up to half a day in the fridge (although twenty minutes for the modern rushed mum is more than adequate!).

Thread your lamb on to some metal skewers and either grill for seven minutes, turning once, or place in the oven for twenty minutes.

Simple, eh?

Oh-so-easy Fish

I have cooked this dish (with various types of fish) so many times I could do it with my eyes closed. The reason I love it is simple: it's as quick as a flash to make, it's stuffed full of goodness, and it's delicious enough to eat for lunch with the kids or for a dinner party of hard-working, knackered grown-ups. How many dishes can you say that about? I tend to serve it with steamed broccoli and sweet-potato crush (literally sweet potato, carrot and a tiny knob of butter crushed together) or just a salad of cherry tomatoes and fresh basil.

Ingredients
Serves two.

2 salmon or monkfish steaks or two cod loins (skinless and boneless if possible)

4 strips of Parma ham (trim off the fat if you're watching the calories) a handful of fresh dill

Preheat the oven to 180°C/350°F/gas mark 5.

Wrap each fish steak/loin in a couple of strips of Parma ham, chop the dill and sprinkle over the dish. Cook for around fifteen minutes. It really is as easy as that!

Stuffed Chicken Surprise

I'm a big fan of chicken. I love the fact that without the skin it's a pretty low-fat option, and the smell of cooking chicken always reminds me of my mum's house on a lazy Sunday afternoon. The added bonus is that most kids love chicken (well, one out of my two isn't bad!) and teamed with homemade chips and some mangetout with a dash of sesame oil (and a sprinkling of sesame seeds if you're feeling brave), you're sorted for a good all-round family-pleaser. (Just remember to go easy on the homemade chips, or exchange for sweet-potato wedges if you're really feeling sensible!)

Ingredients
Serves two.

1 packet of mozzarella	sea salt
10 sweet cherry plum	black pepper
tomatoes	2 skinless chicken breasts
a handful of basil	(preferably organic, or free-
1 tbsp of olive oil	range at least)

Preheat your oven to 180°C/350°F/gas mark 5.

Chop your mozzarella, your cherry plum tomatoes and your basil, and give them a good stir, adding in the olive oil, salt and pepper. Slice your chicken breasts down the centre and stuff with your delicious-smelling filling. (I don't know about you, but I'm a sucker for the aroma of fresh basil.) You may need skewers to keep it all together, but I tend to leave it to spill over in the oven – I love all that gooey, hot mozzarella bubbling as it's served! Cook it for twenty-five minutes and serve piping hot.

Grace's Sweet-and-Savoury Salad

Anyone who has spent any time in my company will tell you that there's not a lot about salad innovation that I haven't tried at one point or another. I've been through stages of green salad with apple and prosciutto ham, I've been obsessed with cherry tomatoes, avocado and mozzarella (when I was pregnant with my first, I ate this at least twice daily), and I've been known to toast mushrooms with every oil under the sun to give oomph to a spinach salad. However, my sweet-and-savoury salad has to be the ultimate winner. It's so quick to prepare, it's got great kick and goes wonderfully with a whole host of other lunchtime hits. Chicken breast, organic ham, a flash-fried tuna steak and a heap of couscous cooked in vegetable stock, they are all ideal accompaniments to my sweet-and-savoury salad.

Ingredients
Serves two.

1 bag of rocket, spinach and watercress salad
Parmesan shavings
a handful of walnuts or pine nuts, chopped to suit
(and toasted if you fancy)
2 ripe peaches
a dash of olive oil
a dash of balsamic vinegar

Line a nice big bowl with the salad and add the Parmesan shavings and nuts. Peel and slice your peaches and add these to the mix. Pour your olive oil and balsamic vinegar over the salad and toss. It's a five-minute wonder!

Ladies' Lunch

I call this a 'ladies' lunch' because every time I whip it up for brunch with fellow mums and our kids, it is guaranteed to go down a treat. The mums love the fact it's filling (but not stodgy), low in fat and great for sustained afternoon energy, and the kids love the fact they've got grapes for their main course! Ideally, I make it in the morning (and occasionally I make the chicken the night before while cooking supper) and then forget about it until lunchtime, but it's so quick and easy it can usually be prepared with three toddlers at your feet and two fellow mums gassing at the kitchen table. (I even get them to seed and halve the grapes!)

Ingredients
Serves three.

100g grapes or 35g raisins	2 skinless, boned chicken
4 sticks of celery	breasts
1/2 cucumber	sea salt
3 spring onions	black pepper
1 tbsp fresh parsley	4 tbsp olive oil
20g almonds (omit these	120g brown rice or basmati
from the kids' portions if	and wild rice
under the age of five)	1 tbsp lemon juice

Preheat your oven to 180°C/350°F/gas mark 5.

Halve and seed the grapes, slice the celery, cucumber and spring onions, and chop the parsley. Chop the almonds (keep them separate and add these just before you serve). The rest of the salad ingredients (grapes, celery, cucumber, onions and parsley) can be placed in a bowl and tossed together. Season the chicken with some salt, pepper and olive oil, and cook it in the oven. (It should take around twenty to twenty-five minutes, depending on the thickness of the chicken breasts.)

Meanwhile, place the rice in 250ml of water, bring to the boil and simmer until tender (around fifteen minutes), then drain any remaining water and, once cooled, add to your salad mixture. Once the chicken has cooled down, slice it and add to the rice and salad mix. Add your remaining olive oil, the lemon juice and salt and pepper to taste. A whole meal in one dish. Perfect!

Virtuous Pizza

Like a lot of nutrition-conscious mums, I'm always looking for speedy, healthy meals that the kids may be tempted to enjoy too. Say 'pizza' and 'virtuous' together and you'd be forgiven for thinking there'd been a misprint. Admittedly, it's not as angelic as a green salad, 'hold the dressing', but this version is a pretty healthy option and one you can make with the children, allowing them to pick their toppings (cheese, cherry tomatoes, ham, sweetcorn, pineapple, olives, etc.).

Ingredients
Serves six.

Base:
2 tsp dried yeast

1/2 tsp caster sugar
215g plain flour

a pinch of salt
1/2 tsp dried oregano
1 tbsp olive oil

Salad topping:
60g ready-made sun-dried-
tomato pesto
125g goat's cheese
assorted toppings (ham,
pineapple, sweetcorn, etc.)
100g mixed lettuce leaves

(I love rocket, but it can be
pricey)
1/2 cucumber
10 cherry tomatoes
1 tbsp balsamic vinegar
2 tbsp olive oil
40g toasted pine nuts
100g olives (either black or
those stuffed with anchovies
work well)

Mix the yeast and sugar together in a bowl. Stir in 170ml of cool water (not too cold), then cover with a tea towel and leave at room temperature for around fifteen minutes. Sift your flour, salt and oregano together and make a small hole in the centre of the mix; pour in the yeast mixture and olive oil. Knead all this together on a floured surface to form a soft dough. (Kids love this, just don't let them get too carried away with making *Star Wars* figurines from the dough!) Place the dough into an oiled bowl and leave in a warm room for thirty minutes. (You'll know it's been enough time when the dough has doubled in size.)

Divide the dough into six flat portions. Press each portion into a thin, round pizza-base shape and place on a lightly oiled tray. (Brush with a dash more olive oil if you remember.) Prick several times with a fork and grill for two minutes; they should be puffy and golden, so you'll know to turn them over and repeat on the other side.

The next bit is the fun bit. Lightly spread your pizza with the pesto and goat's cheese, and grill again until the cheese is nice and melted. Then let the kids go wild with their ingredients, even encouraging them to make faces from ham and pineapple or the letter of their name with sweetcorn!

Toss your salad ingredients (lettuce, cucumber and tomatoes) with your olive oil and balsamic and place over the hot cheese. Sprinkle with the pine nuts, arrange the olives at random and eat *en famille*!

Mr and Mrs Mixed-Vegetable Medley

Sometimes even the thought of a cold salad makes me groan with indifference. If the weather's dreary and you need a yummy, aromatic lunch to inspire you to get through the afternoon chores, then a hot salad can be the best alternative. My husband and I love this dish, and I often use it as a salad for lunch, keep it in the fridge overnight and thread with chicken on skewers as a kebab for supper.

Ingredients
Serves two.

150g pumpkin	1 orange pepper
1 courgette	3 garlic cloves, crushed
1 red onion	2 tbsp pesto
4 button mushrooms	2 tbsp olive oil
1 red pepper	black pepper
1 yellow pepper	

Cut the pumpkin into really thick slices, slice the courgette, cut the onion into moons and halve the mushrooms; leave all these ingredients to one side. Cut the peppers into large strips, discard all the pith, seeds and stems. Cook skin side up under a hot grill until the skin blackens and peals. Leave them to cool in a small plastic bag.

Immediately afterwards, grill the rest of the veg and the garlic for around fifteen minutes (or until cooked through and soft). Once you've peeled the skin from the peppers, mix them up with the rest of the hot vegetables. Toss with your pesto and olive oil, and season with a little black pepper.

Simple Snack Attacks

- oatcakes with hummus
- a corn cake with low-fat cream cheese and a slither of ham
- a small bowl of porridge, quinoa or millet with hot skimmed milk, soya milk or Rice Dream. Top with half a banana and a small handful of raisins.
- oatcakes with a small dollop of sugar-free peanut butter and four slices of banana
- a handful of dried sulphur-free apricots, coconut shavings and pecan nuts
- a slice of rye bread toasted and spread with reduced-fat cream cheese and sliced fresh apricot
- a bowl of blueberries topped with goat's yoghurt, a small handful of dry muesli and a few pecan nuts
- raw vegetable fingers (carrot, cucumber, red pepper, cauliflower, sugar-snap peas) dipped in hummus or tzatziki
- some chopped fruit (an apple, half a banana, four

strawberries) and a dollop of live yoghurt. Sprinkle with cinnamon.

- a small bowl of salted popcorn
- half a papaya. Scoop out the seeds and replace with raspberries and a dollop of raspberry bio yoghurt.

Fruit Smoothies

I blend the following combinations for a yummy breakfast or snack for the kids and me. They really are so easy to prepare, and I keep them in the fridge to last a few days. Each of the smoothie combinations serves four.

- 150g blueberries, 150g strawberries, four bananas, 400ml fresh apple juice
- the juice from four oranges, two peaches, six fresh apricots, two bananas
- one papaya (peel and deseed), one banana, 150g raspberries, 300g natural yoghurt.

Useful Addresses for Fabulous Mums

Nutrition

Arkhill Farm Shop
Tel: 028 2955 7920
www.arkhillfarm.co.uk
As well as selling a vast range of organic products, this farm in County Londonderry, Northern Ireland, is a great day out for the kids.

Blooming Awful
Tel: 07020 969 728
www.hyperemesis.org.uk
For victims of the wretched hyperemesis, this information-packed organisation will be a lifeline.

Borough Market
(8 Southwark Street, London SE1 1TL)
www.boroughmarket.org.uk
Good-quality and well-priced fresh produce, most of which is organic. Stallholders also have a nice policy of letting kids try and taste new foods.

British Association for Nutritional Therapists

Tel: 0870 606 1284

www.bant.org.uk

This is the UK's registered governing body for nutritional therapists. If you're thinking of seeing a nutritionist, start here.

Farm Around

Tel: 0207 627 8066

www.farmaround.co.uk

Organic food delivery in London and the north of England, plus great nutritious recipes to cook with all your delicacies!

Food Revolution

Tel: 0800 169 6673

www.foodrevolution.com

A whole website dedicated to selling the best-quality produce on the market. Most of their goodies come from small organic sources that use traditional methods.

Fresh and Wild

Tel: 0207 229 1063 (Nothing Hill branch)

www.wholefoods.com

Supplies a wide selection of organic food, vitamins and cosmetics.

Fresh Food Company

Tel: 0208 749 8778

www.freshfood.co.uk

The UK's first nationwide organic delivery service.

The Nutri Centre
Tel: 0207 436 5122
www.nutricentre.com
This shop sells a vast quantity of nutritional supplements together with sound books on nutrition and eating well.

Penrhos Court
Tel: 01544 230 720
www.greencuisine.org
A beautiful Herefordshire hotel offering cooking and nutrition courses for the new mum.

Sainsbury's Well-being Eating for Pregnancy Helpline
Tel: 0845 130 3646
The latest research on food safety during pre-conception and pregnancy.

Spitalfields Organic Market
(Old Spitalfields Market, Brushfield Street, London E1 6AA)
Head here on Sundays between 10 a.m. and 5 p.m. and pick up London's largest selection of organic produce. (Beware, the cheeses and breads are to die for.)

Stoneground
Tel: 0117 974 1260
This vegetarian, GM-free shop in Bristol is stuffed with healthy produce that all tastes delicious.

Max Tomlinson

Tel: 0207 385 6001

Max's expertise in naturopathy and nutrition can give run-down, tired mums a new lease of life.

The Vegetarian Society

Tel: 0161 928 2000

www.vegsoc.org

Can advise on the best vegetarian diet to follow when pregnant.

Victoria Health

Tel: 0800 389 8195

www.victoriahealth.com

A great place to source health foods and supplements (and a good stockist of Floradix).

Waitrose

Tel: 0207 700 3717

www.ocado.com

Online food delivery with a huge choice of organic stock.

Zita West Products Limited

Tel: 0870 166 8899

www.zitawest.com

Brilliant nutritional products designed especially for the pregnant and new mum.

Exercise and the Body

Absolute Fitness
Tel: 0207 834 0000
www.absolutefitness.co.uk
Eighteen personal trainers ready to come to your home and help you get back into shape.

Fiona Allen
Tel: 07976 403 949
The best personal trainer in town, and because she comes to your home and has pre- and post-natal training, she's ideal for new mums.

Anniluce
Tel: 0208 924 5200
www.anniluce.co.uk
Co-ordinated lightweight gym clothes.

Art of Swimming
Tel: 0208 446 9442
www.artofswimming.com
London-based teacher Steven Shaw converts the principles of the Alexander technique to swimming. Ideal if you want to maximise the toning, relaxing and meditative qualities of swimming.

Birth Light

Tel: 0771 458 6153

www.birthlight.com

Details of holistic exercise classes around the country. Also useful for yoga and Pilates books and videos.

British Wheel of Yoga

Tel: 01529 306 851

www.bwy.org.uk

The governing body for yoga in the UK provides a list of yoga teachers and classes around the country.

Bush Baby

Tel: 0161 474 70976

www.bush-baby.com

Offers a range of products for mums who want to get active with their baby in tow.

David Lloyd

Tel: 01582 844 899

www.davidlloydleisure.co.uk

Forty-five clubs around the country, all offering crèches for the under-fives.

Esporta

Tel: 0800 0377 678

www.esporta.com

A nationwide sports club most with crèches and kids' activities.

The Hale Clinic
Tel: 0870 676 667
www.haleclinic.com
With over a hundred practitioners, this is one of the best examples of integrating conventional and complimentary medicine. Alexander technique, counselling, homeopathy, massage, nutrition and osteopathy are just a few of the treatments on offer here.

Massage for Mums
Tel: 07946 268 217
www.massageformums.com
Sophie Kingsley brings everything to your home and tailors a massage specifically for your needs as a new mum. Based in London.

Neal's Yard Remedies
Tel: 0845 262 3145
www.nealsyardremedies.com
A large selection of wonderful aromatherapy oils and great pregnancy massage lotions.

The Pilates Foundation
Tel: 07071 781 859
www.pilatesfoundation.com
For an up-to-date listing of all good Pilates instructors and classes in your area.

Powerpramming
Tel: 07976 778 413
www.powerpramming.co.uk
Call Liz Stuart for more information on the power-pramming phenomenon.

Proactive
Tel: 0870 848 4842
www.proactive-health.co.uk
Brilliant home gym equipment, gym balls and weights.

Return to Glory
Tel: 0207 993 8063
www.returntoglory.co.uk
Therapists come to your home to do tailor-made massage and beauty therapies to pamper and restore new mums.

Rojo
Tel: 0208 731 8485
Stockist of the MBT shoes (that apparently aid in cellulite reduction). Available by mail order.

Speedo
www.speedo.com
Get your swimming costume, goggles and swim hat here and you've no excuse not to hit the pool!

Lolly Stirk
Tel: 0208 674 6997
The ultimate pre- and post-natal yoga guru. (She also runs great classes in birth preparation.)

Unlisted London

Tel: 0870 225 5007

www.unlistedlondon.com

Therapists specialising in massage, hair, make-up, personal training, yoga and nutrition who will work with mums from their own home.

Virgin Active

Tel: 01908 546 600

www.virginactive.co.uk

Sports clubs around the UK, most with crèches and kids' classes.

Well Women

www.rwh.org.au/wellwomens/which.cfm/doc_id=3458

A good, easy-to-use website for post-natal exercise advice.

World of Health

Tel: 0207 357 9393

www.worldofhealth.co.uk

Suppliers of a whole host of fitness and yoga DVDs.

Sleep

Association of Breastfeeding Mothers

Tel: 0870 401 7711

www.abm.me.uk

Advice and support groups for breastfeeding mothers.

Avent Tel: 0800 289 064

www.avent.com

All the kit you need for bottlefeeding, expressing and weaning.

The Breastfeeding Helpline

Tel: 0870 444 8708

An NCT-run helpline that will put you in touch with a breastfeeding counsellor.

Cry-sis

Tel: 0207 404 5011

A self-help and advice group for parents of children with severe sleep problems.

Andrea Grace

Tel: 0208 348 6959 or 07717 324 377

Andrea comes to your home and provides comprehensive sleep solutions to fit your family's needs.

Grobag

Tel: 0870 420 4920

www.grobag.com

Online sales of nursing pillows, pregnancy support pillows and babies' sleeping bags.

Marshall and Gurney

Tel: 0208 444 0040

www.mill-pond.co.uk

Tracey Marshall and Mandy Gurney are two registered nurses who offer comforting support and solutions for families with disturbed-sleep problems.

NCT Maternity Sales

Tel: 0870 444 8708

www.nctms.co.uk

A good selection of books on breastfeeding, sleep and parenting.

Night Nannies

Tel: 0207 731 6168

www.nightnannies.com

One of the top agencies for finding a nanny to cover the hellish night shift, plus advice and tips on how to get your baby to sleep well.

Nutkin

Tel: 01628 778 856

A small company offering the new mum help with sleep, routines, shopping and even nursery design.

The Sleep Council

www.sleepcouncil.com/consumer_room/leaflets.cfm

Log on to obtain the Sleep Council's leaflet 'The Good Night Guide For Children'.

Urban Escapes

Tel: 07976 701 041

Massage and relaxation techniques for the mum-to-be and new mum.

Fashion

Accessorize

Tel: 0207 313 3000

Reasonably priced and fashion-forward accessories to spruce up a mum's wardrobe.

Barnet Lawson

Tel: 0207 636 8591

www.bltrimmings.com

A fabulous selection of over ten thousand haberdashery items, trimmings and ribbons, great for altering or giving new life to clothes. Based in London.

Blooming Marvellous

Tel: 0845 459 7400

www.bloomingmarvellous.co.uk

The UK's leading maternity store. Great for basics, but avoid the attempts at 'high fashion'.

Buba

Tel: 0207 384 4540

www.bubalondon.com

Hand-crafted and exquisitely appliquéd with sequins and coral; these are the fashionista's baby bag of choice.

Change of Heart
Tel: 0208 341 1575
They will sell your unwanted designer and high-street clothes, giving you the freedom to reinvest. Based in London.

eBay
www.ebay.co.uk
An ideal place to pick up or sell second-hand clothes.

Elias & Grace
Tel: 0207 499 0574
www.eliasandgrace.com
In vogue London-based boutique for mother and baby. If you can't stretch to the luxury goodies, console yourself by picking up a few basics and popping next door for an indulgent hot chocolate.

Fantasy Cleaners
Tel: 0207 820 8203
www.fantasycleaners.com
Speedy and efficient, these dry-cleaners will collect and deliver dry-cleaning from any address in London.

Figleaves Maternity
www.figleaves.com/babybook
The best place to buy maternity underwear.

Formes
Tel: 0208 689 1133
www.formes.com
Chic French maternity clothes.

French Sole
Tel: 0207 730 3771
www.frenchsole.com
The only place to go for the ultimate flat pumps. Based in London.

Ghost
Tel: 0208 960 3121
www.ghost.co.uk
Beautiful clothes to carry you through the early stages of pregnancy, the birth and beyond.

H&M
Tel: 0207 323 2211
www.hm.com
Cheap and cheerful maternity wear and great basics for the busy mum.

The Home Laundering Consultative Council
Tel: 0207 636 7788
www.care-labelling.com
Confused about washing instructions? Address your queries here and you'll get the best results every time.

I Love Jeans
www.ilovejeans.com
Brilliant website for selecting the perfect jeans to fit your changing shape. Input your body shape and they'll tell you the jeans to suit you best.

The Invisible Menders of Knightsbridge
Tel: 0207 373 0514
Top dog Nina will work wonders on hems, buttons and holes, restoring clothes to their former glory.

Jojo Maman Bébé
Tel: 0870 241 0560
www.jojomamanbebe.co.uk
A wide selection of maternity wear and underwear; also check out the wooden-toy selection.

Kurt Geiger
Tel: 0207 794 4290
www.kurtgeiger.com
A large selection of designer shoes and the less expensive but equally stylish KG line.

The Maternitywear Exchange
Tel: 01628 851 187
www.maternityexchange.co.uk
New and nearly new maternity clothes with up to 80 per cent discount.

Muji
Tel: 0207 239 3500
www.muji.co.uk
Brilliant ideas for wardrobe storage. Clear shoeboxes, adjustable hangers and clothes covers are amongst their winning stock.

Net-à-Porter

www.netaporter.com

The best way to get designer trends (especially bags) without leaving the living room!

9 London

Tel: 0207 352 7600

www.9london.com.uk

The chicest maternity wear on the market. Expect to share a fitting room with A-list mums!

Selfridges

Tel: 0870 837 7377

www.selfridges.co.uk

You can't beat it for its selection of fashionable clothes, shoes, bags and accessories. Also comes with a feeding room, so ideal for shopping with baby in tow.

Top Shop

Tel: 0207 636 7700

www.topshop.com

Great clothes, shoes and accessories for pregnancy and beyond. It also offers a brilliant style advisory service for the stressed-out new mum.

What's Mine Is Yours

www.whatsmineisyours.com

A swap shop where you list and then trade in your unwanted designer goodies for an item of equal value.

Interiors

Auro Organics Paint Supplies
Tel: 01452 772 020
www.auro.co.uk
Specialists in organic and hypoallergenic emulsion and gloss paints – great for the eco-friendly nursery.

Baby Concierge
Tel: 0208 964 5500
www.babyconcierge.co.uk
Private consultation, expert advice and delivery of all your baby equipment.

Baby Equipment Complete
Tel: 01788 832 219
www.babyequipmentcomplete.co.uk
A huge selection of baby equipment with the bonus of online and phone sales.

Bump to 3
Tel: 0870 606 0276
www.bumpto3.com
A good range of practical products for pregnancy and beyond, specialises in great developmental toys and state-of-the-art high chairs.

Chairworks

Tel: 0208 247 3700

www.chairworks.info

Brilliant big baskets to store toys, wellies and general children's junk.

Chic Shack

Tel: 0208 785 7777

www.chicshack.net

My dream wish list for nursery furniture, warn the bank manager before you visit!

Daisy & Tom

Tel: 0207 352 5000

www.daisyandtom.com

Gorgeous baby equipment and toys, many of which are made from wood.

Designers Guild

Tel: 0207 893 7400

www.designersguild.com

A vast selection of wallpaper, bed linen and curtain fabrics.

Escor Toys

Tel: 01202 591 1081

www.escortoys.com

Award-winning traditional wooden toys. Toys 'R' Us eat your heart out!

FK Domestics
Tel: 0870 919 3014
www.fastclean.co.uk
A hard-working company who will send domestic cleaners
to get your home shipshape.

Nicky Grace
Tel: 0208 883 1564
www.nickygrace.co.uk
Nicky has a wonderful selection of vintage nursery furniture, quilts, toys and kids' accessories.

The Great Little Trading Company
Tel: 0870 850 6000
www.gltc.co.uk
Amongst other baby equipment and toys, this company has
great storage solutions for all that kids' paraphernalia.

Habitat
Tel: 0845 601 0740
www.habitat.net
Habitat is always worth checking out for storage solutions
(they do great rattan toy chests in three different sizes) and
simple deco inspirations.

The Handy Squad
Tel: 0800 012 1212
www.handysquad.com
These efficient and chirpy handymen will fix shelves, lay
floorboards or put up the most complex pirate-ship-cum-
bed.

The Holding Company

Tel: 0207 352 1600

www.theholdingcompany.co.uk

Storage solutions, organisation tools, cute boxes and great shelving all beautifully made – ideal for making a clutter-free home.

Ikea

Tel: 0845 355 1141

www.ikea.co.uk

You'll be surprised at how many good storage solutions or simple kids' furniture items you can pick up here. Avoid the Sunday crush, though!

John Lewis

Tel: 0845 604 9049

www.johnlewis.co.uk

Brilliant for baby basics and essential nursery equipment.

Cath Kidston

Tel: 0870 850 1084

www.cathkidston.co.uk

Beautiful nursery wallpaper and cushions.

Lilliput

Tel: 0207 720 5554

www.lilliput.com

Stockists around the UK offering a good selection of baby equipment; one of the few places to hire out specific items as well.

Little Green Earthlets
Tel: 0845 072 4462
www.earthlets.co.uk
Many eco-friendly toys and stylish baby equipment (including the Tripp Trapp high chairs).

Lizzilu
Tel: 0161 929 6610
www.lizzilu.co.uk
Lizzilu will hand-paint any item of furniture or interior décor in any design that takes your fancy.

The Natural Mat Company
Tel: 0207 985 0474
www.naturalmat.com
The best made-to-measure natural-fibre mattresses and nursery furniture.

Oka
Tel: 0870 160 6002
www.okadirect.com
Great, simple and economical toy storage ideas.

Pramsdirect
Tel: 0870 442 2545
www.pramsdirect.co.uk
Get your chosen pram delivered straight to the door.

The Stencil Library
Tel: 01661 844 844
www.stencil-library.com
Thousands of beautiful stencil designs and equipment – a brilliant alternative to 100 per cent Barbie coverage!

Top Stitch
Tel: 0208 455 4045
Beautiful personalised linen, cushions and bedspreads.

Unto This Last
Tel: 0207 613 0882
www.untothislast.co.uk
Great for affordable, innovative and good-quality slat shelving – ideal for the short-of-space family home.

Work

Au pairs
www.aupairs.co.uk
A good place to advertise if you're looking for an au pair.

Best Bear
Tel: 0870 720 1277
www.bestbear.co.uk
The definitive guide to the country's best childcare agencies.

Citizens Advice Bureau

Tel: 0870 128 8080

www.nacab.org.uk or www.adviceguide.org.uk

Free advice on work-related problems or queries.

Domestic Solutions

Tel: 0207 225 1550

www.nannyworld.co.uk

This is the leading agency for supplying nannies, cleaners and housekeepers.

The Equal Opportunities Commission (EOC)

Tel: 0845 601 5901

www.eco.org.uk

Confidential advice for mums who feel they have been discriminated against at work. Go to a section called 'Know Your Rights' on www.eoc-law.org.uk and you'll find all you need to know about your legal rights as a working mum.

Full-time Mothers

Tel: 0208 670 2525

www.fulltimemothers.org

Support and advice for full-time mothers.

Geeks on Wheels

Tel: 0800 107 4110 (London area) or 0800 107 4111 (Sussex area)

www.geeks-on-wheels.com

The must-have number for the mum working from home; uniformed gents offer twenty-four-hour computer assistance over the phone or straight to your home.

Gum Tree

www.gumtree.com

A website packed full of childcare professionals looking for work. You can also advertise your needs.

The Lady

Tel: 0207 379 4717

www.lady.co.uk

A weekly magazine with childcare small ads.

Mum and Working

www.mumandworking.co.uk

Online nationwide job directory listing family-friendly part-time jobs.

Nannyjob

www.nannyjob.co.uk

Simple but efficient website offering a notice board for finding or posting a childcare position.

Nannysearch

Tel: 0208 348 4111

www.nanny-search.co.uk

A top-notch nanny placement agency, which also offers babysitters and mother's help.

The Nanny Sharers

www.thenannysharers.co.uk

Enter your postcode and link up with a compatible family near you.

Nannytax
Tel: 0845 226 2203
www.nannytax.co.uk
Payroll service designed specifically for nannies.

National Association of Children's Information Services
Tel: 0207 515 9000
www.nacis.org.uk
Information on childminders, nurseries, nannies, crèches, play-groups and parent-toddler groups.

Office of Standards of Education (OFSTED)
Tel: 0845 640 4040
www.ofsted.gov.uk
Check out government reports of your prospective nurseries here.

Simply Childcare
Tel: 0207 701 6111
www.simplychildcare.com
A childcare listings magazine, which also offers a helpful pack with example contracts and interview questions.

Working Families
www.workingfamilies.org.uk
Log on for more information on flexi-time.

Grown-up Time

Baby Centre
www.babycentre.co.uk
This website offers useful advice on sex after giving birth.

The Blue Kangaroo
Tel: 0207 371 7622
www.thebluekangaroo.co.uk
One of the few restaurants where you can sit with your partner or friends, eat and relax while your kids are entertained in the 'playzone'.

Gingerbread
Tel: 0800 018 4318
www.gingerbread.org.uk
Supportive self-help organisation for lone-parent families.

Kasimira
Tel: 0207 581 8313
www.kasimira.com
Kasimira will provide trustworthy and enthusiastic babysitters within the London area with almost no notice at all.

Meet-a-Mum Association
Tel: 0845 120 3746
www.mama.co.uk
The best UK network for meeting new mums in your area.

Mr & Mrs Smith Hotel Collection
Tel: 0207 978 1000
www.mrandmrssmith.com
This is the place to find a real blow-the-budget treat hotel.

Myla
Tel: 0870 745 5003
www.myla.com
Beautiful and tasteful underwear and sex aids.

Relate
Tel: 01788 573 241
www.relate.org.uk
Support, advice and counselling for relationships under strain.

Restaurant Guide
www.restaurant-guide.com
Thousands of restaurants nationwide listed and reviewed. Find the best Italian near you and book it up!

Restaurant Reservations
Tel: 0870 850 8454
www.toptable.co.uk
If you're too busy and frazzled to book a romantic night out, give them a call and they'll do all the work for you.

Sitters
Tel: 0800 389 0038
The most professional and thorough organisation for helping you find a babysitter. Saturday nights on the razzle may be an option once more!

Special Places to Stay

www.specialplacestostay.com

Babysitter in place? Why not log on and book a mini-break with your partner or best friend?

Theatre Tickets

theatre-tickets.top-uk.co.uk

Surprise your partner with theatre tickets at the click of a finger.

Thank You

There are so many thank-yous for making this book happen I suppose the best place to start is at the beginning . . .

Thanks to

My amazing husband, Michael. The depth of your love, patience and support never ceases to amaze me. Not only do you make my dreams come true, you also happen to cook the best lobster this side of the Atlantic. I couldn't love you more.

Our beautiful, wonderful, unique and often hysterical children, Bella and Gabriel. You make us the proudest parents in the world.

Mum, for being the original fabulous mum, and Dad, who is, of course, the role-model writer.

To my Nan, the matriarch.

My stepfather, Will, for making my dream feel it could become a reality.

Sister bliss Fleur, for her support, love and ability to travel across London most weekends to face-paint, read stories and bake cookies with her adoring niece and nephew. They love you just as much as I do.

My best buddy Clare – from secondary school to the grave, you are the most astonishing person to share life with.

All my wonderful, wonderful mummy friends – you are a constant source of inspiration, camaraderie, humour and love (Jennie, Katie, Gayle, Lyn, Esme, Tanith, Ros, Kate, Luella, Amy, Danni, Cat, Danielle, Kym, Paula, Lucie, Sara, Lisa, Sonia, Sophie, Carolina, Rainbow, Elaine, you know who you are). A big thanks, too, for letting me publish some of your unique and often hilarious stories.

Jools, for talking bumps, babies and 'where has our groove gone?' with me way before our friends had even settled down. And for putting me in touch with the team at Fresh Partners who kick-started this whole project.

A big thanks to Helen, for putting the kids to bed on the odd occasion I was up late to finish a chapter, for taking them to the park whilst I interviewed yet another guru and for entertaining them with your crazy dancing while I swam to keep sane. You will always be one of the family.

My amazing babysitter Gillian, who gave Mike and me Saturday nights off to feel like a dating couple again, and therefore inspired the chapter 'Grown-up Time'.

Those truly fabulous work colleagues Sarah Bailey, Paula Whiteman, Rosie Green, Claudia Navone, Lucie Kearney, Sue Ward-Davis, you helped me believe in myself (not to mention life after *Elle*).

My agent Lorella Belli, for taking me (and my endless rants about motherhood) under her wing and for all her hard work in making this book happen. Have I ever said how much I value our early-morning cappuccinos at the Electric?

My wonderful, inspiring gurus, you were all a pleasure to work with and I hope mums all over the country gain as much from your wisdom as I did. You are brilliant!

To all those mums who offered up their anecdotes for 'Mother knows best', thank you, they made me laugh and cry and contributed to making this book a breadth of women's voices.

To Lindsay Smith, for being the first mum to read and make judgement on the book. Your comments were a life-saver!

A massive thank-you to Nikola Scott – my editor at Random House – for taking me on and sharing my confidence in the book. Without our endless emails on sleep deprivation, childcare solutions and methods for toy storage, I think I would have gone mad.

Thanks, too, to all at Random House who have helped this dream become a hardback reality.

Last, but by no means least, a massive thank-you to my late mother-in-law, Valerie. You always believed I could make it as an author. I know somewhere you are smiling proudly.

Index

Notes

Notes

Notes

Notes

Notes